Triple Decker Sandwich

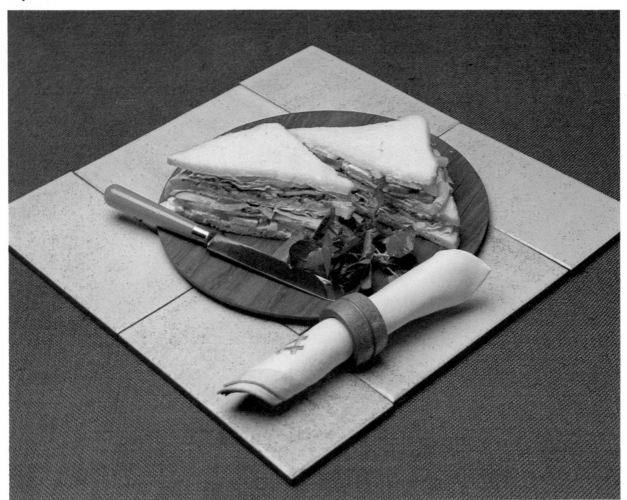

Weight Watchers*
NEW FOOD PLAN COOKBOOK

NEW ENGLISH LIBRARY

ACKNOWLEDGMENTS

Photoset by South Bucks Photosetters Ltd.

Printed and Bound by Hazell, Watson and Viney Ltd., Aylesbury

ISBN: 0 450 04922 1

The creation of a cookbook is never the work of one individual. This book is no exception and many people have helped in its preparation. Numerous hours were spent in the test kitchens of Weight Watchers International creating and testing recipes. Countless members and staff of Weight Watchers U.K. added their own enthusiasm and ideas to the project. To all these people we say 'Thank you'.

We also wish to acknowledge the contribution of Felice Lippert, Advisor and Consultant to the Food Research and Development Department, for her inspiration and conception of this series of Weight Watchers cookbooks.

Dr Lelio G. Parducci
Vice President
Food Research & Development
Department.

For more information about this cookbook, its recipes and the Weight Watchers Classroom Programme, contact:
Weight Watchers U.K.
635/637 Ajax Avenue
Slough
Berkshire

CONTENTS

INTRODUCTION

Dear Friend,

Many of us dreamed that in some idyllic life we'd be able to enjoy such delights as bacon and ice cream and still lose weight.

With the 1982 revision of our Food Plan, this fantasy became a reality. On the famous Weight Watchers Food Plan you can now eat food never believed possible on a weight-loss regime. You can even toast your pound-shedding efforts with wine! And you can use such popular cooking methods as sauteeing with oil and stir-frying.

Why was a Food Plan that was already so successful changed? Partly because the Weight Watchers organisation has never been content to stand still. Partly because we wanted our Food Plan to have increased flexibility and offer even greater freedom.

The medical consultants and nutritionists who staff our Food Research and Development Department evaluated the most up-to-date nutritional findings and produced this new Food Plan, which opened kitchen doors to a vast range of culinary possibilities.

For months, our expert home economists and chefs worked in the test kitchens of Weight Watchers International testing recipes individually and evaluating them to meet our exacting standards. This book is the result of their work.

It offers more than 500 easy ways to serve delectable dishes that blend with equally pleasing weight losses. To ease your way, the recipes are grouped according to Food Plan categories. Whether you're serving a routine family meal, a lavish spread, or a simple snack, you'll find invaluable recipes on every page of this book.

We are frequently asked how it is possible to include such an incredible array of foods. The answer takes us into another area of Weight Watchers, for we offer more than a Food Plan. We include invaluable eating-management techniques that help Weight Watchers members learn various strategies, including portion control. That is why we felt confident about expanding the choices on our Food Plan.

I have watched the Weight Watchers organisation grow from a handful of members in one American town to hundreds of thousands around the world. If our new foods seem like a dream come true, the more meaningful dreams come true are the incredible transformations of the overweight men, women and teenagers all over the world who have come through our doors to find not just a new eating style but new lives. In almost every language, the Weight Watchers name has come to stand for quality help.

You'll find that kind of quality between the covers of this book. If you're just beginning to lose weight, if you are already at goal weight, if you never had a weight problem but simply want to learn how to prepare nutritious, well-balanced meals, I can't think of a more helpful friend to have in the kitchen than this book.

Jean Nidetch
Founder Weight Watchers International

We hope that you will find this book interesting and enjoy the recipes we give you.

The following information may help you understand the menu plan on page 5. This plan represents the Full Choice Plan in the Food Plan. You will find that the recipes relate to the food group list on the menu plan.

Wherever specific amounts are given in these recipes they relate to the women's plan. To make the adaptations for men and teenagers, refer to the menu plan on page 5.

You will see the word 'serving' in recipes and on our menu plan. A serving is a portion of food which equates to the amount of food allowed on the Food Plan.

You will find it useful to keep a daily food diary so that you know exactly what you have eaten and that you have fulfilled all the requirements of the Full Choice Plan.

Artificial Sweeteners

The use of artificial sweeteners on the Weight Watchers Food Plan has always been optional. Natural sweeteners are available in the form of fruits, honey, molasses and syrup. Your use of artificial sweeteners is completely optional, and we believe that the decision about using them should be made by you.

Caution

Weight Watchers strongly advise you to consult your doctor while participating in the Food Plan.

Menu Plan (Full Choice)

	Food		Quantity	Food Group
Morning Meal				
	Fruit or Fruit Juice		1 serving	Fruits
Choice of	Egg		1	Protein
Or	Cheese, soft		2½ oz (75 g)	Protein
Or	Cheese, semisoft or hard		1 oz (30 g)	Protein
Or	Cereal		¾ oz (20 g) with Milk	Grains, Milk
Or	†Peanut Butter		1 tbsp	Protein
Or	*Dried Peas/Beans		3 oz (90 g)	Protein
Or	*Poultry, Meat or Fish		1 oz (30 g)	Protein
	Beverage, if desired			Optional
Midday and Evening Meal				
Choice of	*Poultry, Meat or Fish	**Women**	3-4 oz (90-120 g)	Protein
		Men	4-5 oz (120-150 g)	Protein
		Teenagers	3-4 oz (90-120 g)	Protein
Or	Eggs		2	Protein
Or	Cheese, soft		5 oz (150 g)	Protein
Or	Cheese, semisoft or hard		2 oz (60 g)	Protein
Or	‡Peanut Butter		3 tbsps	Protein
Or	*Dried Peas/Beans	**Women**	6 oz (180 g)	Protein
		Men	8 oz (240 g)	Protein
		Teenagers	6 oz (180 g)	Protein
	Beverage, if desired			Optional
Daily, at any time				
	**Fruits	**Women**	3 servings	Fruits
		Men	4-6 servings	Fruits
		Teenagers	4-6 servings	Fruits
	Vegetables		2 servings (minimum)	Vegetables
	Milk	**Women**	2 servings	Milk
		Men	2 servings	Milk
		Teenagers	3-4 servings	Milk
	Bread	**Women**	2-3 servings	Grains
		Men	4-5 servings	Grains
		Teenagers	4-5 servings	Grains
	Fats		3 servings	Fats

†Omit 1 serving Fat ‡Omit 2 servings Fat
*Cooked Weight **Includes fruit at Morning Meal

tbsp=tablespoon   tsp=teaspoon   g=grammes   ¾ oz=20 grammes

Metric Conversion Table

Liquids		Solids		Liquids		Solids	
		¼ oz	7 g	14 fl oz	420 ml	16 oz (1 lb)	480 g
		½ oz	15 g	15 fl oz	450 ml	17 oz	510 g
¼ fl oz	7 ml	1 oz	30 g	16 fl oz	480 ml	18 oz	540 g
½ fl oz	15 ml	2 oz	60 g			19 oz	570 g
1 fl oz	30 ml	3 oz	90 g	20 fl oz (1 pint)	600 ml	20 oz (1¼ lb)	600 g
2 fl oz	60 ml	4 oz	120 g	24 fl oz	720 ml	24 oz (1½ lb)	720 g
3 fl oz	90 ml	5 oz	150 g	30 fl oz (1½ pints)	900 ml	28 oz (1¾ lb)	840 g
4 fl oz	120 ml	6 oz	180 g	32 fl oz	960 ml	32 oz (2 lb)	960 g
5 fl oz	150 ml	7 oz	210 g			36 oz (2¼ lb)	1 kg 80 g
6 fl oz	180 ml	8 oz	240 g	35 fl oz	1 litre	40 oz (2½ lb)	1 kg 200 g
7 fl oz	210 ml	9 oz	270 g	40 fl oz (2 pints)	1 litre 200 ml	48 oz (3 lb)	1 kg 440 g
8 fl oz	240 ml	10 oz	300 g	45 fl oz (2¼ pints)	1 litre 250 ml	56 oz (3½ lb)	1 kg 680 g
9 fl oz	270 ml	11 oz	330 g	50 fl oz (2½ pints)	1 litre 500 ml	64 oz (4 lb)	1 kg 920 g
10 fl oz	300 ml	12 oz	360 g	60 fl oz (3 pints)	1 litre 800 ml	68 oz (4¼ lb)	2 kg 40 g
11 fl oz	330 ml	13 oz	390 g	70 fl oz (3½ pints)	2 litres	72 oz (4½ lb)	2 kg 160 g
12 fl oz	360 ml	14 oz	420 g	80 fl oz (4 pints)	2 litres 250 ml	80 oz (5 lb)	2 kg 400 g
13 fl oz	390 ml	15 oz	450 g				

FRUITS

Apples, peaches, berries, dried fruits and dozens of others are listed in the first category in the Food Plan. You may enjoy them just as fruit or include them in prepared dishes, such as Apple Crumble, Rich Fruit Pudding and Orange Jelly Cream. However you use them, they are satisfying and nutritious components of our Food Plan

One fruit must be taken at the morning meal, the others at any time. Choose at least one daily from those marked with an asterisk (*) and be sure to vary your selections. These fruits supply almost all of the Vitamin C required daily. If you cook this asterisked fruit, one of your remaining fruit selections should be another one, because some Vitamin C is lost in the cooking. You can use fresh, dried, canned or frozen fruit or fruit juice with no sugar added. The serving size for canned fruit is 4 oz (120 g) or the fresh equivalent with 2 tablespoonfuls of juice.

Women	3 servings daily
Men	4-6 servings daily
Teenagers	4-6 servings daily

Fruit Juice

	Serving
apple juice	2½ fl oz (75 ml)
grape juice	2½ fl oz (75 ml)
* grapefruit juice	4 fl oz (120 ml)
* orange juice	4 fl oz (120 ml)
pineapple juice	2½ fl oz (75 ml)
prune juice	2½ fl oz (75 ml)
* tomato juice	8 fl oz (240 ml)
mixed vegetable juice	8 fl oz (240 ml)

Fruits

	Serving
apple	1 medium
apricots	3 medium
banana	½ medium
berries:	
blackberries	5 oz (150 g)
blueberries	5 oz (150 g)
boysenberries	5 oz (150 g)
cranberries	5 oz (150 g)
gooseberries	5 oz (150 g)
loganberries	5 oz (150 g)
raspberries	5 oz (150 g)
strawberries	5 oz (150 g)
* cantaloupe melon	½ medium or 5 oz (150 g) chunks
cherries	4 oz (120 g)
* currants, black, red, white	5 oz (150 g)
damsons	5 oz (150 g)
dates	3
figs	1 large
fruit cocktail or salad	4 oz (120 g)
* grapefruit	½ medium
* grapefruit sections	4 oz (120 g)
grapes	3 oz (90 g)
* honeydew (or similar) melon	2″ (5 cm) wedge or 5 oz (150 g) chunks
mandarin	1 large
mandarin sections	4 oz (120 g)
nectarine	1 medium
* orange	1 medium
* orange sections	4 oz (120 g)
peach	1 medium
pear	1 medium
pineapple	¼ small or 4 oz (120 g)
plums	2 medium
pomegranate	½
tangerine	2 small
watermelon	3″ x 1½″ (8 x 4 cm) triangle

In addition: rhubarb may be used as desired.

Dried Fruits

	Serving
apples	1 oz (30 g)
apricots	1 oz (30 g)
currants	2 tbsps
dates	2
peaches	1 oz (30 g)
pears	1 oz (30 g)
prunes	1 oz (30 g)
raisins	2 tbsps
sultanas	2 tbsps

Minted Summer Delight

1 medium cantaloupe melon

3 x 1½-inch (8 x 4 cm) triangle watermelon, seeded and cut into chunks

bunch of fresh mint

5 oz (150 g) strawberries

5 oz (150 g) honeydew melon chunks

5 oz (150 g) blackberries

Cut cantaloupe in half. Remove seeds. Cut skin from fruit, keeping pulp intact. Cut each cantaloupe half lengthwise into about 6 crescent shaped slices. Arrange sprigs of mint on serving dish, reserving 6 sprigs for garnish. Arrange cantaloupe slices over mint, with the points of the melon slices meeting in the centre of the dish, like spokes of a wheel. Arrange remaining fruit between cantaloupe slices. Chop remaining mint and sprinkle over fruit. Divide evenly.
Makes 6 servings.

Grilled Spiced Peaches

4 oz (120 g) canned sliced peaches, no sugar added, drain and reserve juice

pinch allspice

4 teaspoons dry white wine

Arrange sliced peaches on a heatproof dish. Sprinkle with allspice and put under hot grill and cook until heated through. Gently warm juice and wine. Place peaches in serving dish and pour over warmed wine/juice and serve at once.
Makes 1 serving.

Dorset Apple Cake

1 tablespoon self-raising flour

1 tablespoon margarine

1 teaspoon baking powder

1 egg

2 slices (2 oz/60 g) white bread, made into crumbs

2 medium apples, cored and finely chopped

½ teaspoon cinnamon

artificial sweetener to taste

Cream flour, margarine and baking powder together. Add egg yolk and beat. Add breadcrumbs, apple and cinnamon and mix. In separate bowl beat egg white, until stiff; add sweetener and gently fold into the rest of the ingredients. Pour into a small cake tin and bake in oven, 350°F, 180°C, Gas Mark 4, for 25 minutes or until brown and firm to the touch. Divide evenly.
Makes 2 midday or evening meal servings. Add protein as required.

Glazed Melon

1 medium cantaloupe melon, seeded and cut into 8 wedges

4-inch (10-cm) wedge honeydew melon, cut into 4 wedges

4 teaspoons honey

1 tablespoon lime juice

mint sprigs to garnish

Arrange melon wedges on a platter. Combine honey and lime juice in a bowl and spoon evenly over melon. Garnish with mint sprigs.
Makes 4 servings.

Baked Apples

4 medium cooking apples, cored

4 fl oz (120 ml) water

1 teaspoon lemon juice

½ teaspoon vanilla flavouring

½ teaspoon cinnamon

Peel apples halfway down. Place in shallow casserole. Add water, lemon juice and vanilla. Sprinkle apple with cinnamon. Cover; bake at 400°F, 200°C, Gas Mark 6, for 20 minutes or until apples are tender. Divide evenly.
Makes 4 servings.

Raspberries and Apricots in Red Wine

10 oz (300 g) raspberries

6 medium apricots, peeled, stoned and sliced

8 fl oz (240 ml) red wine

2 teaspoons sugar

In medium bowl combine all ingredients; cover and refrigerate. Allow to marinate for 20 minutes before serving. Divide evenly.
Makes 4 servings.

FRUITS

Crispy Peach Foam

8 oz (240 g) canned sliced peaches, no sugar added; drain and reserve juice

10 fl oz (300 ml) natural unsweetened yogurt

2 eggs, separated

artificial sweetener to taste

1 tablespoon unflavoured gelatine

1 tablespoon hot water

2 digestive biscuits, made into crumbs

nutmeg to taste

Dice and reserve 4 peach slices; combine remaining slices, yogurt and egg yolks in blender container and blend until smooth. Add artificial sweetener to taste. Sprinkle gelatine over reserved peach juice and let stand to soften; add hot water and stir to dissolve. Add juice mixture to blender container and blend until combined. Pour into a basin. Whisk egg whites until stiff and fold peach into mixture. Arrange diced peach slices in bottom of a 1-pint (600-ml) souffle dish. Pour in peach mixture and sprinkle with biscuit crumbs and nutmeg. Chill until set. Divide evenly.
Makes 2 midday or evening meal servings. Add protein as required.

Banana Mousse

1 tablespoon unflavoured gelatine

2 fl oz (60 ml) cold water

4 fl oz (120 ml) boiling water

1 very ripe medium banana, diced

2 oz (60 g) non-fat dry milk

1 teaspoon sugar

1 teaspoon lemon juice

6 to 7 drops yellow food colouring

4 to 6 ice cubes

In blender container sprinkle gelatine over cold water to soften; add boiling water. Blend to dissolve. Add ¾ of diced banana, milk, sugar, lemon juice and food colouring. Blend until smooth. Add ice cubes, one at a time, blending after each addition. Pour into bowl. Fold in remaining banana. Divide mousse evenly into 2 dessert glasses.
Makes 2 servings.

'Special' Red Berry Salad

5 oz (150 g) blackberries

5 oz (150 g) raspberries

5 oz (150 g) redcurrants

5 oz (150 g) blackcurrants

5 oz (150 g) strawberries

7½ teaspoons caster sugar

lemon juice

Combine berries in a large bowl and sprinkle with sugar and lemon juice to taste. Divide evenly.
Makes 5 servings.

'Special' Red Berry Salad

FRUITS

Fruit Medley

½ medium apple, cored and finely chopped, sprinkled with ¼ teaspoon lemon juice

2 oz (60 g) pineapple pieces

2½ oz (75 g) strawberries, sliced

2 tablespoons low-calorie orange drink diluted with 2 tablespoons water

Combine all ingredients in a bowl. Mix well and place in refrigerator to chill.
Makes 1 serving.

Jellied Orange Cups

1 tablespoon unflavoured gelatine

12 fl oz (360 ml) water

5 teaspoons sugar

1 teaspoon orange flavouring

4 medium oranges

mint sprigs to garnish

In bowl soften gelatine in 2 fl oz (60 ml) water. Heat remaining water; add to gelatine and stir to dissolve. Add sugar and flavouring. Cut off top of each orange in a zigzag fashion. Carefully remove all pulp. Chop roughly and return an equal amount to each orange shell. Fill each shell with 4 tablespoons of gelatine mixture and set aside remainder in another dish to be diced. Chill orange cups and remaining gelatine mixture until set. To serve, place crushed ice in each of 4 dessert dishes. Place 1 orange cup in each dish. Dice remaining orange jelly. Spoon an equal amount into each orange cup. Garnish with mint sprigs.
Makes 4 servings.

Spiced Pear Salad

6 canned pear halves with 6 tablespoons juice, no sugar added

2 fl oz (60 ml) red wine

¼ cinnamon stick

1 clove

4½ oz (135 g) lettuce, shredded

3 tablespoons mayonnaise

Combine pear juice with wine, cinnamon stick and clove in medium saucepan. Bring to the boil; cook until mixture is reduced to about 2 fl oz (60 ml). Place pear halves in medium bowl. Pour hot juice over pears and chill for several hours, turning fruit occasionally. Drain pears, strain and reserve liquid. Arrange pear halves on shredded lettuce. Combine liquid with mayonnaise and serve over pears as salad dressing. Divide evenly.
Makes 6 servings.

Pineapple Peach Sorbet

1 medium peach, peeled, stoned and quartered

2 slices canned pineapple with 2 tablespoons juice, no sugar added

5 fl oz (150 ml) natural unsweetened yogurt

¼ teaspoon raspberry flavouring

Combine all ingredients in blender container. Blend until smooth. Place in freezer container and freeze until firm, about 20 minutes. Remove from freezer and beat with a hand beater or electric mixer. Refreeze until icy. Divide evenly into 2 dessert glasses.
Makes 2 servings.

Peach Custard

1 slice (1 oz/30 g) currant bread, torn into small pieces

1 medium peach, peeled, stoned and sliced

10 fl oz (300 ml) skim milk

1 egg

½ teaspoon vanilla flavouring

pinch cinnamon

Make a layer of bread in 1-pint (600-ml) baking dish. Arrange peach slices over bread. Combine remaining ingredients in blender container and blend; pour over peach slices and bread. Bake at 325°F, 160°C, Gas Mark 3, for 30 minutes or until custard is set.
Makes 1 morning meal serving.

Strawberry-Orange Water Ice

1¼ lbs (600 g) fresh or frozen strawberries, no sugar added

12 fl oz (360 ml) water

2 tablespoons granulated sugar

2 tablespoons lemon juice

¼ teaspoon orange flavouring, or to taste

Hull and wash strawberries and reduce to a puree in the blender. Gradually add remaining ingredients and continue blending until well mixed. Pour into shallow container and freeze until crystals begin to form. Remove from freezer, turn into a bowl and beat well to break up crystals. Cover, return to freezer until firm. Divide evenly.
Makes 4 servings.

Glazed Strawberries

5 oz (150 g) strawberries

2 teaspoons water

1 teaspoon sugar

½ teaspoon arrowroot

To prepare glaze: crush ⅓ of the strawberries in a small saucepan. Place rest in dessert bowl. Add water, sugar and arrowroot to strawberries in saucepan. Bring to the boil and cook until thickened, about 1 minute. Spoon over strawberries in bowl. Chill thoroughly before serving. *Makes 1 serving.*

Strawberry Divine

5 oz (150 g) strawberries, fresh or frozen, no sugar added

1½ teaspoons unflavoured gelatine

1 tablespoon hot water

1 teaspoon lemon juice

2 drops red food colouring

artifical sweetener to taste

2½ fl oz (75 ml) natural unsweetened yogurt

Reserve 1 strawberry for garnish. Place remainder into blender container; puree. Dissolve gelatine in hot water, add to strawberries with lemon juice and food colouring. Add sweetener to taste. Pour into one tall sundae glass. Leave to set. Add yogurt and garnish with strawberry. Chill and serve. *Makes 1 serving.*

Pineapple Water Ice

1 very ripe small pineapple

8 fl oz (240 ml) water

1 tablespoon lemon juice

Prepare pineapple container according to directions below and set aside; dice pineapple. In medium saucepan combine diced pineapple, water and lemon juice. Cook about 5 minutes. Place in blender container and blend, in 2 batches if necessary, until smooth. Place in freezer container. Freeze until firm. Remove from freezer and beat until fluffy. Spoon into pineapple shell and freeze until ready to serve. Divide evenly. *Makes 4 servings.*

Pineapple Container

Cut off crown about 2 inches (5 cm) from the top and set aside. Hold the fruit upright and with a long, sharp knife remove the pineapple pulp, cutting close to the rind. Don't pierce through the rind, or it will leak.

Red Mary Mix

1 pint 4 fl oz (720 ml) tomato juice

4 teaspoons Worcester sauce

1 teaspoon lime juice

hot sauce to taste

salt and freshly ground pepper to taste

1 lime or lemon, cut into wedges

Combine all ingredients except lime or lemon wedges in cocktail shaker. Shake; divide evenly into 4 glasses, over ice. Garnish each with lime or lemon wedge. *Makes 3 servings.*

Cinnamon Peaches

2 canned peach halves with 2 tablespoons juice, no sugar added

¼ teaspoon lemon juice

¼ cinnamon stick

1 clove

1 teaspoon cornflour dissolved in 1 teaspoon water

1 teaspoon low-fat spread

In shallow grill pan grill peach halves, cut-side up, about 4 inches (10 cm) from source of heat, for 5 minutes or until peaches begin to brown. While peaches are grilling, combine peach juice, lemon juice, cinnamon stick and clove in a small saucepan. Bring to the boil. Reduce heat; simmer for 2 to 3 minutes. Discard cinnamon stick and clove. Add cornflour and cook, stirring, until thickened. Remove from heat, stir in low-fat spread. Divide juice mixture evenly into peach cavities. Grill for 1 minute longer. *Makes 1 serving.*

Rich Fruit Pudding

Serve with Custard or Rum Sauce (see page 172 or page 39)

4 slices (4 oz/120 g) brown bread, made into crumbs
3 oz (90 g) self-raising flour
12 tablespoons natural bran
8 tablespoons raisins
4 tablespoons dried currants
4 tablespoons sultanas
grated rind of 1 lemon
grated rind of 1 orange
2 to 3 teaspoons mixed spice
8 fl oz (240 ml) skim milk
8 teaspoons low-fat spread
2 teaspoons rum flavouring
1 teaspoon gravy browning (use more for darker pudding)
4 oz (120 g) canned carrots, mashed
artificial sweetener to taste

Combine first 9 ingredients in a large basin. Toss thoroughly to distribute mixture evenly throughout. Put skim milk, 8 teaspoons low-fat spread, rum flavouring and gravy browning into a saucepan. Gradually heat milk and stir until all the low-fat spread has melted. Remove from heat and let cool slightly; pour into a blender container and add the carrots and artificial sweetener to taste. Blend until contents are smooth. Pour this mixture onto the dry ingredients and beat thoroughly. Rub 1 teaspoon of low-fat spread around the bottom and sides of a 2-pint (1-litre 200-ml) pudding basin, with clip on lid. Pour mixture into the greased basin; clip on lid and then cover tightly with foil or use greaseproof paper and then foil. Put pudding into the top of a double steamer and cook for 4½ to 5 hours. Allow pudding to stand for at least 5 minutes before turning out. Divide evenly.

Makes 8 servings.

Rich Fruit Pudding

FRUITS

Blackberry Dessert

1¼ lbs (600 g) blackberries

1 tablespoon cornflour

pinch salt

2 fl oz (60 ml) water

3 teaspoons sugar

pinch ground cloves

4 tablespoons low-fat spread

8 slices (8 oz/240 g) currant bread

10 fl oz (300 ml) natural unsweetened yogurt

In medium saucepan toss blackberries with the cornflour and salt. Add water and sugar, simmer, constantly stirring, until blackberries are cooked but still whole (about 5 minutes). Add cloves. Remove from heat and cool slightly. Spread 1½ teaspoons low-fat spread on each slice of bread. Arrange 4 slices, spread side up in 10 x 8 x 2-inch (25 x 20 x 5-cm) serving dish. Spread half the blackberry mixture over bread. Top with remaining 4 slices of bread, fat side up. Spread with remaining blackberry mixture. Cover and refrigerate for several hours or overnight. Serve with yogurt. Divide evenly.
Makes 8 meal servings.

Rhubarb-Strawberry Dessert

1 lb (480 g) rhubarb

10 oz (300 g) strawberries

6 teaspoons sugar

Combine rhubarb and strawberries in 3-pint (1 litre 750 ml) casserole. Cover and bake at 300°F, 150°C, Gas Mark 2, for 1 hour or until rhubarb is tender. Remove from oven; cool. Add sugar; mix well. Chill if desired. Divide evenly.
Makes 4 servings.

Pineapple-Cherry Dessert with Whipped Topping

16 oz (480 g) canned crushed pineapple, no sugar added

8 oz (240 g) frozen, stoned, sweet cherries, no sugar added, partially thawed

¼ teaspoon cherry flavouring

¼ teaspoon pineapple flavouring

2 teaspoons sugar

Whipped Topping (see following recipe)

Place 12 oz (360 g) pineapple in blender container; blend until smooth. Pour into 3-pint (1 litre 750 ml) bowl. Cut all but 6 cherries into quarters over bowl to catch juice. Combine cut cherries and remaining pineapple with pureed pineapple. Stir in flavourings and sugar. Divide evenly into 6 dessert glasses. Top each with 1 serving of Whipped Topping and 1 cherry. Refrigerate or serve immediately.
Makes 4 servings.

Whipped Topping

1 tablespoon unflavoured gelatine

2 fl oz (60 ml) cold water

4 fl oz (120 ml) boiling water

2 oz (60 g) non-fat dry milk

2 teaspoons sugar

½ teaspoon vanilla flavouring

6 to 8 ice cubes

Sprinkle gelatine over cold water in blender container, to soften. Add boiling water. Blend until dissolved. Add remaining ingredients except ice cubes. Blend until smooth. Add ice cubes, one at a time, blending after each addition, until topping sets. Divide evenly.
Makes 4 servings.

Watermelon Froth

3 x 1½-inch (8 x 4-cm) triangle watermelon, seeded and cut into chunks

¼ small pineapple, peeled and diced, or 4 oz (120 g) canned crushed pineapple, no sugar added

3 ice cubes (optional)

2 mint sprigs

Blend fruit in blender container until pureed. If desired, add ice cubes, one at a time, blending after each addition until all ice is crushed. Divide evenly into 2 glasses. Garnish with mint sprigs.
Makes 2 servings.

Banana Dessert

½ medium banana, peeled

2½ fl oz (75 ml) skim milk

artificial sweetener to taste

1 to 2 drops vanilla flavouring

1 teaspoon unflavoured gelatine

2 tablespoons hot water

pinch cinnamon

Place banana, milk, artificial sweetener and vanilla in blender container. Run at low speed until smooth. Dissolve gelatine in hot water, add to contents of blender and run for ½ minute. Pour into a dessert dish. Chill in refrigerator until set. Sprinkle with cinnamon before serving.
Makes 1 serving.

Pineapple with Meringue Topping

8 oz (240 g) canned pineapple chunks, no sugar added

few drops each orange and coconut flavourings

1 egg white

2 teaspoons sugar

¼ teaspoon cream of tartar

pinch salt

Divide pineapple chunks into 2 small oven-to-table casseroles. Sprinkle each with flavourings. In medium bowl beat egg white with sugar, cream of tartar and salt until it stands in peaks. Pile half of mixture on top of each portion of pineapple. Bake at 350°F, 180°C, Gas Mark 4 for 10 to 12 minutes or until topping begins to brown.
Makes 2 servings.

Hot Tomato-Beef Drink

8 fl oz (240 ml) tomato juice

6 fl oz (180 ml) beef stock, made with ½ cube

⅛ teaspoon hot sauce

lemon slices to garnish

In medium saucepan combine tomato juice, stock and hot sauce. Bring to the boil. Serve, evenly divided, in mugs. Garnish with lemon slices.
Makes 2 servings.

Peach Upside Down Cake

8 canned peach halves, no sugar added, with 8 tablespoons juice

4 eggs separated

artificial sweetener to taste

2 slices (2 oz/60 g) white bread made into crumbs

12 teaspoons self-raising flour

Preheat oven to 425°F, 220°C Gas Mark 7. Arrange peach halves in the base of a 7-inch cake tin. Mix the juice, egg yolks, sweetener, breadcrumbs and flour. Beat egg whites until stiff and fold into yolk mixture. Pour over peach halves and bake for 25 minutes or until risen and golden brown. Turn out onto serving dish, divide into 4 equal portions and serve.
Makes 4 midday or evening meal servings. Add protein as required.

Apricot Almond Mousse

12 canned apricot halves with 4 tablespoons juice, no sugar added

1 tablespoon unflavoured gelatine

2 fl oz (60 ml) boiling water

2 oz (60 g) non-fat dry milk

1 teaspoon sugar

1 teaspoon lemon juice

¼ teaspoon almond flavouring

3 to 4 ice cubes

Pour apricot juice into blender container. Sprinkle gelatine over juice and let stand a few minutes to soften. Add boiling water and blend until gelatine is dissolved. Add 10 apricot halves, milk, sugar, lemon juice and flavouring. Blend until combined. Add ice cubes, one at a time, blending after each addition, until smooth. Pour mousse immediately into 2 large dessert dishes, dividing evenly. Garnish each serving with 1 apricot half, diced or sliced.
Makes 2 servings.

FRUITS

Orange Jelly Cream

2 tablespoons unflavoured gelatine

1 pint (600 ml) water, divided

16 fl oz (480 ml) orange juice; no sugar added

1 teaspoon lemon juice

2 oz (60 g) non-fat dry milk

pinch nutmeg (optional)

In saucepan sprinkle gelatine over 8 fl oz (240 ml) water and let stand to soften. Heat, stirring constantly until gelatine is dissolved. Stir in orange juice, 4 fl oz (120 ml) water and lemon juice. Chill until syrupy, but do not allow to set. Meanwhile, mix non-fat dry milk with remaining 8 fl oz (240 ml) water in measuring jug. Turn gelatine mixture into large bowl and whisk, preferably with electric mixer, until light and frothy. Still whisking, gradually add milk. Continue whisking for a few minutes longer. Pour into wetted mould or divide evenly into 4 individual moulds. Chill until set, turn out and sprinkle with nutmeg if desired.

Makes 4 servings.

Apple and Pear Flan
Filling

2 medium cooking apples, peeled, cored and sliced

2 medium pears, peeled, cored and sliced

pinch cinnamon

1 tablespoon cornflour, dissolved in 1 tablespoon water

2 tablespoons low-fat spread

Pastry

4½ oz (135 g) plain flour

4 tablespoons low-fat spread

To Prepare Filling: In medium saucepan combine fruit, cinnamon and enough water to cover; cook over medium heat for 7 minutes. Add cornflour, stirring constantly. Cook until thickened. Remove from heat. Stir in low-fat spread.

To Prepare Pastry: In bowl rub low-fat spread into flour; add enough water to make up to a thick dough. Roll out pastry between 2 sheets of greaseproof paper. Line baking dish with pastry, saving some to make a lattice top for pie.

To Prepare Flan: Fill pastry base with cooked fruit mixture; decorate with pastry lattice. Bake in moderate oven, 375°F, 190°C, Gas Mark 5, until pastry is golden, 30 to 40 minutes. Divide evenly.

Makes 4 servings.

Apple and Pear Flan

VEGETABLES

Hundreds and thousands of edible plants flourish around the world, but only a few kinds are ordinarily used as food. Our section on vegetables includes both popular and less well-known ones. Do, please, try the strange and exotic vegetables which you might be lucky enough to find at your greengrocers. They will cheer up your menu. For the same reason, cook some of those which you normally eat raw— celery, cucumbers, tomato, and, in reverse, try eating raw some of those which are usually cooked, such as broccoli, cauliflower or courgettes.

One serving of raw or cooked vegetables is equal to 3 oz (90 g) and you must have a minimum of 2 servings daily. Don't forget that some vegetables are restricted to 3 oz (90 g) daily and these are listed for you. Corn and potato belong to the Grains section. See page 46. The Avocado Pear, of course, is a forbidden fruit (and vegetable) until you get to goal!

Because vegetables differ so much in nutritional content it is important that you vary your selections. Cook them until barely tender and use the cooking water too, because it contains much of the goodness which has come out of the vegetables.

Women ....2 servings daily (minimum)

Men...2 servings daily (minimum)

Teenagers ....2 servings daily (minimum)

One serving of raw or cooked vegetables is equal to 3 oz (90 g)

The following vegetables are LIMITED to 3 oz (90 g) combined total daily:—

beetroot	parsnips
broad beans	peas
mange tout peas	water chestnuts

In addition you may select appropriate servings of any other vegetables. Do not include vegetables from the Grain section.

Vegetables may be selected at any time. Vary selections.

Courgettes with Lemon Dressing

Courgettes

1 lb (480 g) courgettes, peeled and cut into slices	
salt	

Dressing

2 tablespoons white vinegar

1 tablespoon lemon juice

½ small garlic clove, crushed

½ teaspoon Worcester sauce

½ teaspoon Dijon style mustard

4 tablespoons vegetable oil

2 teaspoons chopped fresh parsley

1 teaspoon chopped chives

salt and freshly ground pepper to taste

To Prepare Courgettes: Put courgettes in a medium saucepan with salted water to cover. Bring to the boil and continue cooking until vegetable is just done and becomes translucent, about 5 minutes. Transfer to colander, pour cold water over courgettes, drain and dry with paper towels.
To Prepare Dressing: Combine vinegar, lemon juice, garlic, Worcester sauce and mustard in a mixing bowl. Mix well with fork or wire whisk. Add oil, a spoonful at a time, stirring constantly. Add parsley, chives and seasoning to taste.
To Serve: Pour dressing over courgettes and chill until ready to serve. Divide evenly.
Makes 4 servings.

Chilled Summer Soup

1½ oz (45 g) green pepper, seeded and chopped

1 oz (30 g) onion, chopped

3 oz (90 g) tomato, skinned and chopped

1½ oz (45 g) red pepper, seeded and chopped

½ garlic clove, crushed

1 teaspoon vegetable oil

1 teaspoon cider vinegar

salt and pepper to taste

Reserve 1 tablespoon each green pepper and onion. Combine remaining vegetables and garlic in blender container with a little water and puree until smooth. Pour into serving bowl and add oil and vinegar; add salt and pepper and stir. Chill well and garnish with the reserved vegetables.
Makes 1 serving.

Minty Spring Salad

6 oz (180 g) green beans, blanched

3 oz (90 g) tomato, quartered

2½ fl oz (75 ml) natural unsweetened yogurt

1½ oz (45 g) carrot, grated

1 oz (30 g) spring onion, chopped

2 teaspoons chopped fresh mint

½ garlic clove, chopped (optional)

pinch each salt and pepper

lettuce leaves

In a bowl combine all ingredients except lettuce. Toss to combine. Let stand for 15 minutes. Serve on lettuce leaves. Divide evenly.
Makes 2 servings.

Ratatouille

8 oz (240 g) courgettes, cut into ¼-inch (5-mm) thick slices

6 oz (180 g) onions, sliced

6 oz (180 g) green pepper, seeded and cut into ½-inch (1-cm) dice

4 oz (120 g) aubergine, peeled and cut into ½-inch (1-cm) dice

1 teaspoon chicken stock powder

1 garlic clove, crushed

8 oz (240 g) canned tomatoes, coarsely chopped

4 tablespoons tomato puree, mixed with 4 fl oz (120 ml) water

1 teaspoon basil

1 teaspoon oregano

salt and freshly ground pepper to taste

Combine first 6 ingredients in saucepan; cook for 5 minutes. Add all remaining ingredients and cook over medium heat, stirring often, for about 1¼ hours or until vegetables are tender. Divide evenly.
Makes 4 servings.

VEGETABLES

Sauteed Vegetable Mix

4 teaspoons vegetable oil

8 oz (240 g) bean sprouts

5 oz (150 g) cabbage, shredded

4 oz (120 g) celery, sliced diagonally

4 oz (120 g) drained canned water chestnuts, sliced

2 oz (60 g) spring onions, finely chopped

8 fl oz (240 ml) chicken stock, made with 1 stock cube

2 tablespoons soy sauce

½ teaspoon dry mustard, dissolved in 1 tablespoon water (optional)

Heat oil in non-stick frying pan; add next 5 ingredients and saute for 3 minutes. Add stock and simmer, stirring often, until most of the liquid has evaporated. Stir in soy sauce and mustard if desired. Divide evenly.
Makes 4 servings.

Spinach and Mushroom Salad

4 oz (120 g) spinach leaves, thoroughly washed, dried and cut into bite-size pieces (discard tough stems)

1½ oz (45 g) sliced mushrooms

1 tablespoon vegetable oil

2 teaspoons wine vinegar

1 teaspoon Dijon-style mustard

1 garlic clove, crushed

Place spinach leaves and mushrooms in medium bowl. In small bowl combine oil, vinegar, mustard and garlic; add to vegetables and toss.
Makes 1 serving.

Hearty Vegetable Soup

6 oz (180 g) courgettes, sliced

4 oz (120 g) celery, sliced

4 oz (120 g) carrots, sliced

4 oz (120 g) spring onions or onions, trimmed and diced

3 oz (90 g) cabbage, shredded, or cauliflower, coarsely chopped

4 teaspoons chicken stock powder

1 garlic clove, crushed

1¾ pints (1 litre) water

3 tablespoons tomato puree, mixed with 4 fl oz (120 ml) water

½ teaspoon basil

¼ teaspoon thyme

2 peppercorns, crushed

8 oz (240 g) cooked elbow macaroni

In large saucepan combine courgettes, celery, carrots, spring onions, cabbage, stock powder and garlic. Simmer for 3 to 5 minutes over medium heat, stirring occasionally. Add all remaining ingredients except macaroni. Bring to the boil; cover. Reduce heat and simmer for 20 minutes or until vegetables are tender. Stir in macaroni; cook until thoroughly heated. Divide evenly.
Makes 4 servings.

Hearty Vegetable Soup

VEGETABLES

Grecian Style Vegetables with French Dressing

Vegetables

2 pints (1 litre 200 ml) water

4 fl oz (120 ml) lemon juice

1 teaspoon salt

½ teaspoon thyme

½ teaspoon rosemary

½ teaspoon savory

10 peppercorns

2 garlic cloves, crushed

1 bay leaf

12 oz (360 g) vegetables (cauliflower, carrots, celery, green beans, broccoli etc.)

Dressing

4 tablespoons vegetable oil

2 fl oz (60 ml) red wine vinegar or tarragon vinegar

¼ teaspoon salt

pinch white pepper

To Prepare Vegetables: In saucepan combine first 9 ingredients and simmer for 15 minutes. Add vegetables, return water to the boil, reduce heat and simmer until vegetables are tender-crisp. Allow vegetables to cool in liquid; drain. Toss vegetables with dressing. Chill. Divide evenly.

To Prepare Dressing: Combine all ingredients in a jar with tight-fitting cover. Shake vigorously before using.

Makes 4 servings.

Chili Mushrooms

1 lb (480 g) mushrooms

3 small dried chili peppers, chopped, or ½ teaspoon ground red pepper

2½ fl oz (75 ml) chicken stock, made with ¼ stock cube

salt to taste

Wipe mushrooms clean. Slice them through stems and caps and brown in non-stick frying pan over moderate heat; add chopped chili peppers and cook with mushrooms, stirring often, for about 1 minute. Pour in chicken stock and salt to taste. Simmer, uncovered, for 3 to 4 minutes, and serve hot. Divide evenly.

Makes 8 servings.

Mushroom Casserole

3 oz (90 g) mushrooms, sliced

2 oz (60 g) tomato, skinned and sliced

2 oz (60 g) onion, cut into rings

1 oz (30 g) celery, chopped

seasoning to taste

1 teaspoon chopped fresh parsley

2 tablespoons chicken stock, made with ¼ stock cube

Fill a casserole with alternate layers of mushrooms, tomato, onion and celery, reserving some mushrooms. Season each layer well, and finish with a layer of reserved mushrooms. Sprinkle with parsley, add liquid and bake in oven, 350°F, 180°C, Gas Mark 4, until tender—about ½ hour.

Pack the vegetables closely to allow for shrinkage whilst cooking.

Makes 1 serving.

'Hot' Cauliflower and Pepper Salad

6 oz (180 g) cos lettuce

6 oz (180 g) cauliflower florets, thinly sliced

6 oz (180 g) green pepper, seeded and cubed

2 tablespoons vegetable oil

1 tablespoon plus 1 teaspoon chili sauce

1 tablespoon lemon juice or red wine vinegar

1 tablespoon water

½ teaspoon grated horseradish

pinch each salt and ground red pepper

Separate lettuce leaves, wash and dry well. Stack leaves and cut crosswise to make ¼ (5-mm) to ½-inch (1-cm) shreds. Place in large salad bowl; add cauliflower and green pepper. Combine all remaining ingredients in small jar with tightly fitting lid; cover and shake well. Pour over vegetables; toss to combine. Divide evenly.

Makes 4 servings.

Brussels Sprouts with Basil and Tarragon Dressing

1 lb (480 g) Brussels sprouts

salt to taste

2 fl oz (60 ml) chicken stock made with ¼ stock cube, hot

4 teaspoons margarine

1 tablespoon chopped fresh basil or ½ teaspoon dried

pinch tarragon

Wash Brussels sprouts in cold salted water. Remove wilted leaves if necessary. Cut a cross in stem ends. Place in saucepan and cover with boiling water; add salt and bring to the boil. Simmer, uncovered, for 10 to 12 minutes, or until just tender. Drain. Combine hot stock, margarine, basil and tarragon and pour over Brussels sprouts. Divide evenly.
Makes 4 servings.

Tomato, Cauliflower and Tarragon Soup

3 oz (90 g) onion, chopped

15 fl oz (450 ml) water (preferably water left over from cooking vegetables)

8 oz (240 g) cauliflower pieces

7 oz (210 g) canned tomatoes

4 teaspoons white wine

1 teaspoon dried tarragon

seasoning to taste

artificial sweetener to taste (optional)

'Sweat' onion in a little vegetable water for 5 minutes. Add all remaining ingredients. Bring to the boil for 45 minutes. Rub through sieve or liquidise. Correct seasoning and add a little artificial sweetener if desired. Divide evenly.
Makes 2 servings.

Crisp Cheesed Beans

12 oz (360 g) tomatoes

4 oz (120 g) onions, thinly sliced

parsley and thyme sprigs

1 bay leaf

artificial sweetener to taste

salt and pepper to taste

12 oz (360 g) French beans, sliced

4 oz (120 g) hard cheese, grated

Dip tomatoes in boiling water, drain and skin. Coarsely chop tomatoes and place in saucepan with onion, herbs, sweetener and seasoning. Cook gently until tender. Rub mixture through sieve. Reheat gently. Cook beans in boiling, salted water for 6 to 8 minutes or until tender but still crisp. Drain and mix with tomato sauce. Place in a heatproof serving dish and cover with grated cheese. If desired, place under grill for 1 minute before serving. Divide evenly.
Makes 2 midday or evening meal servings.

Vegetable Soup

1½ oz (45 g) celery, diced

1½ oz (45 g) carrot, sliced

1 oz (30 g) onion, diced

½ beef stock cube

pinch basil

pinch oregano

pinch garlic powder

10 fl oz (300 ml) water

1½ oz (45 g) green beans, cut into chunks

1 tablespoon tomato puree

In saucepan combine first 7 ingredients and cook for 5 minutes, stirring frequently. Add remaining ingredients and bring to the boil. Reduce heat and simmer for 40 minutes.
Makes 1 serving.

Fresh Bean Salad

12 oz (360 g) fresh runner beans

6 oz (180 g) celery, diced

6 oz (180 g) green pepper, seeded and chopped

6 oz (180 g) pickled cucumbers, chopped

6 oz (180 g) fresh cucumber, sliced

3 tablespoons tarragon vinegar

3 tablespoons white wine vinegar

½ teaspoon dried onion flakes

artificial sweetener to taste

freshly ground pepper to taste

Mix all ingredients except sweetener and pepper in a large bowl, season well. Cover and chill overnight in refrigerator. Divide evenly.
Makes 4 servings.

VEGETABLES

Creamy Cucumber Soup

1 lb 2 oz (540 g) cucumbers

salt to taste

4 tablespoons margarine

2 tablespoons flour

1 pint (600 ml) hot skim milk

¼ teaspoon dill weed

18 fl oz (540 ml) chicken stock, made with 1 stock cube

¼ teaspoon white pepper

chopped chives to garnish

Cut half of one cucumber into 6 even slices. Reserve for garnish. Peel, seed and grate remaining cucumbers. Sprinkle with salt and let stand for 20 minutes. Drain and set aside. In non-stick saucepan melt margarine, stir in flour and simmer for 5 minutes. Add milk, dill and grated cucumber. Simmer for 30 more minutes. Remove from heat; allow to cool, then place in blender container and blend until smooth. Transfer to bowl and add stock, salt and pepper. Refrigerate for 3 hours or until well chilled. Stir; divide evenly into 4 bowls. Garnish each with chives and one cucumber slice.
Makes 4 servings.

Hot Cucumber and Orange Salad

1½ lbs (720 g) cucumbers

4 fl oz (120 ml) orange juice, no sugar added

1 tablespoon grated orange rind

¼ teaspoon salt

⅛ teaspoon freshly ground pepper

4 teaspoons margarine

Peel cucumbers. Cut a thin slice off both ends of each cucumber. Score each lengthwise with a fork on all sides and cut into ½-inch (1-cm) slices. In saucepan cover slices with water; cook for 15 minutes. Drain cucumbers and set aside. In small saucepan combine orange juice, rind, salt and pepper. Heat and add to cooked cucumber slices. Stir in margarine. Serve as a vegetable. Divide evenly.
Makes 4 servings.

Mushroom Starter

3 oz (90 g) mushrooms, quartered

1½ teaspoons lemon juice

1 tablespoon low-fat spread

½ teaspoon paprika

1 oz (30 g) onion, chopped

2 teaspoons flour

4 fl oz (120 ml) skim milk

⅛ teaspoon salt

1 slice (1 oz/30 g) white bread, toasted

In a medium saucepan combine mushrooms and lemon juice. Add boiling water to cover and simmer for 3 minutes. Drain mushrooms and set aside. In a non-stick saucepan melt low-fat spread. Add paprika and then onion; saute until onion is tender. Add flour and stir to combine. Gradually stir in milk. Cook, stirring constantly, until sauce thickens. Add salt and mushrooms. Serve on the toast.
Makes 1 serving.

Baked Aubergine Casserole

2 lbs (960 g) aubergines, peeled and cut into 1-inch (2.5-cm) slices

2 tablespoons salt

6 oz (180 g) onion, sliced

1 lb (480 g) tomatoes, peeled and sliced

1 lb 2 oz (540 g) green peppers, seeded and cut into ¼-inch (5-mm) thick slices

½ oz (15 g) chopped fresh parsley

2 garlic cloves, crushed

6 tablespoons tomato puree, mixed with 6 fl oz (180 ml) water

Sprinkle aubergines with salt and let stand for 20 minutes. Rinse, drain and dry with paper towels. In a large casserole make layers using half of each ingredient, in order given, beginning with aubergines. Repeat layers using remaining ingredients. Bake at 425°F, 220°C, Gas Mark 7, for 40 minutes or until vegetables are soft. Divide evenly.
Makes 6 servings.

Baked Aubergine Casserole

VEGETABLES

Gazpacho

8 oz (240 g) tomatoes, chopped

3 oz (90 g) cucumber, peeled and chopped

3 oz (90 g) green pepper, seeded and chopped

1 oz (30 g) onion, diced

½ slice (½ oz/15 g) white bread, torn into pieces (optional)

3 tablespoons water

1 tablespoon vegetable oil

2 teaspoons red wine vinegar

½ teaspoon chili powder, or to taste

1 garlic clove

pinch cumin

salt and pepper to taste

Combine all ingredients in blender container; blend to desired consistency. Add more water to adjust consistency if necessary. Chill. Divide evenly.
Makes 2 servings.

Summer Salad

2½ fl oz (45 ml) natural unsweetened yogurt

1 oz (30 g) grated carrot

1 oz (30 g) minced spring onion

1 teaspoon chopped fresh dill

pinch minced fresh garlic

pinch each salt and pepper

1½ oz (45 g) celery, sliced into 1-inch (2.5-cm) pieces

1½ oz (45 g) green beans, blanched

1½ oz (45 g) tomatoes, quartered

lettuce leaves

In a bowl combine the first 6 ingredients and mix well. Add remaining ingredients, except lettuce, and toss to combine. Serve on lettuce leaves.
Makes 1 serving.

Buffet Tomatoes

4 x 3 oz (90 g) tomatoes

4 oz (120 g) onions, minced

1 tablespoon chopped fresh parsley

2 tablespoons vegetable oil

2 tablespoons cider vinegar

¼ teaspoon pepper

¼ teaspoon salt

1 teaspoon dry mustard

artificial sweetener to taste

Halve tomatoes and arrange on a serving dish. Mix onion and parsley and place an equal portion on top of each tomato half. Combine remaining ingredients and spoon ⅛ of mixture over each tomato half.
Makes 4 servings. 2 tomato halves each.

Lemon Carrot Soup

1 lb (480 g) carrots

4 oz (120 g) onions, chopped

1½ pints (900 ml) beef or chicken stock, made with 2 stock cubes

pepper to taste

grated rind of 1 lemon

1 tablepoon lemon juice

lemon slices and parsley sprigs for garnish

In non-stick saucepan gently cook carrots and onions together until onions start to soften. Add stock, pepper and lemon rind. Bring soup to the boil, partially cover and simmer for 30 minutes or until carrots and onions are soft; let cool slightly. Blend soup in blender container and then re-heat with the lemon juice. Adjust seasoning. Divide evenly and serve garnished with slices of lemon and parsley sprigs.
Makes 4 servings.

Swede and Potato Mash

3 oz (90 g) peeled cooked swede, mashed

3 oz (90 g) peeled cooked potato, mashed

1 teaspoon margarine

Combine swede and potato in saucepan and heat. Remove from heat, add margarine and serve.
Makes 1 serving.

Tomato and Orange Salad

3 oz (90 g) tomato, sliced

1 medium orange, peeled and sliced

2 oz (60 g) spring onions, finely chopped

1 tablespoon chopped fresh parsley

2 teaspoons vegetable oil

2 teaspoons wine vinegar

artificial sweetener to taste

salt and pepper to taste

Place sliced tomato and orange in a bowl; sprinkle with onions and parsley. Combine the rest of the ingredients in a small bowl and pour over orange and tomato; toss to mix. Chill and serve.
Makes 1 serving.

Chinese Asparagus Salad

6 asparagus spears, approximately 3 oz (90 g)

1 tablespoon water

2 teaspoons soy sauce

2 teaspoons cider vinegar

1 teaspoon sesame oil

shredded lettuce

In saucepan or perforated steamer, steam asparagus for approximately 12 minutes or until tender. In a shallow dish combine water, soy sauce, vinegar and oil; add asparagus and marinate for 1 hour in refrigerator, turning occasionally. Serve asparagus and marinade over shredded lettuce.
Makes 1 serving.

Mushroom and Celery Soup

15 oz (450 g) canned celery hearts, reserve liquid

1 pint (600 ml) beef stock, made with 1 stock cube

3 oz (90 g) button mushrooms, sliced

2 teaspoons paprika

¼ teaspoon dried tarragon

salt and pepper to taste

Place celery hearts and can liquid in blender container and blend at high speed until smooth. (Alternatively, mash very well with a fork.) In saucepan combine stock, mushrooms, paprika, tarragon, salt and pepper and simmer until mushrooms are tender. Add blended celery hearts and bring to the boil; reduce heat and simmer for 2 to 3 minutes. Adjust seasonings. Divide into 4 equal portions and serve hot.
Makes 4 servings.

Split Pea Soup

2 oz (60 g) onion, chopped

2 oz (60 g) celery, diced

2 oz (60 g) carrot, chopped

15 fl oz (450 ml) chicken stock, made with 1 stock cube

3 oz (90 g) cooked split peas

1½ oz (45 g) diced cooked ham

pepper to taste

Place onion, celery and carrot in saucepan with stock and simmer until celery and carrot are tender but still crisp. Add peas, ham and pepper to taste and cook until thoroughly heated, about 5 minutes more. Serve piping hot.
Makes 1 midday or evening meal serving.

Pickled Mushrooms

8 oz (240 g) button mushrooms

10 fl oz (300 ml) cider vinegar

½ teaspoon salt

½ teaspoon celery salt

¼ teaspoon dried onion flakes

1 parsley sprig

1 bay leaf

6 peppercorns

Wash mushrooms and discard stems; place caps in bowl and set aside. In saucepan combine all other ingredients and boil for 10 minutes. Pour over mushroom caps and let cool. When cool, transfer to a jar, cover tightly and shake well. Refrigerate for at least 24 hours before using. Drain off liquid before serving. Divide evenly.
Makes 2 servings.

VEGETABLES

Chilled Beetroot Soup

6 oz (180 g) drained canned beetroot, with 2 fl oz (60 ml) liquid

12 fl oz (360 ml) beef or chicken stock, made with 2 stock cubes

1 teaspoon lemon juice

10 fl oz (300 ml) natural unsweetened yogurt

3 oz (90 g) cucumber, peeled and diced

2 lemon wedges

Combine beetroot with liquid, stock, and lemon juice in blender container and blend until smooth. Chill. Before serving, stir in 5 fl oz (150 ml) of yogurt and cucumber. Serve with additional yogurt on the side and garnish with lemon wedges. Divide evenly.
Makes 2 servings.

Mixed Vegetable Salad

4 oz (120 g) tomato, diced

2½ oz (75 g) cooked green beans

2½ oz (75 g) cooked mushrooms

2 oz (60 g) carrot sticks

1 tablespoon vegetable oil

1 tablespoon red wine vinegar

1 teaspoon tarragon

1 teaspoon Worcester sauce

1 teaspoon chopped fresh parsley

½ teaspoon sugar

salt and pepper to taste

Arrange tomatoes, green beans, mushrooms and carrots on a serving plate. In a small bowl combine remaining ingredients. Pour over salad.
Makes 1 serving.

Onion Soup

12 oz (375 g) Spanish onions, thinly sliced

1 pint 16 fl oz (1 litre 80 ml) beef stock, made with 4 stock cubes

1 teaspoon Worcester sauce

pinch each celery salt and pepper

4 slices (4 oz/120 g) white bread, toasted

4 oz (120 g) hard cheese, grated

Combine all ingredients except toast and cheese in large saucepan. Cover and bring to the boil. Reduce heat and simmer for 20 minutes or until onions are soft. Cover each slice of bread with 1 oz (30 g) grated cheese and grill until golden and bubbly. Divide soup equally between 4 large soup bowls and top each with 1 slice toasted cheese.
Makes 4 midday or evening meal servings. Add protein as required.

Onion Soup

VEGETABLES

Baked Leek Special

3 oz (90 g) leeks

1 teaspoon margarine

2 teaspoons flour

¼ teaspoon nutmeg

1½ oz (45 g) thinly sliced boiled ham

3 oz (90 g) potato, baked or boiled in skin, sliced

1 oz (30 g) Swiss cheese, grated

Preheat oven to 350°F, 180°C, Gas Mark 4. Wash leeks thoroughly, cut into 4 to 5-inch (10 to 12-cm) lengths. Boil in salted water for about 5 minutes, or until tender. Drain and reserve liquid. Melt margarine in non-stick saucepan and stir in flour. Add 6 fl oz (180 ml) cooking liquid from leeks and cook until thickened, stirring occasionally. Add nutmeg. Wrap boiled ham round leeks and place in oven-proof dish. Cover with potatoes, then with sauce and sprinkle with grated cheese. Bake in oven for 15 to 20 minutes.
Makes 1 midday or evening meal serving.

Sweet-Sour Red Cabbage with Apple

1 lb 2 oz (540 g) red cabbage, shredded

12 fl oz (360 ml) water

3 fl oz (90 ml) cider vinegar

artificial sweetener to taste

1 teaspoon lemon juice

1 teaspoon caraway seeds

3 medium apples, peeled, cored and sliced

In a saucepan combine all ingredients except apples. Cover and cook over medium heat for 20 minutes. Add apples and cook for 30 minutes longer. Divide evenly.
Makes 6 servings.

Spiced Beetroot

6 oz (180 g) cooked beetroot, thinly sliced

2½ fl oz (75 ml) cider vinegar

2 bay leaves

2 teaspoons pickling spice

½ teaspoon salt

pepper to taste

Place beetroot in serving dish and set aside. Combine remaining ingredients in small saucepan; bring to the boil. Strain vinegar mixture over beetroot. Garnish with bay leaves. Serve immediately or chill. Divide evenly.
Makes 2 servings.

'Cream' of Mushroom Soup

1 pint 4 fl oz (720 ml) water

4 teaspoons chicken stock powder

6 oz (180 g) mushrooms, finely chopped

1 tablespoon dried onion flakes

¼ teaspoon chopped fresh dill

2 oz (60 g) non-fat dry milk, reconstituted with 8 fl oz (240 ml) water

1 teaspoon Worcester sauce, or to taste

salt and white pepper to taste

Combine water, stock powder, 4½ oz (135 g) of the mushrooms, onion flakes and dill in a saucepan. Simmer for 10 minutes; let cool slightly. Transfer to blender container; blend until smooth. Return to saucepan, add remaining ingredients. Heat thoroughly. Do not boil. Divide evenly.
Makes 4 servings.

Thick Carrot Soup

8 fl oz (240 ml) chicken stock, made with ½ stock cube

6 oz (180 g) sliced carrots

1½ oz (45 g) sliced celery

1 oz (30 g) diced onion or 2 teaspoons dried onion flakes

1 oz (30 g) non-fat dry milk, reconstituted with 5 fl oz (150 ml) water

2 fl oz (60 ml) water

1 parsley or thyme sprig, chopped, or ⅛ teaspoon dried

freshly ground pepper to taste

Heat stock, carrots, celery and onion to boiling in a medium

saucepan. Reduce heat, cover and simmer until carrots are tender; let cool slightly. Place in blender container and blend at medium speed until smooth. Return to saucepan, stir in milk and water and heat. Sprinkle top with parsley and freshly ground pepper. Divide evenly.
Makes 2 servings.

Mushroom Relish

2 tablespoons vegetable oil

1 tablespoon red wine vinegar

1 tablespoon Dijon-style mustard

1½ teaspoons chopped fresh parsley

½ garlic clove, crushed

½ teaspoon sugar

1 tablespoon chopped chives

salt and pepper to taste

12 oz (360 g) drained canned sliced mushrooms

In medium bowl combine oil, vinegar, mustard, parsley, garlic, sugar, chives, salt and pepper; mix well. Add mushrooms and let marinate overnight. Divide evenly.
Makes 4 servings.

Baked Vegetable Rice

2 oz (60 g) cooked rice

1½ oz (45 g) diced courgette

1½ oz (45 g) green beans, sliced

1½ oz (45 g) carrot, sliced

1½ oz (45 g) cooked broccoli, cut into pieces

2 fl oz (60 ml) boiling water

½ chicken stock cube

pinch chopped mint

pinch garlic powder

2 teaspoons margarine

In ½-pint (300-ml) casserole mix rice, courgette, green beans, carrot and broccoli. In small cup combine boiling water, stock cube, mint and garlic powder; stir until dissolved. Pour over rice mixture, dot with margarine and bake in oven, 325°F, 160°C, Gas Mark 3, for half an hour.
Makes 1 serving.

Broad Bean Soup

16 fl oz (480 ml) chicken stock made with 1 stock cube

3 oz (90 g) cooked fresh broad beans, reserve cooking liquid

2 oz (60 g) finely chopped carrot

1½ oz (45 g) green pepper, finely chopped

1 oz (30 g) chopped celery

1 oz (30 g) onion, chopped

pinch basil

pinch thyme

½ oz (15 g) non-fat dry milk, reconstituted with 2½ fl oz (75 ml) water

salt and pepper to taste

Place stock and beans (with liquid) in blender container. Blend until smooth. Pour into saucepan; add carrot, pepper, celery, onion and herbs. Simmer for 20 minutes or until vegetables are tender. Add milk; reheat (do not boil). Season to taste and serve.
Makes 1 serving.

Chicory-Radish Salad

2 teaspoons vegetable oil

2 teaspoons lemon juice

½ teaspoon water

pinch chopped fresh dill

pinch garlic powder

1½ oz (45 g) lettuce leaves

3 oz (90 g) chicory, cut into ¾-inch (2-cm) pieces

3 oz (90 g) radishes, sliced

1 oz (30 g) onion rings, quartered

freshly ground pepper to taste

Combine first 5 ingredients in small jar. Cover, shake vigorously and place in refrigerator. Line salad bowl with lettuce leaves. In another bowl combine rest of vegetables and pour over chilled dressing. Toss well to thoroughly coat vegetables and transfer to other bowl with lettuce; season to taste.
Makes 1 serving.

VEGETABLES

Spanish Salad

4 tablespoon vegetable oil

4 tablespoon wine vinegar

¼ teaspoon pepper

12 oz (360 g) cucumber, peeled, seeded and diced

salt to taste

2 lbs 4 oz (1 kg 80 g) green peppers, seeded and cut into quarters

6 oz (180 g) tomatoes, peeled, seeded and diced

½ garlic clove (optional)

1 tablespoon dried onion flakes, reconstituted

In small bowl mix oil, vinegar and pepper for a dressing and set aside. Place diced cucumber in bowl, sprinkle with salt and let stand for 20 minutes. Liquid will accumulate. Drain and dry on paper towels. Remove to small bowl and toss with half the dressing. Grill pepper 4 inches (10 cm) from source of heat until skin browns and puckers, about 15 minutes. Watch carefully. Skin will look burnt when peppers are ready. Peel skin and dice peppers. Place in small bowl, sprinkle with salt and let stand for 15 minutes. Place tomatoes in separate bowl, sprinkle with salt and let stand for 15 minutes also. Drain peppers and toss with remaining dressing. Drain tomatoes. Rub salad bowl with garlic if desired. Place cucumbers, green peppers, tomatoes and onion flakes in salad bowl and toss lightly; chill. Divide evenly.
Makes 8 servings.

Courgette Salad

Vegetables

12 oz (360 g) courgettes, thinly sliced

8 oz (240 g) tomatoes, cut into wedges

3 oz (90 g) mushrooms, thinly sliced

4 oz (120 g) onion, thinly sliced

1 medium head lettuce

Dressing

4 tablespoons vegetable oil

2 fl oz (60 ml) red wine vinegar or tarragon vinegar

¼ teaspoon salt

pinch white pepper

To Prepare Salad: In bowl combine all vegetables except lettuce. Arrange lettuce on serving dish. Top with vegetable mixture. Serve with dressing. Divide evenly.
Makes 4 servings.

To Prepare Dressing: Combine all ingredients in jar with tight-fitting cover. Cover and shake vigorously before using.

Courgette Salad

VEGETABLES

Bean Sprout Curry

2 tablespoons vegetable oil

1 medium apple, peeled and diced

4 oz (120 g) celery, diced

4 oz (120 g) onion, finely diced

2 teaspoons chicken stock powder

2 teaspooons curry powder

12 fl oz (360 ml) hot water

6 tablespoons raisins

12 oz (360 g) bean sprouts

2 tablespoons cornflour, dissolved in 2 tablespoons water

Heat oil in non-stick frying pan; add apple, celery, onions, stock powder and curry powder. Saute over medium heat, stirring frequently, until onions are translucent. Add water and raisins. Bring to the boil; reduce heat and simmer for 15 minutes. Add bean sprouts and cook for 5 minutes or until vegetables are tender-crisp. Stir in cornflour; simmer, stirring constantly, until thickened. Divide evenly.
Makes 4 servings.

Stir-Fried Broccoli and Water Chestnuts

1½ lbs (720 g) broccoli

4 teaspoons vegetable oil

4 oz (120 g) drained canned water chestnuts, sliced

2 fl oz (60 ml) chicken stock, made with ¼ stock cube

2 tablespoons soy sauce

1 garlic clove, crushed

Cut broccoli into florets and cut stems into pieces about the same size as the florets. Place in large saucepan; cover with water. Bring to the boil; reduce heat and simmer for about 3 minutes. Drain. In a wok or large non-stick frying pan heat oil and saute broccoli and water chestnuts until tender-crisp. Add stock, soy sauce and garlic. Cook, stirring, for 2 minutes. Divide evenly.
Makes 4 servings.

Broccoli and Potato Soup

12 fl oz (360 ml) chicken stock, made with 2 stock cubes

6 oz (180 g) broccoli, cut up

3 oz (90 g) peeled potato, diced

1 oz (30 g) onion, sliced

Combine all ingredients in saucepan; cover and cook until potato is tender. Allow to cool, then place in blender container and puree. Reheat and serve. Divide evenly.
Makes 2 servings.

Vegetable and Fish Soup

10 fl oz (300 ml) stock, made with 1 stock cube

4 fl oz (120 ml) tomato juice

4 oz (120 g) onions, coarsely chopped

3 oz (90 g) mushrooms, sliced

1½ oz (45 g) fennel, sliced

2 garlic cloves, chopped

1 bay leaf

3 oz (90 g) any boned firm white fish, cut into chunks

2 oz (60 g) peeled prawns

2 tablespoons chopped fresh parsley

squeeze lemon juice

1 slice (1 oz/30 g) bread

Place stock in saucepan with tomato juice, onions, mushrooms, fennel, garlic and bay leaf and simmer until vegetables are tender. Add fish and prawns. When fish is cooked, add chopped parsley. Pour into soup bowl and serve with a squeeze of lemon juice and slice of bread.
Makes 1 midday or evening meal serving.

Watercress Roulade with Vegetable Filling

Filling

1 oz (30 g) onion, roughly chopped

1 oz (30 g) mushrooms, sliced

salt to taste

3 oz (90 g) canned tomatoes

2 teaspoons tomato puree

pepper and artifical sweetener to taste

Roulade

½ bunch of watercress

2 teaspoons chopped fresh parsley

2 eggs, separated

salt and pepper to taste

Garnish

3 oz (90 g) tomato, cut into wedges

To Prepare Filling: In non-stick saucepan, combine onion, mushrooms and salt and dry-fry gently for a few minutes. Add canned tomatoes and break up well with a wooden spoon. Stir in tomato puree, sweetener and pepper. Bring to the boil and boil rapidly for about 10 minutes, until well reduced and pulpy.
To Prepare Roulade: Line a non-stick swiss roll tin, 7 inches x 11 inches (18 x 28 cm), with non-stick silicone paper sprayed with non-stick cooking spray. Wash watercress; pat dry on kitchen paper, trim feathery stalks, then chop finely. Place in a bowl and add parsley. Place egg yolks in bowl with watercress. Beat well and season lightly. Whisk egg white until stiff and fold in lightly with a metal spoon. Turn into prepared tin and smooth surface. Cook, near top of oven, 400°F, 200°C, Gas Mark 6, for 8 to 10 minutes, until lightly golden and firm to the touch.
To Serve: Turn Roulade onto a clean sheet of greaseproof paper and carefully remove paper from base of Roulade. Spread tomato mixture over Roulade and roll up swiss roll fashion. Serve warm or cold in slices, with tomato wedges.
Makes 1 midday or evening meal serving.

Three-Bean Salad

4 tablespoons vegetable oil

2 fl oz (60 ml) cider vinegar

4 teaspoons tomato puree, mixed with 2 tablespoons water

1 tablespoon chopped fresh parsley

1 tablespoon chopped chives

1 teaspoon sugar

1 teaspoon tarragon

⅛ teaspoon garlic powder

8 oz (240 g) cooked young broad beans

12 oz (360 g) cooked cut French beans

12 oz (360 g) cooked cut runner beans

salt and white pepper to taste

In large bowl combine oil, vinegar, tomato puree, parsley, chives, sugar, tarragon and garlic powder. Add beans, salt and pepper; toss lightly. Chill lightly before serving. Divide evenly.
Makes 4 servings.

Baked Stuffed Mushrooms Florentine

8 oz (240 g) large mushrooms

6 oz (180 g) cooked spinach, chopped

2 teaspoons dried onion flakes, reconstituted in 1 tablespoon water

2 teaspoons vegetable oil

½ teaspoon chicken stock powder

½ teaspoon Worcester sauce

salt and pepper to taste

Wash mushrooms. Remove and finely chop stems; reserve caps. In bowl combine chopped stems and remaining ingredients. Stuff mushroom caps with spinach mixture. Place mushrooms, stuffed side up, in an 8 x 8-inch (20 x 20-cm) baking tin; cover. Bake at 375°F, 190°C, Gas Mark 5, for 10 minutes. Remove cover, bake for 10 minutes longer or until mushrooms are tender. Divide evenly.
Makes 4 servings.

VEGETABLES

Creamy Cole Slaw

1 lb (480 g) shredded cabbage

8 oz (240 g) carrots, grated

5 fl oz (150 ml) natural unsweetened yogurt

4 tablespoons mayonnaise

1 teaspoon sugar

½ teaspoon salt

¼ teaspoon onion powder

¼ teaspoon dried onion flakes

⅛ teaspoon celery seed

pinch white pepper

In large bowl combine cabbage and carrots. In small bowl combine remaining ingredients. Pour over cabbage mixture. Toss lightly. Chill. Divide evenly.
Makes 4 servings.

Sauerkraut with Sultanas

12 oz (360 g) canned sauerkraut, rinsed

6 fl oz (180 ml) chicken stock, made with 1 stock cube

4 oz (120 g) onions, finely chopped

8 tablespoons sultanas

pinch white pepper

Combine sauerkraut, stock and onions in a medium saucepan. Bring to the boil; reduce heat and simmer for 20 minutes or until onions are tender. Add sultanas; cook about 10 minutes longer or until most of the liquid has evaporated. Season with pepper. Divide evenly.
Makes 4 servings.

'Squeak and Bubble'

3 oz (90 g) peeled potato, mashed

1½ oz (45 g) cooked cabbage, chopped

1½ oz (45 g) cooked carrot, diced

2 pinches freshly ground nutmeg

2½ fl oz (75 ml) natural unsweetened yogurt

½ teaspoon chopped fresh parsley

½ teaspoon finely chopped chives

salt and pepper to taste

Combine potato, cabbage, carrot and nutmeg in a bowl and let stand for half an hour. Mix yogurt, parsley and chives and season with salt and pepper to taste. Spray non-stick frying pan with non-stick cooking spray, making certain to cover surface evenly. Mix all ingredients together and cook slowly until brown, turning to cook the other side.
Makes 2 servings.

'Squeak and Bubble'

MILK

Milk Shakes? Mousses? Puddings? The names sound sinful on the Weight Watchers Food Plan, but they're all here, prepared in our own way and all with lots of delicious flavours.
We've brought you recipes such as Orange Custard, Strawberry Orange Souffle and Apple Strawberry Whisk.

You may use fresh skim milk or dried skim milk (made up according to the directions on the packaging) and the serving size is 10 fl oz (half a pint (300 ml)). You need 2 servings (one pint (600 ml)) each day and can take them at any time.

Milk is a particularly good source of essential nutrients and skim milk lacks only calories when compared with full cream milk.

Women	2 servings daily
Men	2 servings daily
Teenagers	3-4 servings daily

	Serving
milk, non-fat dry	1 oz (30 g)
milk, skim	10 fl oz (½ pint) (300 ml)
buttermilk	8 fl oz (240 ml)
yogurt, natural unsweetened	5 fl oz (150 ml)

Iced Coffee

8 fl oz (240 ml) freshly brewed coffee

8 fl oz (240 ml) chilled coffee

5 fl oz (150 ml) skim milk

2 teaspoons sugar, optional

Pour the freshly brewed coffee into ice cube tray and freeze until solid. Remove cubes and divide into 2 tall glasses. Pour chilled coffee evenly into two glasses over the cubes. Serve each portion with 2½ fl oz (75 ml) skim milk and 1 teaspoon sugar if desired.
Makes 2 servings.

Honeycomb Mould

1 egg, separated

grated rind of ¼ lemon

artificial sweetener to taste

10 fl oz (300 ml) skim milk

2 tablespoons hot water

1½ teaspoons unflavoured gelatine

put yolk in bowl; beat in lemon rind and sweetener. Heat milk to just boiling and pour over yolk, stirring. Rinse saucepan and put yolk and milk mixture into it. Dissolve gelatine in hot water and fold into yolk mixture. Beat egg white until stiff and add to mixture, folding in carefully. Place over heat and bring to the boil without stirring. Pour into mould and leave to cool. Add protein as required.
Makes 1 midday or evening meal serving.

Homemade Yogurt

2 pints (1 litre 200 ml) less 2 tablespoons skim milk (or reconstituted non-fat dry milk)

1 tablespoon natural unsweetened yogurt

In a large saucepan, heat milk to lukewarm 110° to 115°F (40° to 45°C) over direct heat. (For better control, use the top of a double boiler over boiling water). Add yogurt and mix well with a wire whisk. Divide evenly into yogurt-maker containers and blend, following manufacturer's instructions. When thick and creamy, place in refrigerator until chilled. Divide evenly.
Makes 4 servings.

Hot Lemon Custard

2 eggs, well beaten

1 teaspoon sugar

¼ teaspoon lemon flavouring

1 oz (30 g) non-fat dry milk

8 fl oz (240 ml) water

In bowl combine eggs, sugar and flavourings; mix well. Combine milk and water in saucepan and heat until milk forms tiny bubbles round the edges. Gradually stir milk into beaten eggs. Return to saucepan and heat until mixture thickens. Do not overcook. Divide evenly. Add protein as required.
Makes 2 midday or evening meal servings.

Rum Sauce

2 pints (1 litre 200 ml) skim milk

artificial sweetener to taste

½ teaspoon rum flavouring

12 teaspoons cornflour

Put all ingredients into a saucepan and bring to the boil, stirring constantly. Cook for 2 minutes. Serve with Rich Fruit Pudding (see page 12). Divide evenly.
Makes 8 servings.

Banana Milk Shake

10 fl oz (300 ml) skim milk

1 teaspoon sugar

½ medium banana

½ teaspoon vanilla flavouring

3 ice cubes

Combine all ingredients except ice cubes in blender container; blend until frothy. Add ice cubes one at a time, blending after each addition. Serve in tall glass.
Makes 1 serving.

Apple-Strawberry Whisk

1 tablespoon unflavoured gelatine

2 fl oz (60 ml) cold water

3 fl oz (90 ml) boiling water

2 oz (60 g) non-fat dry milk

2½ oz (75 g) strawberries (reserve 2 strawberries)

2 teaspoons sugar

¼ teaspoon strawberry flavouring

8 to 10 ice cubes

½ medium apple, peeled, cored and sliced

In blender container sprinkle gelatine over cold water to soften. Add boiling water; blend until dissolved. Add milk, strawberries, sugar and flavouring. Blend until smooth. Add ice cubes, two at a time, blending after each addition. Fold apple into mixture; divide evenly into 2 dessert glasses. Top each with a whole strawberry and chill.
Makes 2 servings.

Pears with Chocolate Sauce

4 teaspoons unsweetened cocoa

2 tablespoons water

2 teaspoons cornflour

1½ oz (45 g) non-fat dry milk, dissolved in 6 fl oz (180 ml) water

3 teaspoons sugar

12 canned pear halves with 12 tablespoons juice, no sugar added

Combine cocoa, water and cornflour in small saucepan and stir until completely dissolved. Add milk and cook, stirring constantly, until mixture comes to the boil. Remove from heat; add sugar. Cover and chill. Place 2 pear halves and 2 tablespoons juice in each of 6 dessert dishes. Top each with equal amounts of sauce.
Makes 6 servings.

Banana Yogurt Delight

1 medium banana, very ripe

10 fl oz (300 ml) natural unsweetened yogurt

cinnamon or instant coffee, if desired

Mash banana in bowl; add yogurt. Spoon equal amounts of mixture into each of 2 dessert dishes. Chill in freezer. Before serving, sprinkle with cinnamon or coffee.
Makes 2 servings.

MILK

Courgette Soup

1½ lbs (720 g) courgettes, diced

4 oz (120 g) onions, diced

1 tablespoon chicken stock powder

½ bay leaf

2 pints (1 litre 200 ml) water

4 oz (120 g) non-fat dry milk

1 teaspoon Worcester sauce

pinch nutmeg

salt and white pepper to taste

In large saucepan combine courgettes, onions, stock powder and bay leaf. Stir together over low heat for 10 minutes. Add water. Bring to the boil. Reduce heat. Simmer 10 minutes. Remove from heat. Discard bay leaf. Place in blender container; blend until smooth. Return mixture to saucepan. Bring to the boil. Add dry milk, Worcester sauce and nutmeg. Stir until dry milk has dissolved. Season to taste. Heat thoroughly but do not boil. Divide evenly.
Makes 4 servings.

Blackberry Pudding

1 tablespoon unflavoured gelatine

2 fl oz (60 ml) cold water

2 fl oz (60 ml) boiling water

10 oz (300 g) fresh or frozen blackberries, no sugar added

5 fl oz (150 ml) buttermilk

2 teaspoons sugar

few drops lemon or vanilla flavouring

In blender container sprinkle gelatine over cold water to soften. Add boiling water and blend until dissolved. Add 5 oz (150 g) berries and remaining ingredients; blend until smooth. Fold in remaining berries. Divide evenly into 2 dessert glasses. Chill.
Makes 2 servings.

Brown Rice Pudding

8 oz (240 g) cooked brown rice, hot

16 fl oz (480 ml) skim milk

4 eggs

8 tablespoons sultanas

2 tablespoons brown sugar

4 to 5 drops vanilla flavouring

¼ teaspoon cinnamon

¼ teaspoon nutmeg

cinnamon to garnish

In a mixing bowl, combine all ingredients. Pour into a baking dish, cover tightly with aluminium foil and bake at 350°F, 180°C, Gas Mark 4, for 40 minutes or until set. Sprinkle with cinnamon and divide evenly.
Makes 4 midday or evening meal servings. Add protein as required.

Brown Rice Pudding

Tropical Mousse

2 tablespoons unflavoured gelatine

1 pint 4 fl oz (720 ml) water

3 oz (90 g) non-fat dry milk

½ teaspoon rum flavouring

¼ teaspoon vanilla flavouring

2 tablespoons shredded coconut

2 teaspoons sugar

12 oz (360 g) canned crushed pineapple, no sugar added

In medium saucepan sprinkle gelatine over 8 fl oz (240 ml) water; heat, stirring until gelatine is dissolved. Pour gelatine mixture into blender container; add remaining water, dry milk, flavourings, coconut and sugar. Blend at low speed until smooth. Add pineapple, blend at medium speed until smooth. Pour into 3-pint (1 litre 750 ml) mould. Chill. Turn out. Divide evenly.
Makes 6 servings.

Yogurt Milk Shake

5 fl oz (150 ml) skim milk

5 oz (150 g) blackberries

2½ fl oz (75 ml) natural unsweetened yogurt

1 teaspoon sugar

¼ teaspoon vanilla flavouring

3 ice cubes

Combine all ingredients except ice cubes in blender container. Blend until smooth. Add ice cubes. Blend until frothy. Serve at once.
Makes 1 serving.

Creamy Pear Conde

1½ teaspoons unflavoured gelatine

1 tablespoon hot water

2 oz (60 g) cooked rice

2½ fl oz (75 ml) skim milk

2½ fl oz (75 ml) natural unsweetened yogurt

artificial sweetener to taste

2 canned pear halves with 2 tablespoons juice, no sugar added

1 teaspoon lemon juice

2 teaspoons arrowroot

2 to 3 drops red food colouring

In a small bowl dissolve gelatine in hot water. Stir in rice, milk, yogurt and artificial sweetener to taste. Mix well. Pour into dessert dish; top with pear halves and place in refrigerator to chill thoroughly. Place pear juice, lemon juice, arrowroot and food colouring in small saucepan. Bring to the boil, stirring all the time and cook for 1 minute or until liquid is clear and syrupy. Spoon over pear and rice mixture and serve at once.
Makes 1 serving.

Strawberry Milk Shake

10 fl oz (300 ml) skim milk

1 teaspoon sugar

5 oz (150 g) strawberries

½ teaspoon vanilla flavouring

3 ice cubes

Combine all ingredients except ice cubes in blender container; blend until frothy. Add ice cubes one at a time, blending after each addition. Serve in tall glass.
Makes 1 serving.

Tangy Strawberry Shake

5 fl oz (150 ml) buttermilk

2½ oz (75 g) strawberries

1 teaspoon sugar

¼ teaspoon lemon juice

Combine all ingredients in blender container. Blend until smooth. Pour into a tall glass. Serve immediately.
Makes 1 serving.

Hot Cocoa

12 fl oz (360 ml) water

2 teaspoons unsweetened cocoa

2 oz (60 g) non-fat dry milk

1 teaspoon sugar

Bring water to the boil in small saucepan; stir in cocoa until dissolved. Remove from heat. Stir in remaining ingredients, using a wire whisk, or transfer to blender container and blend until smooth. Divide evenly.
Makes 2 servings.

Apple 'Cream' Jelly

1 medium apple

few drops lemon juice

artificial sweetener to taste

½ oz (15 g) non-fat dry milk

½ teaspoon unflavoured gelatine

Peel and slice apple and sprinkle with lemon juice. Put in saucepan and just cover with water. Simmer for 5 minutes. When cooked, put apple and juice into blender; add sweetener, dry milk and gelatine. Blend for three seconds. Put in dish and put in cool place to set.
Makes 1 serving.

Cinnamon Peach Dessert

1 oz (30 g) non-fat dry milk

6 fl oz (180 ml) water

1½ teaspoons unflavoured gelatine

1 teaspoon sugar

1 medium peach, peeled, stoned and diced

¼ teaspoon brandy flavouring

pinch cinnamon

Mix dry milk with water. In saucepan sprinkle gelatine over milk to soften; add sugar. Heat, stirring constantly, until gelatine has dissolved. Do not boil. Remove from heat; add peach and flavouring. Cool. When on the point of setting, whisk well with rotary or electric beater. Pour into small dish; sprinkle with cinnamon and chill for 1 hour.
Makes 1 serving.

Strawberry-Orange Souffle

8 fl oz (240 ml) orange juice, no sugar added

12 fl oz (360 ml) water

1 tablespoon unflavoured gelatine

few drops strawberry flavouring

3 teaspoons sugar

2 oz (60 g) non-fat dry milk

2 tablespoons lemon juice

In medium saucepan combine orange juice and 4 fl oz (120 ml) water. Bring to the boil. Remove from heat and sprinkle in gelatine, flavouring and sugar. Stir to dissolve gelatine. Dissolve non-fat dry milk in 8 fl oz (240 ml) water; mix with gelatine and lemon juice. Chill until syrupy, then whisk until thick and foamy. Divide evenly into 4 individual souffle dishes. Chill until set.
Makes 4 servings.

Peach Drink

4 oz (120 g) canned sliced peaches, no sugar added

1 oz (30 g) non-fat dry milk

3 fl oz (90 ml) water

1 tablespoon low-calorie carbonated orange drink

Combine all ingredients in blender container. Blend until well mixed; about 20 seconds. Serve in a tall glass, over ice.
Makes 1 serving.

Minty Yogurt Dip

5 fl oz (150 ml) natural unsweetened yogurt

1 teaspoon sesame oil

1 teaspoon chopped fresh mint

pinch salt

Place yogurt in serving dish. Sprinkle with remaining ingredients. Serve chilled as a dip with raw vegetables.
Makes 1 serving.

Iced Rice Pudding

5 fl oz (150 ml) skim milk

pinch of cinnamon

1 teaspoon cornflour, dissolved in 1 teaspoon water

2 oz (60 g) cooked rice

artificial sweetener to taste

½ teaspoon vanilla flavouring

In non-stick saucepan combine milk and cinnamon and heat. When mixture is hot, stirring constantly, add dissolved cornflour and cook for 5 minutes. Add rice and cook for 25 minutes, stirring occasionally. Transfer to bowl. Add sweetener and vanilla flavouring and stir to combine. Allow to cool then cover and place in refrigerator for at least 3 hours.
Makes 1 serving.

MILK

Cucumber and Yogurt Salad

6 oz (180 g) cucumber, peeled, seeded and diced

10 fl oz (300 ml) natural unsweetened yogurt

1 tablespoon chopped fresh mint

½ garlic clove, crushed

¼ teaspoon salt

Combine all ingredients in a bowl. Divide evenly.
Makes 4 servings.

Orange Custard

2 oz (60 g) non-fat dry milk

16 fl oz (480 ml) water

4 eggs

½ teaspoon grated orange rind

¼ teaspoon cinnamon

⅛ teaspoon nutmeg

3 teaspoons sugar

Scald milk in a saucepan; remove from heat and allow to stand for a few minutes. Add remaining ingredients and whisk well together. Divide evenly into 4 individual ovenproof custard cups. Place in shallow pan containing 1 inch (2.5 cm) water. Bake at 350°F, 180°C, Gas Mark 4 for 25 minutes or until a knife inserted in the centre comes out clean. Add protein as required.
Makes 4 midday or evening meal servings.

Apple Cheese Mousse

2 tablespoons unflavoured gelatine

2 fl oz (60 ml) cold water

2 fl oz (60 ml) boiling water

2 medium red dessert apples

lemon juice

10 oz (300 g) cottage cheese

5 fl oz (150 ml) buttermilk

2 slices (2 oz/60 g) white bread, torn into pieces

1 teaspoon sugar

In blender container sprinkle gelatine over cold water to soften. Add boiling water; blend until dissolved. Peel, core and chop one apple; halve the other apple; peel, core and chop one half. Core and slice remaining half, sprinkle with lemon juice and reserve for decoration. Add chopped apple with remaining ingredients in blender container and blend until smooth. Pour mixture into a small loaf tin. Place in refrigerator until firm; unmould and decorate with reserved apple slices. Divide evenly.
Makes 2 midday or evening meal servings.

Apple Cheese Mousse

GRAINS

You can't live by bread alone, and we've shown you how to use it as a basic ingredient in so many dishes such as shortcrust pastry and bread stuffing. We also offer you many foods to use as alternatives to bread, such as pasta, rice, flour, even biscuits. The amounts of each item are carefully calculated, and they all differ, so be sure to read the list before you make your selection.

Bread and Substitutes
(bread selections)

Women	2-3 servings daily
Men	4-5 servings daily
Teenagers	4-5 servings daily

	Serving
bagel, small	1 oz (30 g)
barley	¾ oz (20 g) uncooked
	2 oz (60 g) cooked
bread, rolls or baps	1 oz (30 g)
breadcrumbs, dried	¾ oz (20 g)
cereal	¾ oz (20 g)
corn:	
corn ear	1 medium
whole kernel	3 oz (90 g)
cream style	3 oz (90 g)
cornmeal	¾ oz (20 g) uncooked
	2 oz (60 g) cooked
cream crackers (plain)	2
crispbreads	¾ oz (20 g)
crumpet	¾ oz (20 g)
currant bread	1 oz (30 g)
digestive biscuit	1
dried peas/beans	1 oz (30 g) uncooked
	3 oz (90 g) cooked
flour	¾ oz (20 g)
matzoh	½ oz (15 g)
melba toast	¾ oz (20 g)
muffin	¾ oz (20 g)
pasta: macaroni, spaghetti,	
noodles	¾ oz (20 g) uncooked
	2 oz (60 g) cooked
pita	1 oz (30 g)
potato	3 oz (90 g)
potato scone	¾ oz (20 g)
rice	¾ oz (20 g) uncooked
	2 oz (60 g) cooked
scone (plain)	¾ oz (20 g)
scotch pancake	1 oz (30 g)
semolina	¾ oz (20 g)
toast breads	¾ oz (20 g)
water biscuits	2

Rice and Liver Pilaf

12 oz (360 g) chicken livers

4 fl oz (120 ml) boiling salted water

4 oz (120 g) cooked rice

4 tablespoons tomato puree

2 fl oz (60 ml) water

1 tablespoon dried onion flakes

parsley sprigs for garnish

Cook liver in 4 fl oz (120 ml) boiling, salted water until done. Do not overcook; liver should stay soft and moist. Drain; if liquid is bitter discard and substitute chicken stock, otherwise reserve liquid. Mince one quarter of the cooled liver using coarse blade of mincer. Return to saucepan with 2 fl oz (60 ml) reserved liquid or stock. Add rice, tomato puree, water and onion flakes. Stir to combine. Add whole livers and simmer gently for 15 minutes. Divide evenly and serve in bowls with parsley to garnish.
Makes 2 midday or evening meal servings.

Apple Pie (with lid)

Filling

4 medium cooking apples, peeled, cored and sliced

1 tablespoon cornflour, dissolved in 1 tablespoon water

2 tablespoons low-fat spread

Pastry

4 tablespoons low-fat spread

4½ oz (135 g) plain flour

To Prepare Filling: In medium saucepan combine apples and enough water to cover. Cook over medium heat for 7 minutes. Add cornflour, stirring constantly. Cook until thickened. Remove from heat. Stir in low-fat spread. Pour fruit mixture into pie dish.

To Prepare Pastry: Rub low-fat spread into flour; add enough water to make up to a thick dough. Between 2 sheets of greaseproof paper roll out dough until it is just large enough to cover pie.

To Prepare Pie: Cover fruit mixture with dough. Bake in moderate oven, 375°F, 190°C, Gas Mark 5, for 30 to 40 minutes or until pastry is golden. Divide evenly.

Makes 6 servings.

Quickie Bean and Meat Stew

4 oz (120 g) diced cooked lamb
1 oz (30 g) onion, chopped
½ garlic clove, crushed
4 fl oz (120 ml) beef stock, made with 1 stock cube
1 tablespoon tomato puree
6 oz (180 g) cooked dried butter beans
1 tablespoon chopped fresh parsley
pinch thyme

In a non-stick saucepan, combine lamb, onion and garlic and saute until onion is browned. Stir in stock and tomato puree. Add beans, parsley and thyme; cook until most of the liquid has evaporated.

Makes 2 midday or evening meal servings.

Potato Lamb Pie

6 oz (180 g) minced lamb
1 tablespoon dried onion flakes
10 fl oz (300 ml) beef stock, made with ½ stock cube
2 tablespoons tomato puree
1½ oz (45 g) green pepper, seeded and finely chopped
1½ oz (45 g) red pepper, seeded and finely chopped
1 oz (30 g) drained canned whole kernel corn
3 oz (90 g) carrot
dash soy sauce
pinch mace
1 teaspoon arrowroot
2 oz (60 g) peeled cooked potato, mashed
1 teaspoon margarine

Form minced meat into 3 to 4 small flat cakes and place under hot grill until cooked through. Mash with a fork before adding to other ingredients. Reconstitute onion flakes in stock. Place all ingredients, except potato, arrowroot and margarine, in bowl and mix together thoroughly. Place in small casserole, cover with foil and place in preheated oven, 375°F, 190°C, Gas Mark 5, for half an hour. Meanwhile mix arrowroot with a tablespoon of water. When contents of casserole are cooked, stir in arrowroot mixture and put back into oven for a further 5 minutes. Spread mashed potato over mince and dot with 1 teaspoon margarine and place under grill for 1 minute. Serve with grilled mushrooms and tomatoes.

Makes 1 midday or evening meal serving.

Apple Matzoh Kugel (Pudding)

2 matzoh boards (2 oz/60 g), broken into pieces
4 eggs, separated
3 medium apples, peeled, cored and grated
4 fl oz (120 ml) orange juice, no sugar added
1 teaspoon lemon juice
1 teaspoon grated lemon rind
2 teaspoons sugar
½ teaspoon salt
¼ teaspoon cinnamon

In small bowl soak matzoh in water until soft. Drain in colander and squeeze dry. Transfer to medium bowl; add egg yolks, one at a time, mixing well after each addition. In a separate bowl, combine grated apples, fruit juices, lemon rind, sugar and seasonings. Add to matzoh mixture and stir well. Beat egg whites, in small bowl, until stiff but not dry; fold into matzoh mixture. Place in 3-pint (1 litre 800 ml) casserole and bake at 350°F, 180°C, Gas Mark 4, for 1 hour or until top is browned. Divide evenly.

Makes 4 midday or evening meal servings. Add protein as required.

Iced Vanilla Buns (Basic Bun Mix)

Buns

4 tablespoons low-fat spread

artificial sweetener to equal 6 teaspoons sugar

2 tablespoons warm water

¼ teaspoon vanilla flavouring

3 oz (90 g) self raising flour

2 egg whites

Icing for Buns

4 teaspoons sifted icing sugar

1 to 2 drops raspberry food colour flavouring

barely 1½ teaspoons water

To Prepare Buns: Preheat oven to 375°F, 190°C, gas mark 5. Put the low-fat spread into a large basin; add artificial sweetener and cream together. Add the warm water, flavouring and half the flour; beat thoroughly together. Beat egg whites into stiff peaks and fold into cake batter; beat in gradually, adding rest of the flour. Spray a 12 portion non-stick cake tray with non-stick cooking spray. Using a small spoon, divide cake batter evenly between each portion on cake tray. Reduce oven temperature to 350°F, 180°C, Gas Mark 4, place buns on middle shelf and cook for 12 to 15 minutes or until brown. Allow buns to cool a little before lifting onto wire cake tray and leave until quite cool.
To Prepare Icing for Buns: Place icing sugar in small basin, mix flavouring with water and add to icing sugar and mix until smooth. Divide evenly over each of the buns. Divide evenly.
Makes 4 servings.

Spicy Raisin Buns
Substitute for the vanilla flavouring—¼ teaspoon allspice and add 4 tablespoons raisins. Omit icing.

Coconut Buns
Substitute for the vanilla flavouring—coconut flavouring and for the raisins—8 teaspoons shredded coconut. Omit icing.

Iced Vanilla Buns

GRAINS

Potato-Yogurt Salad

10 fl oz (300 ml) natural unsweetened yogurt

2 teaspoons prepared mustard

2 teaspoons prepared horseradish

1½ lbs (220 g) cooked potatoes, cubed

6 oz (180 g) cucumber, peeled and sliced

2 oz (60 g) celery, thinly sliced

2 tablespoons dried onion flakes, reconstituted

1 tablespoon chopped chives

In small bowl combine yogurt, mustard and horseradish. Combine remaining ingredients in large bowl. Pour yogurt mixture over salad and toss to combine. Refrigerate until chilled. Divide evenly.
Makes 8 servings.

Roast Potatoes

Use 12 oz (360 g) peeled boiled potatoes or drained canned potatoes. Pat dry and arrange in shallow non-stick baking tin; season with salt, pepper and paprika and brush with 2 teaspoons vegetable oil. Bake at 425°F, 220°C, Gas Mark 7, turning occasionally until brown. Divide evenly.
Makes 4 servings.

Baked Potatoes

Pierce the skin of each 3 oz (90 g) potato in several places with the prongs of a fork. This allows steam to escape and prevents the potato from bursting. Bake potatoes directly on oven rack or use a baking sheet. Oven temperature can range from 325°F,

160°C, Gas Mark 3, to 450°F, 230°C, Gas Mark 8. Potatoes are done when they feel soft. Baked potatoes can be wrapped in foil, frozen and reheated at 350°F, 180°C, Gas Mark 4, for 1 hour.

Creamy Baked Potatoes

6 baked potatoes, 3 oz (90 g) each

6 fl oz (180 ml) buttermilk

1 tablespoon chives

1½ teaspoons margarine, melted

½ teaspoon salt or to taste

pinch white pepper

paprika to garnish

Cut baked potatoes in half lengthwise. From one half of each, scoop out pulp, leaving a thin shell that maintains its shape. From other half, scoop out all the pulp and discard skin. In bowl, mash pulp and add remaining ingredients except paprika. Spoon ⅙ of mixture into each shell; sprinkle with paprika. Place on baking sheet, bake at 350°F, 180°C, Gas Mark 4 for 25 minutes or until hot. Serve immediately.
Makes 6 servings.

Hot Potato Salad

12 fl oz (360 ml) ham stock, made with 1 stock cube

4 fl oz (120 ml) water

1½ lbs (720 g) peeled potatoes, cut into ¼ inch (5 mm) slices

4 oz (120 g) onions, diced

1 oz (20 g) celery, diced

1 tablespoon flour

2 fl oz (60 ml) cider vinegar

2 teaspoons sugar

1½ teaspoons salt

½ teaspoon celery seed

¼ teaspoon pepper

In medium saucepan bring stock and water to the boil. Add potatoes; cook until tender but still firm. Using a slotted spoon, remove potatoes from stock; set aside. Add onions and celery to stock. Cook until vegetables are tender and stock is reduced to approximately 4 fl oz (120 ml). In measuring jug dissolve flour in vinegar; add sugar and seasonings. Stir into stock in saucepan; cook until thickened. Pour over potatoes and toss gently. Serve at once. Divide evenly.
Makes 8 servings.

Potato Soup

12 oz (360 g) peeled potatoes, diced

6 oz (180 g) leeks

approximately 1½ pints (900 ml) water (enough to keep vegetables covered)

10 fl oz (300 ml) skim milk

2 tablespoons chopped fresh dill

1 teaspoon salt

freshly ground pepper to taste

2 tablespoons low-fat spread

chopped chives, parsley or dill for garnish, optional

Cook vegetables in water to cover for about ½ hour or until they are tender. Add milk, dill, salt and pepper. Let soup simmer for another 15 to 20 minutes or until it begins to take on a rather thick consistency and the potatoes begin to fall apart a little; stir in

low-fat spread. Cook until heated through. Serve immediately. Garnish with chives, parsley or dill if desired. Divide evenly.
Makes 4 servings.

Lamb Curry

6 oz (180 g) lean lamb fillet

1 oz (30 g) onion, finely diced

3 oz (90 g) carrot, sliced

6 fl oz (180 ml) chicken stock, made with ½ stock cube

1 tablespoon lemon juice

1 teaspoon curry powder

pinch ground bay leaf

2 teaspoons cornflour, mixed with water to form thin paste

salt and pepper to taste

2 oz (60 g) hot cooked rice

Grill fillet of lamb on a rack, turning frequently until well cooked or, when pierced with a fork, no juices run. Remove and cut into cubes. Meanwhile combine onion, carrot, stock, lemon juice and curry powder in saucepan and cook until vegetables are tender-crisp. Add cooked lamb, cornflour, salt and pepper; bring to the boil and cook for 5 to 10 minutes. Serve with rice.
Makes 1 midday or evening meal serving.

Macaroni with Vegetable Sauce

12 oz (360 g) green peppers, seeded and diced

6 oz (180 g) diced aubergine

2 oz (60 g) diced celery

1½ oz (45 g) sliced mushrooms

2 tablespoons dried onion flakes

3 garlic cloves, crushed

5 oz (150 g) fresh or frozen cauliflower or broccoli florets

4 tablespoons tomato puree

6 fl oz (180 ml) water

2 fl oz (60 ml) beef stock, made with ¼ stock cube

1 tablespoon chopped fresh parsley

1 teaspoon basil

½ teaspoon oregano

½ teaspoon salt

¼ teaspoon rosemary

¼ teaspoon thyme

½ teaspoon burgundy or sherry flavouring

8 oz (240 g) cooked macaroni

Brown green peppers, aubergine, celery, mushrooms, onion flakes and garlic in a large non-stick fryng pan, stirring constantly. Transfer mixture to a large saucepan; add cauliflower, tomato puree, water, stock, parsley, basil, oregano, salt, rosemary and thyme. Bring to the boil; reduce heat, cover saucepan and simmer for at least 30 minutes, or until sauce is thick and all vegetables are tender. Stir occasionally, bringing up the vegetables on the bottom. Add more stock, if necessary, to prevent scorching.

Remove from heat. Put entire mixture through a food mill or strainer to puree, if desired. Stir in flavouring and mix well. Divide evenly into 4 portions. Serve each portion over 2 oz (60 g) macaroni.
Makes 4 servings.

Meatballs with Rice

12 oz (360 g) lean minced beef

1½ fl oz (45 ml) water

1 teaspoon garlic salt

½ teaspoon dry mustard

½ teaspoon ginger

6 oz (180 g) cooked celery, sliced

4 fl oz (120 ml) orange juice, no sugar added

1 tablespoon soy sauce

1 tablespoon red wine vinegar

1 teaspoon sugar, optional

4 oz (120 g) cooked rice

chopped fresh parsley to garnish

Preheat grill. Combine first 5 ingredients in mixing bowl; blend well. Form into 16 equal balls. Place on rack in grill pan. Grill 3 to 4 inches (8 to 10 cm) from heat source, for 5 to 7 minutes or until brown; turn and brown other side. Place meatballs in saucepan. Combine celery, orange juice, soy sauce, vinegar and sugar if desired in blender container. Blend until smooth. Pour over meatballs. Heat and serve over rice. Garnish with chopped parsley. Divide evenly.
Makes 2 midday or evening meal servings.

GRAINS

Barley and Vegetables

6 fl oz (180 ml) beef stock, made with ½ stock cube

2½ oz (75 g) carrot, diced

2 oz (60 g) white turnip, diced

1 oz (30 g) celery, diced

1 oz (30 g) onion, chopped

2 oz (60 g) cooked barley

salt and pepper to taste

Heat stock in a medium saucepan. Add vegetables and barley and cook. Season with salt and pepper. Continue cooking until vegetables are tender and mixture becomes slightly thickened, stirring frequently. Serve hot. *Makes 1 serving.*

Basic Rice

Rice may be cooked on top of stove or in the oven—cooking times and amounts will vary according to the brand of rice—however, follow package directions. When cooked, be sure to measure 2 oz (60 g) servings. Here is one cooking method.

1¼ (750 ml) pints water

8 oz (240 g) uncooked rice

1 teaspoon salt

In saucepan combine all ingredients. Bring to the boil; reduce heat, cover and simmer for 20 to 30 minutes. Remove from heat and let stand for 15 to 20 minutes. Measure 2 oz (60 g) cooked rice for each serving.

Minted Rice

8 oz (240 g) cooked rice

1 tablespoon chopped fresh parsley

2 teaspoons finely chopped fresh mint or 1 teaspoon dried mint

salt to taste

2 teaspoons margarine

In medium saucepan combine rice, parsley, mint and salt. Cook, stirring constantly, until heated through. Add a little water if necesary to prevent sticking. Remove from heat, stir in margarine. Divide evenly. *Makes 4 servings.*

Petit Pois with Little Shells

6 oz (180 g) mushrooms

½ garlic clove

4 oz (120 g) frozen peas

2 tablespoons water

2 tablespoons chopped fresh parsley

salt and pepper to taste

4 oz (120 g) cooked macaroni shells

2 oz (60 g) grated Parmesan cheese

Brown mushrooms and garlic in non-stick saucepan until mushrooms release their liquid. Add peas, water, parsley, salt and pepper. Cook until peas are tender. Pour over heated macaroni shells. Stir in Parmesan cheese and serve. Divide evenly. *Makes 2 midday or evening meal servings. Add protein as required.*

Petit Pois with Little Shells

GRAINS

Breadcrumbs Au Gratin

1 slice (1 oz/30 g) white bread, made into crumbs

2 oz (60 g) hard cheese, grated

1 teaspoon margarine

In small bowl combine all ingredients. Scatter over your chosen cooked vegetable and bake in oven until browned.
Makes 1 midday or evening meal serving.

Breadcrumbs

The following is the procedure for making breadcrumbs. Cover blender container. Turn blender on high speed. Remove the clear plastic handle in the blender container cover. Tear each slice of bread into about 4 or 5 pieces. Drop each piece, one at a time, through the opening in the cover; place your hand over the opening to prevent crumbs from scattering. Continue until all bread is crumbled. If crumbs stop moving in blender container, empty container into a bowl and continue with remaining bread. Do not over process. For large crumbs, leave blender on for a few seconds; for fine crumbs, process longer.

Seasoned Crumbs

2 slices (2 oz/60 g) white bread, made into crumbs

1 to 2 teaspoons fresh herbs

1 small garlic clove, mashed with 1 teaspoon salt

2 teaspoons margarine, melted

In bowl combine first 3 ingredients. Add margarine and mix well. Divide evenly.
Makes 4 servings.

Italian Breadcrumbs

1 teaspoon salt

¼ teaspoon paprika

¼ teaspoon basil

¼ teaspoon oregano

¼ teaspoon rosemary

pinch garlic powder (optional)

2 slices (2 oz/60 g) white bread, made into crumbs

Combine seasonings in plastic bag. Add breadcrumbs and shake to mix. Divide evenly.
Makes 4 servings.

Cheese and Turkey Open Sandwich

1 slice (1 oz/30 g) rye bread

2 oz (60 g) skinned and boned cooked turkey, sliced

1 oz (30 g) drained sauerkraut

1 oz (30 g) hard cheese, sliced

2 oz (60 g) pickled cucumber, sliced

watercress and radish roses to garnish

Lightly toast bread. Arrange turkey on toast. Spread sauerkraut over turkey and top with cheese. Place on baking sheet; bake at 450°F, 230°C, Gas Mark 8, or place under preheated grill and heat until cheese is melted. Garnish with pickle slices, watercress and radish roses.
Makes 1 midday or evening meal serving.

Chocolate Currant Cake with Apricot Sauce

Cake

4 eggs, separated

2 fl oz (60 ml) water

1 teaspoon sugar

8 teaspoons unsweetened cocoa, dissolved in 3 tablespoons water

4 slices (4 oz/120 g) currant bread, made into crumbs

Apricot sauce

24 canned apricot halves with 8 tablespoons juice, no sugar added

1 teaspoon sugar

To Prepare Cake: Preheat oven to 350°F, 180°C, Gas Mark 4. Line 9-inch (23 cm) round baking tin with foil; set aside. In mixing bowl combine egg yolks, water and sugar. Beat for 5 minutes or until thick. Add cocoa and beat to combine. Fold in breadcrumbs. In separate bowl beat egg whites until stiff peaks form. Carefully fold whites into yolk mixture. Pour mixture into prepared baking tin; bake for 30 minutes or until firm. Remove from tin and cool on wire rack.

To Prepare Sauce: Dice apricots and set aside. In a small saucepan combine juice and sugar. Boil until liquid is reduced by half. Stir in diced apricots. Cool. Pour three quarters of the sauce over the cake. Divide cake into 4 equal portions. Serve ¼ of remaining sauce with each portion.
Makes 4 midday or evening meal servings. Add protein as required.

Cold Macaroni Salad

8 oz (240 g) cooked small tube macaroni

2 fl oz (60 ml) skim milk

6 oz (180 g) green pepper, seeded and diced

4 oz (120 g) onions, diced

4 oz (120 g) tomato, diced

4 oz (120 g) pickled cucumber, diced (reserve 2 teaspoons brine)

5 fl oz (150 ml) natural unsweetened yogurt

4 tablespoons mayonnaise

1 garlic clove, crushed

¼ teaspoon salt

⅛ teaspoon white pepper

chopped fresh dill or chives to garnish

Place macaroni in large bowl and moisten with milk. Add diced vegetables. In small bowl combine yogurt, mayonnaise, reserved pickle brine, garlic, salt and pepper. Pour over pasta mixture and toss to combine. Cover and refrigerate until chilled. Sprinkle with dill or chives. Divide evenly.
Makes 4 servings.

Cheese Toastie

1 slice (1 oz/30 g) white bread

1 tablespoon tomato puree, mixed with 2 tablespoons water

pinch each oregano, garlic powder and basil or pinch Italian seasoning

2 oz (60 g) hard cheese, grated

Toast bread lightly; spread with puree and sprinkle on seasonings. Top with cheese. Grill until cheese is melted.
Makes 1 midday or evening meal serving.

Triple Decker Sandwich

2 teaspoons low-fat spread

3 slices (3 oz/90 g) bread

1 hard boiled egg, sliced

1½ oz (45 g) sliced tomatoes

1 oz (30 g) cucumber, sliced

lettuce leaves

1¼ oz (37 g) cottage cheese

1 oz (30 g) drained canned sardines mashed and mixed with 2 teaspoons low calorie tomato ketchup

watercress for garnish (optional)

Spread low-fat spread onto both sides of 1 slice of bread and on one side of each of the other 2 slices. Using one slice of bread that has fat on only one side, arrange slices of egg on spread side; top with half of each of the tomato slices, cucumber slices and lettuce. Top with bread that has low-fat spread on both sides; spread with cottage cheese, then sardine mixture. Top with remaining tomato, cucumber and lettuce. Place last slice of bread on top, spread side down, and carefully cut sandwich into

desired shape; decorate with watercress if desired.
Makes 1 midday or evening meal serving.

Savoury Cheese on Toast

1 slice (1 oz/30 g) white bread

1 teaspoon margarine

1 oz (30 g) hard cheese

prepared mustard to taste

½ teaspoon sesame, poppy or caraway seeds, or curry powder to taste

salt and pepper to taste

Spread bread with ½ teaspoon margarine. Top with cheese. Spread cheese with remaining margarine and mustard. Sprinkle with seeds or curry powder and salt and pepper. Bake at 375°F, 190°C, Gas Mark 5, until cheese melts. Cut into 8 pieces.
Makes 1 morning meal serving.

Toast Cups

3 slices (3 oz/90 g) white bread

2 fl oz (60 ml) water

½ teaspoon vanilla flavouring

1 teaspoon sugar

Using a very sharp knife, cut each slice of bread in half horizontally, forming 6 thin slices. Press each thin slice into a patty tin 3-inch [8-cm] diameter. Combine remaining ingredients. Sprinkle bread with flavoured water. Bake for 12 to 14 minutes at 350°F, 180°C, Gas Mark 4, or until golden brown.
Makes 3 servings.

GRAINS

Spaghetti Bolognaise

10 fl oz (300 ml) chicken stock made with 1 stock cube

4 tablespoons tomato puree

8 oz (240 g) cooked minced beef

¼ teaspoon dried oregano

1 bay leaf

pinch garlic granules

4 oz (120 g) hot cooked spaghetti

parsley for garnish

Place the stock and tomato puree in a saucepan with the minced meat, oregano, bay leaf and garlic granules. Bring to the boil, cover and simmer for 25 minutes. Discard the bay leaf. Arrange the hot, freshly cooked spaghetti on a serving dish. Pour the sauce over the spaghetti. Divide evenly and serve garnished with parsley.
Makes 2 midday or evening meal servings.

Bread Stuffing

2 oz (60 g) celery, diced

8 fl oz (240 ml) chicken stock, made with ½ stock cube

2 slices (2 oz/60 g) day-old white bread, diced

salt and pepper to taste

¼ teaspoon thyme

¼ teaspoon savory

In saucepan cook celery in stock until celery is soft and stock is almost evaporated. Add bread and seasonings. Moisten with additional water if stuffing is too dry. Heat and serve. Divide evenly.
Makes 2 servings.

Sweet Corn and Potato Salad

6 oz (180 g) cooked peeled potatoes, sliced

6 oz (180 g) drained canned whole kernel corn

4 oz (120 g) spring onions, chopped

8 teaspoons low-calorie mayonnaise

Place potatoes, corn and spring onions in bowl. Pour low-calorie mayonnaise over vegetables and toss together. Chill and divide into 4 equal portions.
Makes 4 servings.

Sweet Corn and Potato Salad

GRAINS

'Bath Bun'

2 tablespoons self-raising flour

1 teaspoon baking powder

1 teaspoon mixed spice

¼ teaspoon bicarbonate of soda

2 slices (2 oz/60 g) bread, made into crumbs

grated rind of 1 lemon

2 eggs

1 tablespoon vegetable oil

2 teaspoons lemon juice

artificial sweetener to taste

Preheat oven to 375°F, 190°C, Gas Mark 5. Sieve flour, baking powder, mixed spice and bicarbonate of soda, into the breadcrumbs. Add grated rind of the lemon. Beat eggs well; add oil, lemon juice and sweetener and beat again. Gradually add flour mixture to the egg mixture and beat thoroughly. Spray 4 small patty tins with non-stick cooking spray. Spoon mixture evenly into tins and bake for 25 to 30 minutes, until well-risen and firm to the touch. Before eating, sprinkle with artificial sweetener (powdered type) to taste. Divide evenly.
Makes 2 midday or evening meal servings. Add protein as required.

Sponge Cake

4 eggs, separated

4 fl oz (120 ml) water

2 oz (60 g) non-fat dry milk

2 tablespoons sugar

1 teaspoon grated lemon rind

1 teaspoon vanilla flavouring

1½ oz (45 g) self-raising flour

Preheat oven to 350°F, 180°C, Gas Mark 4. In large bowl beat egg yolks until thick and lemon-coloured. Slowly add water, continuing to beat. One at a time, add milk, 1 tablespoon sugar, lemon rind and vanilla, beating after each addition. Fold in flour. In medium bowl beat egg whites with remaining sugar until stiff but not dry; fold into yolk mixture. Pour into 10-inch (25-cm) non-stick loaf tin. Bake for 35 minutes or until lightly browned, Remove from tin. Cool on wire rack. Divide evenly.
Makes 4 midday or evening meal

Cinnamon Toast

1 slice (1 oz/30 g) white bread, lightly toasted

2 teaspoons low-fat spread

1 teaspoon sugar, or to taste

¼ teaspoon cinnamon

pinch nutmeg (optional)

Spread low-fat spread on toast. In small cup combine sugar, cinnamon and nutmeg, if desired. Sprinkle on toast. Place under the grill for about ½ minute.
Makes 1 serving.

Crunchy Rice and Tangerine Salad

Salad

4 oz (120 g) cooked rice

2 small tangerines, peeled and sectioned

2 oz (60 g) cooked peas

2 oz (60 g) diced celery

salt to taste

Dressing

4 fl oz (120 ml) tomato juice

1 tablespoon cider vinegar

1 teaspoon chicken stock powder

1 teaspoon dried onion flakes

¾ teaspoon Worcester sauce

½ teaspoon prepared mustard

pinch each garlic powder and cinnamon

To Prepare Salad: Layer all ingredients in a bowl, in the order given; pour dressing over salad. Divide evenly.
To Prepare Dressing: Combine all ingredients in blender container and blend until well mixed.
Makes 2 servings.

Matzoh Omelette

1 oz (30 g) matzoh board

2 eggs, well beaten

2 tablespoons water

¼ teaspoon salt

pinch pepper

cinnamon to taste (optional)

Break matzoh into 2-inch (5-cm) pieces and place in colander. Pour boiling water over matzoh and drain quickly to prevent sogginess. In bowl combine eggs, water, salt, pepper and matzoh. Heat a 7-inch (18-cm) non-stick frying pan. Add matzoh-egg mixture and cook over low heat until golden brown on one side, then turn carefully and brown the other side. Sprinkle with cinnamon, if desired. Divide evenly.
Makes 2 morning meal servings.

Oatmeal-Currant Crunchies

3 oz (90 g) self-raising flour

artificial sweetener to taste

½ teaspoon baking powder

¼ teaspoon bicarbonate of soda

¼ teaspoon cinnamon

3 oz (90 g) uncooked porridge oats

4 tablespoons low-fat spread, melted

2 egg whites

4 tablespoons dried currants

2 teaspoons golden syrup

Preheat oven to 375°F, 190°C, Gas Mark 5. Sieve first 5 ingredients into a large basin; add oats and melted low-fat spread, stirring to combine. In another bowl beat egg whites until stiff; fold into oat mixture. Mix in currants and golden syrup. Spray a non-stick baking tray with non-stick cooking spray. Make 16 biscuits by dropping teaspoonfuls of mixture on to tray, leaving ½-inch (1-cm) space between each. Bake until biscuits are brown, about 8 to 10 minutes. Using a spatula, transfer cooked biscuits on to a wire cooling tray. Divide evenly.
Makes 4 servings.

Instant 'Pizza'

2 tablespoons tomato puree

2 tablespoons water

1 muffin (1½ oz/45 g) split and toasted

¼ teaspoon oregano or Italian seasoning, or to taste

2 slices Mozzarella, Cheddar, or other hard cheese, 1 oz (30 g) each

Mix tomato puree and water. Spread cut side of each muffin half with half of the tomato mixture. Sprinkle each with ⅛ teaspoon oregano and top each with 1 oz (30 g) cheese. Place under grill; grill just long enough to melt cheese.
Makes 1 midday or evening meal serving.

Curried Toast or Croutons

1 teaspoon margarine

⅛ teaspoon curry powder

pinch salt and pepper

1 slice (1 oz/30 g) white bread

In small bowl combine margarine, curry powder, salt and pepper. Spread over bread slice. Place on baking sheet; bake at 375°F, 190°C, Gas Mark 5, for 7 minutes or until bread is crisp and golden. Serve hot, or cut into cubes and store in airtight container. When ready to use, reheat in oven to crisp.
Makes 1 serving.

Fruit Cake

4 oz (120 g) non-fat dry milk

12 oz (360 g) canned crushed pineapple, no sugar added, drained (reserve juice)

4 fl oz (120 ml) orange juice, no sugar added

10 oz (300 g) cranberries, chopped

2 medium apples, peeled, cored and grated

4 teaspoons sugar

1 tablespoon lemon juice

1 teaspoon vanilla flavouring

8 slices (8 oz/240 g) currant bread, made into crumbs

¼ teaspoon cinnamon

Combine milk, pineapple juice and orange juice in a large bowl. Beat until frothy. Add remaining fruit, sugar, lemon juice and vanilla flavouring. Combine breadcrumbs and cinnamon. Add to fruit mixture and mix well. Pour into 8 x 8 x 3-inch (20 x 20 x 8-cm) non-stick tin and bake at 350°F, 180°C, Gas Mark 4, for 1 hour. Divide evenly.
Makes 8 servings.

GRAINS

Shortcrust Pastry

4½ oz (135 g) plain flour

4 tablespoons low-fat spread

In a bowl rub together flour and low-fat spread until mixture resembles breadcrumbs. Add enough water to make a thick dough.
Makes 6 servings.

Shortcrust Pastry (Oil)

4½ oz (135 g) plain flour

2 tablespoons vegetable oil

Mix together flour and oil, until the ingredients are well combined. Add enough water to make a thick dough.
Makes 6 servings.

Apple Crumble

4 medium cooking apples, peeled, cored and sliced

4 fl oz (120 ml) water

1 tablespoon cornflour

½ teaspoon cinnamon

3 oz (90 g) plain flour

2 tablespoons low-fat spread

Layer apples in 8 x 8 x 2-inch (20 x 20 x 5-cm) non-stick baking tin. Combine water, cornflour and cinnamon in measuring jug; stir to dissolve cornflour. Pour over apples. In bowl combine flour and low-fat spread, mixing with hands until crumbly. Sprinkle over apples. Bake at 350°F, 180°C, Gas Mark 4, for 40 to 45 minutes. Divide evenly. Serve warm or cool.
Makes 4 servings.

Bread and Fruit Pudding

4 teaspoons margarine

4 slices (4 oz/120 g) bread

8 tablespoons raisins

1 pint (600 ml) skim milk

4 eggs, beaten

artificial sweetener to taste

nutmeg to garnish

Spread 1 teaspoon margarine on each bread slice and cut slices into small squares. Layer bread squares and raisins in ovenproof dish; finishing with bread. Warm the milk and add to beaten egg, add sweetener to taste and pour over raisins and bread. Sprinkle with nutmeg and place in hot oven, 375°F, 190°C, Gas Mark 5, and bake for 30 minutes or until pudding is set and top is golden brown. Divide evenly.
Makes 4 midday or evening meal servings.

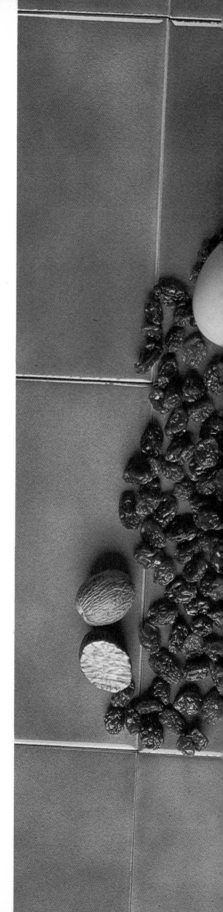

Bread and Fruit Pudding

GRAINS

Banbury Cakes

2 slices (2 oz/60 g) currant bread

1½ oz (45 g) carrot, grated

3 tablespoons dried currants

½ medium apple, grated

1 teaspoon cinnamon

1 teaspoon lemon juice

1 teaspoon grated lemon rind

1 teaspoon grated orange rind

artificial sweetener to taste

2 to 3 drops gravy browning

Cut thick crust from currant bread and make into crumbs for the filling. Roll out currant bread slices and set aside. Mix together the breadcrumbs and rest of the ingredients. Place half of the mixture onto each slice of flattened currant bread. Damp edges of bread with water, fold over to form a triangle and press edges firmly together. Place under hot grill until golden brown, turning once during cooking.
Makes 2 servings.

Banana Pudding

2 matzoh boards (2 oz/60 g) broken into 2-inch (5-cm) pieces

4 eggs, beaten

12 fl oz (360 ml) water

2 oz (60 g) non-fat dry milk

2 teaspoons sugar

½ teaspoon vanilla flavouring

⅛ teaspoon cinnamon

½ teaspoon salt

2 medium bananas, sliced

Pour hot water over matzoh in colander; drain. In medium bowl combine eggs, water, milk, sugar, vanilla, cinnamon and salt. Fold in matzoh and banana. Pour into 8 x 8 x 2-inch (20 x 20 x 5-cm) non-stick baking tin. Bake at 350°F, 180°C, Gas Mark 4, for 50 minutes or until knife inserted in centre comes out clean. Serve warm or chilled. Divide evenly.
Makes 4 midday or evening meal servings. Add protein as required.

Coconut Bread Pudding

10 fl oz (300 ml) skim milk

1 egg

2 teaspoons sugar

2 teaspoons shredded coconut

½ teaspoon vanilla flavouring

1 slice (1 oz/30 g) white bread, cut into cubes

cinnamon to taste

Combine all ingredients except bread and cinnamon in blender container; blend until frothy. Pour mixture into small baking dish. Press bread cubes into mixture. Sprinkle with cinnamon. Set baking dish in a pan containing approximately ½ inch (1 cm) of hot water. Bake at 350°F, 180°C, Gas Mark 4, for about 50 minutes or until knife inserted in centre comes out clean.
Makes 2 midday or evening meal servings. Add protein as required.

Prune Bread Pudding

2 slices (2 oz/60 g) white bread, cut into cubes

10 fl oz (300 ml) skim milk

2 eggs, beaten

2½ fl oz (75 ml) prune juice

1 teaspoon vanilla flavouring

pinch salt

1 oz (30 g) prunes, stoned and chopped

cinnamon to taste

Place half the bread cubes in each of 2 individual casseroles. Combine milk, eggs, prune juice, vanilla and salt in medium bowl. Pour half of mixture over each portion of bread. Top each casserole with half of the chopped prunes. Sprinkle with cinnamon. Bake at 350°F, 180°C, Gas Mark 4, for 45 minutes or until pudding is brown and knife inserted in centre comes out clean.
Makes 2 midday or evening meal servings. Add protein as required.

Ginger Currant Cake

3 oz (90 g) self-raising flour

½ teaspoon cinnamon

½ teaspoon ginger

¼ teaspoon nutmeg

2 teaspoons caster sugar

4 tablespoons dried currants

4 tablespoons low-fat spread, melted

5 fl oz (150 ml) skim milk

4 egg whites

Combine all dry ingredients into a large bowl; add melted low-fat spread. Add milk and stir to combine. In separate bowl beat egg whites until stiff peaks form. Fold egg whites into flour mixture and pour into a 7-inch (18 cm) non-stick baking tin. Bake in oven at 350°F, 180°C, Gas Mark 5, for 25 to 30 minutes.
Makes 4 servings.

Bread Sauce

10 fl oz (300 ml) skim milk

large pinch ground cloves

¼ teaspoon salt

freshly ground pepper

1 teaspoon dried onion flakes

4 slices (4 oz/120 g) bread made into crumbs

Put milk in a saucepan with ground cloves, salt, pepper and onion flakes. Bring to boil and simmer until onion is softened. Stir in the breadcrumbs and mix well. Simmer for a further 3 to 4 minutes. Serve with chicken or turkey. Divide evenly.
Makes 4 servings.

Strawberry Pudding

5 oz (150 g) canned strawberries, no sugar added

1½ teaspoons unflavoured gelatine

1 slice (1 oz/30 g) bread, cubed

1 teaspoon lemon juice

artificial sweetener to taste

red food colouring, optional

Drain strawberries and reserve juice. Place berries in blender container. Heat strawberry juice and sprinkle on gelatine; stir until dissolved. Add to blender container with bread, lemon juice, sweetener and colouring if desired. Blend for 1 minute or until mixture is smooth. Pour into dessert dish and refrigerate until set and thoroughly chilled.
Makes 1 serving.

'Cream' of Corn Soup

1 tablespoon margarine

2 oz (60 g) onion, finely diced

1 tablespoon plain flour

⅛ teaspoon salt

pinch pepper and paprika

10 fl oz (300 ml) skim milk

6 oz (180 g) canned cream style corn

1 tablespoon chopped chives

Melt margarine in medium saucepan. Add onion and saute for 4 minutes or until tender. Stir in flour, salt, pepper and paprika. Gradually add milk and cook, stirring constantly, until thickened. Add corn; cook for 5 minutes, stirring frequently. Sprinkle with chives. Divide evenly.
Makes 2 servings.

Lamb and Barley Stew

1½ lbs (720 g) boned lamb, cut into 1-inch (2.5-cm) cubes

6 oz (180 g) carrots, diced

4 oz (120 g) onions, sliced

2 oz (60 g) canned tomatoes

2 chicken stock cubes

½ teaspoon paprika

¼ teaspoon garlic powder

1 bay leaf

salt and pepper to taste

1¼ pints (750 ml) water

6 oz (180 g) peeled potatoes, diced

8 oz (240 g) cut green beans

8 oz (240 g) cooked barley

Grill lamb on rack, turning to brown all sides; set aside. In large non-stick saucepan combine carrots, onions, tomatoes, stock cubes, paprika, garlic powder, bay leaf, salt and pepper; saute 5 minutes, stirring frequently. Add lamb and water. Bring to the boil; reduce heat. Simmer for 30 minutes or until lamb is tender. Add potatoes, green beans and barley, and cook coverd for 1 hour or until potatoes are soft. Divide evenly.
Makes 4 midday or evening meal servings.

GRAINS

Mushroom Risotto

½ oz (15 g) dried mushrooms

6 oz (180 g) onions, diced

2 tablespoons vegetable oil

½ teaspoon turmeric

salt and pepper to taste

12 oz (360 g) cooked rice

In bowl soak mushrooms in hot water to cover for 20 minutes. Drain and reserve liquid. Chop mushrooms. Saute onion in oil in non-stick frying pan. Add chopped mushrooms and mushroom liquid, turmeric, salt and pepper. Stir in rice and reheat. Divide evenly.
Makes 6 servings.

Curried Rice and Sultana Salad

4 oz (120 g) cooked rice

1 teaspoon lemon juice

1 teaspoon vegetable oil

½ teaspoon curry powder

6 oz (180 g) green pepper, seeded and finely diced

4 tablespoons sultanas

5 fl oz (150 ml) natural unsweetened yogurt

5 teaspoons mayonnaise

salt to taste

lettuce leaves or watercress

Combine all ingredients, except lettuce or watercress, in bowl in order given. Mix well; press mixture gently into 1-pint (600-ml) mould; chill. Turn out on plate. Surround with lettuce or watercress. Divide evenly.
Makes 2 servings.

Creamed Potatoes with Horseradish

12 oz (360 g) peeled cooked potatoes, mashed

2 fl oz (60 ml) skim milk

2 tablespoons grated fresh horseradish

4 teaspoons low-fat spread

1 tablespoon chives

4 x 3-oz (90-g) tomatoes, halved

salt, white pepper and nutmeg to taste

Combine first 6 ingredients in a bowl. Beat until fluffy. Place tomato halves in baking dish, season each tomato half with salt and pepper. Top each with an equal portion of potato mixture and sprinkle with nutmeg. Bake at 400°F, 200°C, Gas Mark 6, for 5 to 10 minutes. (2 halves potato each.)
Makes 4 servings.

Creamed Potatoes with Horseradish

CEREAL

We include cereal in our Grains category, of course. Most of us enjoy it at breakfast and it can be a good source of dietary fibre (as can wholemeal bread, too). Remember that your ¾ oz (20 g) of breakfast cereal must be accompanied by at least 5 fl oz (150 ml) of skim milk.

Serving

ready-to-eat (not presweetened) .....¾ oz (20 g)
uncooked ....¾ oz (20 g)

Cereal at the Morning Meal must be eaten with at least ½ milk serving.

Buttermilk Crunch

¾ oz (20 g) wheatflakes

¾ oz (20 g) bran flakes

1 tablespoon sesame seeds, toasted*

2 tablespoons sultanas

2 dried dates, stoned and chopped

8 fl oz (240 ml) buttermilk

Combine wheatflakes, bran flakes and sesame seeds in a large bowl; mix together and divide evenly between 2 cereal bowls. Top each with 1 tablespoon sultanas and half chopped dates and pour 4 fl oz of buttermilk over each serving of fruit and cereal. Serve at once.
Makes 2 morning meal servings.

*To toast sesame seeds, spread on foil and grill for 1 to 2 minutes until golden brown.

Orange Bran Refresher

¾ oz (20 g) bran flakes

4 fl oz (120 ml) orange juice, no sugar added

2½ fl oz (75 ml) natural unsweetened yogurt

Place bran flakes in blender container; add orange juice and puree for 1 to 2 minutes. Add yogurt and puree for a further minute; pour into a tall glass and serve at once.
Makes 1 morning meal serving.

Orange and Grapefruit Cereal

1 medium orange

½ medium grapefruit

¾ oz (20 g) wheatflakes

¾ oz (20 g) porridge oats

1 tablespoon thin honey

5 fl oz (150 ml) natural unsweetened yogurt

Peel and dice orange and grapefruit, place flesh in large bowl and add wheatflakes and porridge oats; mix thoroughly to distribute ingredients evenly. Divide equally between 2 cereal bowls—pour 1½ teaspoons honey over each serving and top each with 2½ fl oz yogurt. Serve at once.
Makes 2 morning meal servings.

Crispy Fruit Breakfast

¾ oz (20 g) puffed rice

5 oz (150 g) raspberries

1½ teaspoons thin honey

2½ fl oz (75 ml) natural unsweetened yogurt

Place puffed rice in tall stemmed glass or in a cereal bowl; add raspberries, spoon over thin honey, top with yogurt and serve at once.
Makes 1 morning meal serving.

Strawberry Cereal

¾ oz (20 g) cornflakes

5 oz (150 g) strawberries, hulled and sliced

1½ teaspoons strawberry jam

2½ fl oz (75 ml) natural unsweetened yogurt

Place cornflakes in cereal bowl, add sliced strawberries; mix jam into yogurt and pour over cornflakes and strawberries. Serve at once.
Makes 1 morning meal serving.

Tropical Munch

2 pineapple rings with 2 tablespoons juice, no sugar added

½ oz (15 g) non-fat dry milk

¾ oz (20 g) cornflakes, crushed

2 teaspoons shredded coconut

½ teaspoon thin honey

Chop pineapple rings and place on bottom of dessert bowl; mix dry milk with juice and pour over pineapple. Prepare cornflakes by placing in a paper or plastic bag and crushing with a rolling pin; add coconut to crushed flakes, sprinkle over pineapple and milk mixture. Trickle honey over top—serve at once.
Makes 1 morning meal serving.

Melon Honey Crunch

2 teaspoons low-fat spread

1½ teaspoons thin honey

¾ oz (20 g) wheat flakes

5 oz (150 g) honeydew melon balls

2½ fl oz (75 ml) yogurt

In small basin over hot water melt low-fat spread and mix with honey; add wheat flakes and turn over gently with a spoon to coat the flakes. Put the coated flakes on a sheet of foil and put under a medium hot grill for 1 to 2 minutes. Meanwhile, place melon balls in dessert bowl—top with yogurt and sprinkle over crunchy wheat flakes.
Makes 1 morning meal serving.

Mandarin Porridge

4 fl oz (120 ml) water

pinch salt

¾ oz (20 g) uncooked porridge oats

4 oz (120 g) canned mandarin sections, no sugar added

artificial sweetener to taste

5 fl oz (150 ml) skim milk

Bring water to the boil in a small saucepan. Add salt and sprinkle in the porridge oats. Cook and stir over moderate heat for 1 minute. Remove from heat, cover and let stand for 30 seconds. Stir mandarin sections and sweetener into cooked cereal. Serve with skim milk.
Makes 1 morning meal serving.

Honey and Oatmeal Breakfast

¾ oz (20 g) coarse ground oatmeal

1 medium dessert apple, cored and grated

1½ teaspoons thin honey

5 fl oz (150 ml) skim milk

Combine oatmeal and apple in cereal bowl and mix thoroughly; spoon over honey and add milk. Serve at once.
Makes 1 morning meal serving.

Pineapple Porridge

4 fl oz (120 ml) water

pinch salt

¾ oz (20 g) uncooked porridge oats

4 oz (120 g) canned crushed pineapple, no sugar added

¼ teaspoon cinnamon

artificial sweetener to taste

5 fl oz (150 ml) skim milk

Bring water to the boil in a small saucepan. Add salt and sprinkle in the porridge oats. Cook and stir over moderate heat for 1 minute. Remove from heat, cover and let stand for 30 seconds. Stir pineapple, cinnamon and sweetener into cooked cereal. Serve with skim milk.
Makes 1 morning meal serving.

Cooked Cereal with Fruit

¾ oz (20 g) uncooked cereal

5 fl oz (150 ml) skim milk

pinch salt

pinch cinnamon

1 oz (30 g) stoned, diced, prunes

Cook cereal in skim milk, adding water as required. Use very low heat and stir constantly to avoid burning. Add salt and cinnamon. Just before cereal is done, stir in prunes. Heat and serve.
Makes 1 morning meal serving.

CEREAL

Oatmeal Cakes

3 oz (90 g) uncooked porridge oats

¼ teaspoon salt

good pinch bicarbonate of soda

2½ fl oz (75 ml) natural unsweetened yogurt

Mix 2 oz (60 g) oats, salt and soda together. Heat yogurt very gently. Combine yogurt and dry ingredients until a thick paste forms; form into a ball. Sprinkle work surface with 1 oz (30 g) oats; roll yogurt ball in oats until well covered. Roll out into a round and transfer to a baking sheet. Cut into quarters and move slightly apart. Sprinkle evenly with any remaining oats. Bake at 400°F, 200°C, Gas Mark 6 for 12 minutes. Toast again for crispness if allowed to go cold. Divide evenly.
Makes 4 morning meal servings.

Bran Cooler

¾ oz (20 g) natural bran

4 fl oz (120 ml) orange juice, no sugar added

5 fl oz (150 ml) skim milk

1 teaspoon honey

2 to 3 ice cubes

Place all ingredients in a blender container and puree for 50 to 60 seconds—or until all the ice cubes have disappeared.
Pour into a tall glass and serve at once.
Makes 1 morning meal serving.

Muesli with Fruit

¾ oz (20 g) uncooked porridge oats

¾ oz (20 g) cornflakes

2 tablespoons raisins

1 medium red eating apple, cored and chopped

2½ fl oz (75 ml) natural unsweetened yogurt

2 teaspoons sesame seeds

5 fl oz (150 ml) skim milk

Mix first 6 ingredients together and serve with the skim milk. Divide evenly.
Makes 2 morning meal servings.

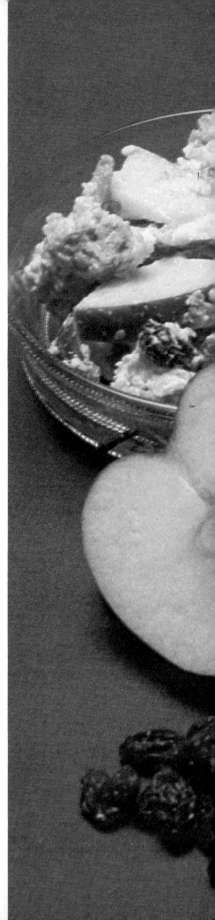

Muesli with Fruit

PROTEIN FOODS

Protein foods are an important part of our eating plan. We can take them at all three meals of the day in appropriate amounts. In many of the recipes you will see the words 'Add protein as required'. Be careful in these cases to make up your protein total to the full amount required in your menu plan on page 5.
Our protein lists include:—

- Eggs
- Cheese
- Peanut Butter
- Poultry, Fish, Meat
- Liver
- Prepared Foods
- Dried Peas & Beans
- Tofu

Eggs

	Serving
Morning Meal	1 egg
Midday and Evening Meal	2 eggs

Select 4 eggs a week

Cheese

Soft Cheese

	Serving
Morning Meal	2½ oz (75 g)
Midday and Evening Meal	5 oz (150 g)

Semisoft and Hard Cheese
Limit to 4 oz (120 g) weekly

	Serving
Morning Meal	1 oz (30 g)
Midday and Evening Meal	2 oz (60 g)

Poultry, Fish, Meat

	Serving
Morning Meal	1 oz (30 g)
Midday and Evening Meal	
Women	3-4 oz (90-120 g)
Men	4-5 oz (120-150 g)
Teenagers	3-4 oz (90-120 g)

Poultry—chicken, turkey
Tripe
Veal
Wild Game

Meat Group—select up to a total of 3 meals weekly, if desired:—

beef	knackwurst
beef sausage	lamb
beef and pork sausage	liver sausage

EGGS

The egg is one of nature's marvels and our test kitchen staff have hatched some marvellous ideas for using it. Make a fluffy souffle or a cheese omelette, enjoy a sweet custard or a meringue topping. You can have 4 eggs each week, taking 1 at a morning meal and 2 at the midday or evening meals. When and where is up to you.

Baked Egg Custard

1 egg, beaten

10 fl oz (300 ml) skim milk

1½ teaspoons sugar

¼ teaspoon vanilla flavouring

pinch salt

pinch cinnamon

Combine all ingredients in blender container; blend. Pour into small ovenproof bowl. Set bowl in baking tin and pour in ½ inch (1 cm) hot water. Bake at 325°F, 160°C, Gas Mark 3, for 1 hour or until knife inserted in centre comes out clean. Serve warm or chilled.
Makes 1 midday or evening meal serving. Add protein as required.

Prawn Omelette

1 egg

2 oz (60 g) shelled prawns, diced

2 tablespoons water

salt, pepper and seasonings to taste

In bowl combine egg, prawns, water and seasonings and beat. Mix well and pour into preheated frying pan. Cook at moderate heat. When edges are firm, lift so uncooked portion flows underneath. When bottom is set and inside almost done to your taste, fold in half. Serve on heated plate.
Makes 1 midday or evening meal serving.

bologna
corned beef
frankfurters
ham

offal
pork
tongue

Liver—select once a week

Fish—select at least 3 meals weekly

Peanut Butter

	Serving
Morning Meal	1 level tbsp
	(Omit 1 serving Fat)
Midday and Evening Meal	3 level tbsps
	(Omit 2 servings Fat)

Prepared Foods

If desired, once a week, in place of the Protein Selection at the Midday or Evening meal, choose one of the following:—

	Serving
fish fingers	4
fish cakes	3
boil-in-the-bag fish in sauce	6 oz (180 g) pack
bacon, lean back (grilled)	2 oz (60 g)

Dried Peas/Beans

	Serving
Midday and Evening Meal	
Women	6 oz (180 g)
Men	8 oz (240 g)
Teenagers	6 oz (180 g)

Beans

butter	lima	soybean
kidney	red	white

Baked Beans (commercial) ....7-8 oz (210-240 g)

Lentils

Peas

  black-eyed (cowpeas)
  chick (garbanzos)
  split

Tofu (soybean curd)—if tofu is selected, increase Dried Peas/Beans serving size by 2 oz (60 g)

Cheese Omelette

1 egg

1 oz (30 g) cheese

2 tablespoons water

salt, pepper and seasonings to taste

In bowl combine egg, cheese, water and seasonings. Mix well and pour into preheated frying pan. Cook at moderate heat. When edges are firm, lift so uncooked portion flows underneath. When bottom is set and inside almost done to taste, fold in half. Serve on heated plate.
Makes 1 midday or evening meal serving.

Tomato Omelette

2 eggs

3 oz (90 g) tomato, chopped

2 tablespoons water

salt, pepper and seasonings to taste

In bowl combine egg, tomatoes, water and seasonings and beat. Mix well and pour into preheated frying pan. Cook at moderate heat. When edges are firm, lift so uncooked portion flows underneath. When bottom is set and inside almost done to your taste, fold in half. Serve on heated plate.
Makes 1 midday or evening meal serving.

Mushroom Omelette

2 eggs

3 oz (90 g) mushrooms, sliced

2 tablespoons water

salt, pepper and seasonings to taste

In bowl combine egg, mushrooms, water and seasonings and beat. Mix well and pour into preheated frying pan. Cook at moderate heat. When edges are firm, lift so uncooked portion flows underneath. When bottom is set and inside almost done to your taste, fold in half. Serve on heated plate.
Makes 1 midday or evening meal serving.

PROTEIN FOODS—EGGS

Savoury Ham Omelette

2 eggs, separated

salt and pepper to taste

3 oz (90 g) diced cooked ham

1 oz (30 g) onion, diced

1½ oz (45 g) green pepper, seeded and diced

½ oz (15 g) celery, diced

2 tablespoons skim milk

4 teaspoons tomato ketchup (optional)

In bowl beat egg whites until stiff but not dry. Set aside. In separate bowl beat egg yolks until frothy. Season with salt and pepper. Add ham, onion, green pepper, celery and skim milk to egg yolks. Fold in whites. Pour into non-stick frying pan with flameproof handle. Cook until bottom is brown and then place frying pan under grill, as close to heat source as possible. Cook until omelette is browned and puffy. Serve with tomato ketchup if desired. Divide evenly.
Makes 2 midday or evening meal servings.

Cheese Souffle

4 tablespoons margarine

1½ oz (45 g) + 4 teaspoons plain flour

2 oz (60 g) non-fat dry milk mixed with 10 fl oz (300 ml) water

4 oz (120 g) mature Cheddar cheese, grated

¼ teaspoon salt

⅛ teaspoon dry mustard

dash hot sauce

4 eggs, separated

Preheat oven to 350°F, 180°C, Gas Mark 4. Melt margarine in saucepan and stir in flour. Gradually add milk and cook over low heat, stirring constantly, until sauce is thick and smooth. Add cheese; stir until cheese melts. Add seasonings. Beat egg yolks in medium bowl. Stir a few tablespoons of hot cheese sauce into yolks, then stir egg yolks into sauce in saucepan and heat for one minute. Remove from heat. In separate bowl beat egg whites until stiff. Stir ⅓ of egg whites into sauce. Gently fold in remaining egg whites. Pour into non-stick 2-pint (1 litre 200 ml) souffle dish. Bake for 45 minutes or until the souffle is set. Serve at once. Divide evenly.
Makes 4 midday or evening meal servings.

Cheese Souffle

PROTEIN FOODS—EGGS

Quick-and-Easy Cheese Souffle

3 slices (3 oz/90 g) white bread, made into crumbs

6 fl oz (180 ml) skim milk

3 oz (90 g) Cheddar cheese, grated

¼ teaspoon salt

dash hot sauce

pinch dry mustard

3 eggs, separated

3 tablespoons margarine

Preheat oven to 375°F, 190°C, Gas Mark 5. In saucepan combine breadcrumbs and milk; simmer over very low heat for 3 minutes. Stir in cheese and seasonings. Heat, stirring often, until cheese is melted. In small bowl beat egg yolks and add to cheese mixture; heat gently for 4 minutes longer. Remove from heat; stir in margarine until melted. Beat egg whites until stiff but not dry. Fold into cheese-yolk mixture. Transfer to 2-pint (1 litre 200 ml) souffle dish that has been sprayed with non-stick cooking spray. Set in pan holding 1 inch (2.5 cm) of water and bake for 30 minutes or until set. Serve at once. Divide evenly. *Makes 3 midday or evening meal servings.*

Currant French Toast

1 egg, beaten

1 tablespoon skim milk

¼ teaspoon vanilla flavouring

pinch salt

1 slice (1 oz/30 g) currant bread

In shallow bowl combine egg, milk, vanilla and salt. Soak bread in mixture, turning at least once. Let stand until as much liquid as possible is absorbed. Place in preheated non-stick frying pan. Pour any remaining egg mixture over bread. Cook until brown on one side; turn to brown other side. Serve hot. *Makes 1 morning meal serving.*

Spring Onion Omelette

1 oz (30 g) sliced spring onion

½ chicken stock cube, crumbled

2 eggs

1 tablespoon water

pinch garlic powder

Spray a 7-inch (18 cm) non-stick frying pan with non-stick cooking spray; heat. Combine spring onion and stock cube in heated frying pan. Cook, stirring occasionally, until spring onion is tender. In bowl, using wire whisk or fork, combine remaining ingredients. Pour egg mixture over spring onion in frying pan. Using a rubber spatula, carefully lift cooked edges of egg mixture and tilt pan so that the uncooked portion flows underneath. When bottom of omelette is lightly browned and top surface is still moist, lift the side nearest the pan handle and fold over about one third of the omelette. Lift opposite side and fold over. Invert omelette onto a warm plate. *Makes 1 midday or evening meal serving.*

Potato-Onion Frittata

1 teaspoon vegetable oil

1 oz (30 g) onion, chopped

3 oz (90 g) peeled potato, cooked and diced

2 eggs, beaten

1 tablespoon water

½ teaspoon chopped fresh parsley

salt and pepper to taste

Preheat grill. Heat oil in small non-stick frying pan and saute onion, stirring frequently until tender. In a bowl combine onion with remaining ingredients. Heat non-stick 7-inch (18-cm) frying pan that has a flameproof handle. Add vegetable-egg mixture, tilting frying pan so that mixture covers bottom. As the edges begin to set, lift edges with spatula and tilt pan, so that the uncooked portion flows underneath. When frittata is firm, place frying pan under the grill for 3 to 5 minutes, or until top of frittata is puffed. Loosen with spatula and remove from frying pan. *Makes 1 midday or evening meal serving.*

Chocolate Meringue Dessert

1 tablespoon unflavoured gelatine

1 pint (600 ml) skim milk

4 teaspoons sugar

¼ teaspoon salt

2 eggs, separated

2 level teaspoons unsweetened cocoa

1 tablespoon water

½ teaspoon vanilla flavouring

⅛ teaspoon cream of tartar

In saucepan sprinkle gelatine over milk to soften. Place over low heat and stir until gelatine dissolves. Remove from heat; add 1 tablespoon sugar and half the salt. In a bowl, beat egg yolks, then stir yolks into milk. Dissolve cocoa in 1 tablespoon water, blend into egg and milk mixture. Cook until mixture thickens slightly; remove from heat. Stir in vanilla. Pour into dessert bowl and refrigerate until firm. Beat egg whites with remaining sugar and salt until frothy. Add cream of tartar and beat until mixture stands in stiff glossy peaks. Spread over chocolate mixture. Grill about 4 inches from heat for 30 seconds, or until meringue is slightly browned. Serve at once or refrigerate and serve well chilled. Divide evenly.
Makes 4 servings. Add protein as required.

Lemon Pancake

1 egg

2 tablespoons skim milk

¾ oz (20 g) flour

1 teaspoon vegetable oil

1 teaspoon lemon juice

1 teaspoon sugar

Combine egg and milk. Beat thoroughly and blend in flour. Heat oil in non-stick frying pan. Pour half pancake mixture into frying pan and cook, turning once, until both sides are golden brown. Transfer to warmed plate and repeat with other half. Sprinkle each pancake with lemon juice and sugar. Roll up and serve at once.
Makes 1 midday or evening meal serving. Add protein as required.

Egg and Potato Pancakes

1 egg, beaten

12 oz (360 g) peeled potatoes, mashed

2 tablespoons fresh parsley, chopped

2 teaspoons Dijon-style mustard

salt and pepper to taste

3 eggs, hard-boiled and chopped

3 oz (90 g) mushrooms

3 oz (90 g) tomato, sliced

Mix beaten egg into mashed potato; add parsley, mustard, salt and pepper. Add chopped hard-boiled eggs. Spray a large frying pan with non-stick cooking spray. Add potato mixture and cook, turning once, until browned on both sides.

Serve with mushrooms and tomatoes. Divide evenly.
Makes 2 midday or evening meal servings.

Orange Peach Meringue

1 slice (1 oz/30 g) bread, made into crumbs

2 teaspoons margarine

4 oz (120 g) canned peach slices, no sugar added

2 teaspoons cornflour

2 fl oz (60 ml) low-calorie orange drink

2 fl oz (60 ml) water

1 egg, separated

Preheat oven to 425°F, 220°C, Gas Mark 7. Put breadcrumbs on a tray and brown in oven. When browned, melt margarine in heatproof container; add crumbs and mix. Press into bottom of small pie dish. Drain juice from peaches into small saucepan. Add cornflour, orange drink and water; bring to the boil, stirring all the time until thickened. Dice peach slices and add, with egg yolk to juice mixture; mix well and then pour over breadcrumb base. Beat egg white until stiff and spoon over peach mixture. Bake in oven for about 5 minutes or until top is golden.
Makes 1 midday or evening meal serving. Add protein as required.

Tuna-Stuffed Eggs

4 eggs, hard-boiled

8½oz (240 g) drained canned tuna, flaked

8 teaspoons vegetable oil

14 capers

¼ teaspoon dry mustard

pinch allspice

freshly ground pepper to taste

1 lb (480 g) tomatoes, sliced

10 oz (300 g) chilled cooked green beans

2 tablespoons red wine vinegar

Cut eggs in half lengthwise. Remove yolks; place in medium bowl and mash. Add 1 oz (30 g) tuna, 2 teaspoons oil, 6 chopped capers, mustard, allspice and pepper. Mix well. Divide evenly and fill egg whites, mounding mixture in the centre. Top each with 1 caper. On each of 4 salad plates, arrange 4 oz (120 g) sliced tomato, 2½ oz (75 g) green beans and 2 filled egg halves. Divide remaining tuna evenly and arrange 1 portion on each plate. Combine remaining oil with vinegar and sprinkle equal amounts over the green beans and tomato on each plate.
Makes 4 midday or evening meal servings.

Russian Egg Salad

4 eggs, hard-boiled and diced

3 oz (90 g) cooked peas

1½ oz (45 g) celery, finely diced

1½ oz (45 g) carrots, finely diced

lettuce leaves

2 tablespoons low-calorie mayonnaise

In bowl combine first 4 ingredients. Chill. Serve on lettuce leaves with low-calorie mayonnaise. Divide evenly.
Makes 2 midday or evening meal servings.

Sweet Pancake with Jam

4 eggs, beaten

1 oz (30 g) non-fat dry milk

8 tablespoons low-fat spread, melted

4 tablespoons water

2 tablespoons plain flour

½ teaspoon vanilla flavouring

2 tablespoons lemon juice (optional)

4 teaspoons strawberry jam

Combine all ingredients except lemon juice and jam in small bowl. Beat until smooth. Pour into a preheated non-stick frying pan and cook until underside is brown and top is set; place under grill to brown top. Sprinkle with lemon juice, if desired. Serve with jam. Divide evenly.
Makes 4 midday or evening meal servings. Add protein as required.

Sweet Pancake with Jam

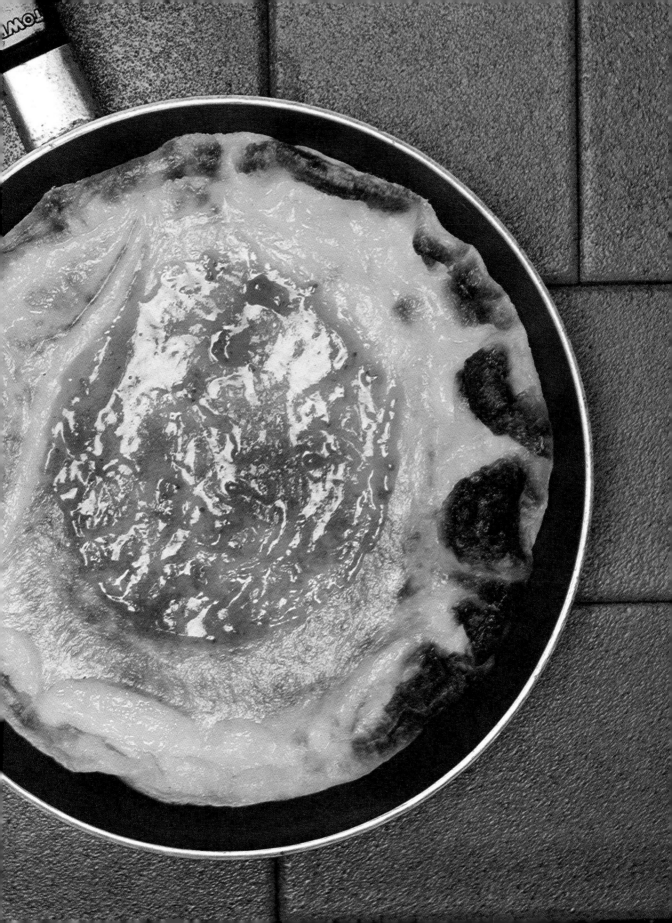

Norfolk Dumplings

1 oz (30 g) non-fat dry milk

10 fl oz (300 ml) water

2 eggs

1 tablespoon plain flour

¼ teaspoon salt

4 teaspoons low-fat spread

Mix together dry milk, water, eggs, flour and salt into a thick batter. Have a saucepan of boiling, salted water ready, into which you drop spoonfuls of this mixture. In fast boiling water the dumplings should be cooked in 2 to 3 minutes. Drain well and serve covered with the low-fat spread. Divide evenly.
Makes 2 midday or evening meal servings. Add protein as required.

Strawberry Omelette

2 eggs, separated

2 tablespoons water

artificial sweetener to taste

5 oz (150 g) strawberries

2½ fl oz (75 ml) natural unsweetened yogurt

Separate eggs. In a small bowl, beat yolks with water until creamy and add sweetener. In another bowl, whisk egg whites until peaks form. Whisk a little white into yolks, then fold in remainder. Heat non-stick pan, spread egg mixture evenly over pan, cook gently until underside is brown. Place under hot grill until top is golden. Mix fruit and sweetener into yogurt. Slide omelette onto heated plate, top with yogurt mixture and fold over. Serve at once.
Makes 1 midday or evening meal serving.

Eggs 'Benedict'

1 muffin, 1½ oz (45 g), split and toasted

1½ oz (45 g) cooked sliced ham

1 egg, poached

2 teaspoons mayonnaise

1 caper or ½ teaspoon chopped fresh parsley

1 teaspoon low-fat spread (optional)

Cover one muffin half with ham. Top with poached egg. Spread with mayonnaise. Place under preheated grill for 1 minute to heat. Garnish with caper or parsley. Serve with remaining muffin half, spread with low-fat spread if desired.
Makes 1 midday or evening meal serving.

Smoked Salmon Scramble

2 tablespoons margarine

6 oz (180 g) green pepper, seeded and diced

4 oz (120 g) onions or spring onions, diced

6 oz (180 g) smoked salmon pieces

4 eggs, beaten

Melt margarine in small non-stick saucepan. Add green pepper and onions. Cover and cook until soft. Add smoked salmon and mix well. Pour in eggs; cook, stirring occasionally, until eggs are done to taste. Divide evenly.
Makes 4 midday or evening meal servings.

'Creamed' Eggs and Mushrooms

12 oz (360 g) mushrooms, sliced

14 fl oz (420 ml) water

1 teaspoon lemon juice

4 teaspoons plain flour, mixed with 2 tablespoons water

¼ teaspoon paprika

pinch ground red pepper

1 oz (30 g) non-fat dry milk

4 eggs, hard-boiled and separated

4 slices (4 oz/120 g) white bread, toasted and cut diagonally into halves

salt and freshly ground pepper to taste

In saucepan combine mushrooms, 10 fl oz (300 ml) water and lemon juice. Simmer for 10 minutes or until mushrooms are tender. Remove mushrooms with slotted spoon and set aside. Reduce mushroom liquid to about 2 fl oz (6 ml) and stir in flour, paprika and red pepper. Add milk and remaining water and cook, stirring constantly, until mixture is smooth and thickened. Chop egg whites. Add egg whites and mushrooms to sauce. Put yolks through a sieve. Serve mushroom sauce on toast, topped with yolks. Season with salt and pepper. Divide evenly.
Makes 2 midday or evening meal servings.

Scrambled Egg and Potato

2 tablespoons margarine

6 oz (180 g) peeled cooked potato, diced

4 eggs, beaten

3 tablespoons liquid (water or potato liquid)

1 teaspoon chopped fresh parsley or chives

½ teaspoon salt

pepper to taste

Melt margarine in small non-stick saucepan. Add potato and heat. Combine eggs with liquid, parsley or chives, salt and pepper. Add to margarine-potato mixture. Cook, stirring frequently, until done to taste. Divide evenly.
Makes 2 midday or evening meal servings.

Yorkshire Pudding

1 tablespoon plain flour

salt and pepper to taste

1 egg, separated

2 tablespoons skim milk

Preheat oven to 500°F, 260°C, Gas Mark 9. In a medium bowl mix flour, salt, and pepper. Add egg yolk and a little milk and mix until creamy. Add the rest of the milk and beat mixture well. Whisk egg white until stiff peaks form. Fold this into the mixture. Spray 2 small patty tins with non-stick vegetable spray. Spoon mixture equally between each patty tin. Reduce oven temperature to 400°F, 200°C, Gas Mark 7

and cook for 15 to 20 minutes, until golden brown.
Makes 1 midday or evening meal serving. Add protein as required.

Egg and Cheese Rice Salad

3 oz (90 g) cooked brown rice, chilled

1 egg, hard-boiled and chopped

1 oz (30 g) Cheddar cheese, diced

1 oz (30 g) minced pickled cucumber

1 oz (30 g) pimiento, diced

1½ teaspoons sesame seeds, toasted

1½ teaspoons Dijon-style mustard

1 tablespoon mayonnaise

⅛ teaspoon salt

dash each white pepper and Worcester sauce

2 large lettuce leaves.

Combine all ingredients except lettuce in large bowl. Chill for at least 2 hours. Serve on lettuce leaves.
Makes 1 midday or evening meal serving.

Picnic Eggs

4 eggs, hard-boiled

2½ fl oz (75 ml) natural unsweetened yogurt

1 teaspoon prepared English mustard

1 teaspoon soy sauce

½ teaspoon curry powder

½ teaspoon Worcester sauce

¼ teaspoon seasoning salt

¼ teaspoon paprika

Slice hard-boiled eggs length-wise. Remove yolks and place in a bowl; add yogurt, mustard, soy sauce, curry powder, Worcester sauce and seasoning salt to egg yolks. Mash with a fork until mixture is smooth. Spoon one eighth of the mixture into each egg white half. Sprinkle with paprika. Chill before serving.
Makes 2 midday or evening meal servings.

Courgette Omelette

4 oz (120 g) onion

3 oz (90 g) courgettes

salt and pepper to taste

2 eggs

Finely chop onion and courgettes. Simmer in a little salted water for 5 minutes. Drain. Beat eggs with seasoning to taste. Stir in cooked vegetables. Heat a non-stick pan; pour in mixture and cook over medium heat until lightly set. Turn carefully to brown second side or finish under a hot grill. Divide into 2 equal portions.
Makes 2 midday or evening meal servings. Add protein as required.

CHEESE

You can do so much with an ounce or two (30 g or 60 g) of cheese—add flavour to an egg, liven up a salad, fill out a sandwich, even create a cheesecake. We have many cheeses on our Food Plan. The soft cheeses, for example, include cottage and curd which can be taken in generous quantities—2½ oz (75 g) at the morning meal and 5 oz (150 g) at the midday or evening meals. Brie, Camembert, Danish Blue and Ricotta are some of the semi-soft cheeses and are limited to 4 oz (120 g) weekly, as are the hard cheeses, such as Caerphilly, Cheddar, Cheshire, Edam, Gruyere and Leicester. Check the menu plan for the amounts at each meal.

Remember that cheese (like eggs) is particularly useful for the person who is eating alone. They both make nutritious and satisfying meals, easily and quickly prepared.

Fruity Cottage Cheese

5 oz (150 g) cottage cheese

5 oz (150 g) blackberries

1½ teaspoons sugar

Blend cottage cheese in blender container until smooth. Transfer to small serving dish. Mash blackberries in small bowl or blend until pureed. Add sugar to blackberries. Gently fold into cheese to give a marble effect. Chill.
Makes 1 midday or evening meal serving.

Cheesecake Pudding

8 oz (240 g) canned pineapple chunks, no sugar added

2 eggs

2 teaspoons lemon juice

¼ teaspoon vanilla flavouring

5 oz (150 g) curd cheese

4 teaspoons low-fat spread

cinnamon to taste

Combine pineapple chunks, egg, lemon juice and vanilla in blender container. Blend until smooth. Add cheese and blend. Pour into 1-pint (600 ml) oven-proof casserole. Dot with low-fat spread; sprinkle with cinnamon and bake at 350°F, 180°C, Gas Mark 4, for 40 minutes. Serve chilled.
Makes 2 midday or evening meal servings.

Savoury Welsh Rarebit

2 oz (60 g) hard cheese

1 tablespoon skim milk

1 oz (30 g) onion, chopped

½ teaspoon sage

1 teaspoon Worcester sauce

salt and pepper to taste

1 slice (1 oz/30 g) wholemeal bread, lightly toasted

3 oz (90 g) tomato, sliced

parsley sprigs to garnish

Grate cheese and mix together with milk. Add onion, sage, Worcester sauce, salt and pepper. Spread mixture evenly onto toast and place under grill on highest setting, until mixture is bubbly and slightly browned. Add tomato slices and parsley to garnish.
Makes 1 midday or evening meal serving.

Pineapple Cheesecake

8 teaspoons low-fat spread

4 digestive biscuits, crumbled

4 teaspoons unflavoured gelatine

1 fl oz (30 ml) warm water

juice and zest of ½ a lemon

5 oz (150 g) curd cheese

5 fl oz (150 ml) natural unsweetened yogurt

4 oz (120 g) canned crushed pineapple (or tidbits)

artificial sweetener to taste

1 to 2 drops vanilla flavouring

lemon twists to garnish

To make base, melt low-fat spread in basin over hot water, add crumbled biscuits and press onto base of loose bottom cake tin. To make filling, dissolve gelatine in warm water; add lemon juice and zest. Add to cheese with the yogurt, pineapple, sweetener, vanilla flavouring. Liquidise thoroughly until all contents are smooth. Pour onto the base and put in refrigerator until set. Garnish with lemon twists. Divide evenly.
Makes 4 midday or evening meal servings. Add protein as required.

Pineapple Cheesecake

PROTEIN FOODS—CHEESE

Harvest Salad with Fruit French Dressing

Salad

2 x 1½ oz (45 g) heads of chicory, cut into ½-inch (1-cm) slices
10 oz (300 g) cottage cheese
*1 medium apple, cored and sliced
2 oz (60 g) canned or fresh orange sections, no sugar added

Dressing

2 fl oz (60 ml) orange juice, no sugar added
1 tablespoon vegetable oil
4½ teaspoons lemon juice or cider vinegar
1 teaspoon chopped fresh mint (optional)
salt and pepper to taste

To Prepare Salad: Arrange 1½ oz (45 g) chicory on each of 2 salad plates. Top each with 5 oz (150 g) cottage cheese. Arrange half of apple slices and 1 oz (30 g) orange sections around each portion of cottage cheese. Place salads in refrigerator to chill.
To Prepare Dressing: Combine all ingredients in small jar with tight-fitting lid. Cover and shake well.
To Serve: Pour half of dressing over each chilled salad.
Makes 2 midday or evening meal servings.

*Apple slices may be dipped in lemon juice to prevent discolouring.

Caesar Salad

1 garlic clove, crushed
1 small lettuce, torn into bite-size pieces
1 oz (30 g) Parmesan cheese, grated
1 egg, softly boiled
2 teaspoons vegetable oil
2 teaspoons lemon juice
dash Worcester sauce
salt and freshly ground pepper to taste
1 slice (1 oz/30 g) white bread, toasted and diced

Rub salad bowl with garlic. Place lettuce in bowl, sprinkle with cheese and top with egg. In small bowl combine oil, lemon juice, Worcester sauce, salt and pepper; pour over salad. Add diced toast. Toss and serve immediately.
Makes 1 midday or evening meal serving.

Cheese Dip

10 oz (30 g) cottage cheese
4 oz (120 g) very mature Cheddar cheese, grated
2 tablespoons water
few drops hot sauce

Combine all ingredients in blender container; blend until smooth. Add more water, a few drops at a time, if necessary. Spoon into small bowl, cover and chill for several hours. Divide evenly. Serve with raw vegetables.
Makes 4 midday or evening meal servings.

Bean and Cheese Salad

2 teaspoons vegetable oil
2 teaspoons lemon juice
hot sauce to taste
salt to taste
3 oz (90 g) fresh bean sprouts, blanched if desired
3 oz (90 g) cooked dried white beans or chick peas
1 oz (30 g) Cheshire cheese, crumbled
½ teaspoon poppy seeds (optional)

In serving bowl combine first 4 ingredients. Add remaining ingredients; toss.
Makes 1 midday or evening meal serving.

Cheese and Egg Stuffed Tomato

4 oz (120 g) tomato
1 egg, lightly scrambled
1 oz (30 g) Cheddar cheese
salt and pepper to taste

Cut a thin slice off the top of the tomato. Scoop out pulp, leaving at least ¼-inch (5-mm) thickness on all sides. Fill cavity with egg and top with cheese. Bake at 350°F, 180°C, Gas Mark 4, until cheese melts. Chop tomato pulp; season with salt and pepper. Spoon over melted cheese.
Makes 1 midday or evening meal serving.

Cheese and Noodle Bake

6 fl oz (180 ml) skim milk

6 oz (180 g) prunes, cooked, stoned and chopped

1 tablespoon plain flour

¼ teaspoon cinnamon

artificial sweetener to taste (optional)

12 oz (360 g) cooked noodles

15 oz (450 g) cottage cheese

In medium bowl combine milk, prunes, flour, cinnamon and sweetener if desired. Set aside. Combine noodles and cottage cheese in large bowl and transfer to 10 x 6 x 1¾ inch (25 x 15 x 4 cm) baking tin. Pour prune mixture over noodles. Bake at 375°F, 190°C, Gas Mark 5, for 1 hour or until hot and bubbly. Divide evenly.
Makes 6 midday or evening meal servings. Add protein as required.

Quick-and-Easy Welsh Rarebit

4 oz (120 g) Cheddar cheese, diced

2 fl oz (60 ml) skim milk

dash Worcester sauce

pinch ground red pepper

salt and pepper to taste

4 slices (4 oz/120 g) white bread, toasted

Combine all ingredients except bread in saucepan. Cook, stirring occasionally, until cheese is melted. Divide evenly. Serve on slices of hot toast.
Makes 2 midday or evening meal servings.

Courgette and Cheese Special

12 oz (360 g) courgettes, sliced

6 oz (180 g) tomatoes, skinned and sliced

8 oz (240 g) onions, sliced

3 tablespoons chicken stock, made with ¼ stock cube

12 oz (360 g) peeled potatoes

8 oz (240 g) Cheddar cheese, grated

4 slices (4 oz/120 g) white bread made into crumbs

salt and freshly ground black pepper

Preheat oven to 350°F, 180°C, Gas Mark 4. Cook courgettes, tomatoes and onions in a non-stick saucepan with the stock for 5 to 10 minutes, stirring constantly. Par-boil potatoes in boiling, salted water for 10 minutes. Drain, cut into ¼-in (5-mm) slices. Mix grated cheese and breadcrumbs together. Arrange layers of vegetables in an ovenproof dish. Sprinkle cheese/breadcrumbs and seasoning between each layer. Finish with layer of potatoes and cheese/breadcrumbs. Bake in oven for 45 minutes. Brown under grill and divide evenly.
Makes 4 midday or evening meal servings.

Ham and Cheese Noodles

8 oz (240 g) cooked broad noodles

10 oz (300 g) cottage cheese

6 oz (180 g) cubed ham

5 fl oz (150 ml) natural unsweetened yogurt

2 teaspoons poppy seeds

½ teaspoon paprika

½ teaspoon Worcester sauce

salt and pepper to taste

Combine all ingredients in medium saucepan. Heat slowly, stirring often, until cheese begins to melt. Divide evenly.
Makes 4 midday or evening meal servings.

Cottage Cheese Pancakes

2 eggs, separated

5 oz (150 g) cottage cheese

2 tablespoons plain flour

1 teaspoon baking powder

¼ teaspoon salt

5 fl oz (150 ml) natural unsweetened yogurt (optional)

In medium bowl combine egg yolks, cottage cheese, flour, baking powder and salt. Beat egg whites in small bowl until stiff but not dry. Fold into yolk mixture. Drop batter from mixing spoon onto preheated non-stick griddle. Brown pancakes on both sides, turning once with spatula. Divide evening. Serve 2½ fl oz (45 ml) yogurt as topping on each portion if desired.
Makes 2 midday or evening meal servings.

PROTEIN FOODS—CHEESE

Yorkshire Curd Cheesecake

Crust

4 slices (4 oz/120 g) bread, made into crumbs and browned in oven or under grill

5 fl oz (150 ml) natural unsweetened yogurt

pinch salt

Filling

5 oz (150 g) curd or cottage cheese

6 teaspoons margarine

artificial sweetener to taste

2 eggs, beaten

grated rind of ½ lemon

4 oz (120 g) prunes, stoned and chopped

¼ teaspoon freshly grated nutmeg

Preheat oven to 350°F, 180°C, Gas Mark 4. Mix breadcrumbs with yogurt and add pinch of salt. Press into 7½-inch (19 cm) flan ring to form flan case. Place curds into a bowl and break into small pieces using a fork. In a separate bowl, cream margarine and artificial sweetener to taste. Add beaten eggs and grated lemon rind. Add curds or cottage cheese and chopped prunes. Mix together and spread over flan case. Sprinkle with grated nutmeg (if preferred, nutmeg can be added to cheese mixture). Bake for 30 to 40 minutes or until firm. Divide evenly.
Makes 4 midday or evening meal servings. Add protein as required.

Chef's Salad

6 oz (180 g) salad greens (e.g. iceberg and cabbage lettuce and endive)

3 oz (90 g) green pepper, seeded and sliced

2 oz (60 g) tomato, cut into 4 wedges

1½ oz (45 g) boneless cooked ham or cooked smoked tongue or 2 oz (60 g) skinned and boned, cooked chicken, cut into thin strips

1 oz (30 g) hard cheese, cut into thin strips

1 tablespoon vegetable oil

1 tablespoon red wine vinegar

salt and pepper to taste

Place salad greens in serving bowl. Arrange vegetables, meat and cheese over greens.
Combine oil, vinegar, salt and pepper in small jar with tight-fitting lid. Cover and shake well. Pour over salad.
Makes 1 midday or evening meal serving.

Grilled Cheese and Ham Sandwich

2 slices (2 oz/60 g) white bread

1½ oz (45 g) sliced cooked ham

1 oz (30 g) hard cheese

Place ham and cheese between bread slices. Place on a rack under grill and toast until brown, turning once, approximately 5 minutes. Serve at once.
Makes 1 midday or evening meal serving.

Macaroni Cheese and Cauliflower

Creamy cheese sauce

2 tablespoons margarine

2 tablespoons plain flour

10 fl oz (300 ml) skim milk

4 oz (120 g) Cheddar cheese, grated

dash Worcester sauce, hot sauce or pinch nutmeg (optional)

Macaroni

10 oz (300 g) cooked cauliflower florets

4 oz (120 g) cooked macaroni

4 oz (120 g) drained canned mushrooms

salt and pepper to taste

paprika to garnish

To Prepare Sauce: Melt margarine in saucepan; blend in flour. Add milk; cook, stirring constantly until thickened. Stir in cheese. Season with Worcester sauce, hot sauce or nutmeg if desired.
To Prepare Macaroni: Mix together cauliflower, macaroni, mushrooms, salt and pepper and cheese sauce. Put into 2-pint (1 litre 200 ml) shallow casserole; sprinkle with paprika. Cover dish and bake at 350°F, 180°C, Gas Mark 4 for 30 minutes. Uncover and bake for 5 minutes until brown.
Makes 2 midday or evening meal servings.

Macaroni Cheese and Cauliflower

PROTEIN FOODS—CHEESE

Sunset Bake

3 oz (90 g) drained cooked butter beans (cooked until very soft)

2 oz (60 g) drained cooked cauliflower (cooked until very soft)

3 oz (90 g) canned tomatoes, drained

1 oz (30 g) hard cheese, grated

1 oz (30 g) finely chopped onion

2 teaspoons low-calorie tomato ketchup

¼ chicken stock cube, crumbled

chopped parsley to garnish (optional)

Combine beans and cauliflower in large bowl. Add tomatoes and grated cheese, keeping a little cheese to one side for topping. Add onion, ketchup and crumbled stock cube. Mash all ingredients together until consistency of mashed potatoes. Place in ovenproof dish and top with remainder of grated cheese and parsley. Bake in moderately hot oven, 375°F, 190°C, Gas Mark 5 for 30 minutes.
Makes 1 midday or evening meal serving.

Green Beans Au Gratin

6 oz (180 g) cooked green beans

3 oz (150 g) mushrooms, sliced

2 oz (60 g) hard cheese, grated

½ teaspoon dried herbs

salt and pepper to taste

2 tablespoons tomato puree, mixed with 1 tablespoon water

1 slice (1 oz/30 g) white bread, made into crumbs

In small ovenproof casserole, layer cooked green beans, mush-rooms, 1½ oz (45 g) cheese and herbs. Sprinkle with salt and pepper. Top with tomato puree mixed with water. Combine remaining cheese and crumbs; sprinkle over casserole. Bake at 350°F, 180°C, Gas Mark 4 for 25 minutes or until hot and bubbly.
Makes 1 midday or evening meal serving.

Cheese Pancakes with Blackberry Topping

Pancakes

1 egg, beaten

2½ oz (75 g) cottage cheese

2½ fl oz (75 ml) skim milk

¼ teaspoon salt

1 slice (1 oz/30 g) white bread, made into crumbs

Topping

5 oz (150 g) blackberries

1 tablespoon water

1 teaspoon sugar

Garnish

1 lemon, cut into 6 wedges

To Prepare Pancakes: In bowl combine egg, cottage cheese, skim milk, salt and bread-crumbs. Using a tablespoon, drop mixture by the spoonful onto a preheated non-stick frying pan. Brown lightly; turn with a spatula to brown other side.
To Prepare Topping: Combine ingredients in saucepan and simmer until blackberries are soft. Serve topping with warm pancakes and garnish with lemon wedges.
Makes 1 midday or evening meal serving.

Cheesy Baked Aubergine

2 aubergines about 8 oz (240 g) each, cut into halves

4 tablespoons tomato puree, mixed with 4 fl oz (120 ml) water

1½ teaspoons chopped fresh parsley

1 teaspoon dried onion flakes, reconstituted in 1 tablespoon water

½ garlic clove, crushed

¼ teaspoon basil

⅛ teaspoon fennel seeds

⅛ teaspoon pepper

4 oz (120 g) Cheddar cheese, grated

4 oz (120 g) cooked rice

Place aubergine halves, cut sides down, in a baking tin. Add ¼ in (5 mm) water and bake at 350°F, 180°C, Gas Mark 4, until soft. Remove and allow to cool slightly. Scoop out pulp leaving a ½-inch (1-cm) shell. Set aside. In saucepan combine next 7 ingredients and simmer for 10 minutes. In bowl combine pulp, cheese, rice and half the tomato mixture. Divide evenly and stuff into aubergine shells. Place in casserole, stuffed side up and cover with remaining tomato mixture. Bake at 375°F, 190°C, Gas Mark 5, for 25 minutes or until stuffing is hot and cheese is melted. Divide evenly.
Makes 2 midday or evening meal servings.

Courgettes au Gratin

6 oz (180 g) courgettes

4 oz (120 g) onions, sliced

2 teaspoons vegetable oil

3 oz (90 g) tomato, chopped

1 tablespoon red wine vinegar

1 teaspoon basil flakes

1 garlic clove, crushed

1 slice (1 oz/30 g) bread, made into crumbs

2 oz (60 g) Cheddar cheese, grated

Top and tail courgettes into rings ¼ inch (5 mm) thick. Put in saucepan with water and cook for 3 to 4 minutes or until tender and crisp. In medium non-stick saucepan, put onion and oil and allow to cook until softened. Add tomatoes, vinegar, herbs and garlic. Cover and cook, stirring occasionally, for 15 to 20 minutes, or until all ingredients are soft. Place courgettes in shallow heatproof dish, spoon tomato and onion mixture over them. Mix breadcrumbs with grated cheese and spread over courgette mixture. Place under hot grill and cook until brown and cripsy.

Makes 1 midday or evening meal serving.

Noodles and Cheese with Ham

2 oz (60 g) hot cooked noodles

1½ oz (45 g) diced cooked ham

1 oz (30 g) grated hard cheese

Mix noodles, ham and cheese together until well combined.

Makes 1 midday or evening meal serving.

Tomato Salad with 'Creamy' Cheese Dressing

Salad

4 x 4½ oz (135 g) tomatoes

4 lettuce leaves

20 oz (600 g) cottage cheese or 10 oz (300 g) cottage cheese and 4 oz (120 g) Danish Blue cheese, crumbled

1 garlic clove, crushed

salt and pepper to taste

1 teaspoon chives

Dressing

1 tablespoon mayonnaise

2 tablespoons blended cottage cheese (see method)

½ teaspoon salt

½ teaspoon paprika

2 tablespoons vegetable oil

4½ teaspoons cider vinegar

To Prepare Salad: Remove core from stem end of each tomato. Make 2 criss-cross cuts through each tomato almost to the bottom, so that tomato opens. Set each tomato on a lettuce leaf. Blend cottage cheese in blender container until smooth. Set aside 2 tablespoons for 'Creamy' Cheese Dressing. Add Danish Blue cheese if used, garlic, salt and pepper and blend until smooth. Stir in chives. Stuff each tomato with ¼ of the cheese mixture. Place in refrigerator until dressing is ready.

To Prepare Dressing: In small bowl, combine mayonnaise, blended cheese, salt and paprika. Slowly add oil, beating con-stantly, until thick. Add vinegar and continue to beat until well blended.

To Serve: Remove tomatoes from refrigerator and pour ¼ of 'Creamy' Cheese Dressing over each.

Makes 4 midday or evening meal servings.

Ham and Cheese Canapes

6 oz (180 g) boneless cooked ham

1 oz (30 g) onion

2 teaspoons prepared mustard

dash hot sauce

4 slices (4 oz/120 g) white bread, toasted

4 oz (120 g) Cheddar cheese, grated

½ teaspoon chopped fresh parsley

Put ham and onion through the mincer. Stir in mustard and hot sauce. Divide evenly into 4 portions and spread 1 portion on each slice of toast. Top each with 1 oz (30 g) cheese and sprinkle with parsley. Place on griller pan and grill until cheese melts. Cut in quarters and serve.

Makes 4 midday or evening meal servings.

PROTEIN FOODS—CHEESE

Vegetable Pasta with Cheese

2 tablespoons margarine

2½ fl oz (75 ml) natural unsweetened yogurt

4 oz (120 g) Parmesan cheese, grated

4 oz (120 g) Cheddar cheese, diced

8 oz (240 g) cooked spaghetti

6 oz (180 g) courgettes, sliced and blanched

salt and freshly ground pepper to taste

parsley sprigs and pimiento strips to garnish

Melt margarine in non-stick saucepan. Add the yogurt and cheese. Cook until cheese melts; add spaghetti and courgettes. Mix well and season with salt and pepper. Serve hot. Garnish with parsley and pimiento. Divide evenly.
Makes 4 midday or evening meal servings.

Macaroni Cheese

5 fl oz (150 ml) skim milk

2 oz (60 g) Cheddar cheese, grated

2 oz (60 g) cooked elbow macaroni

3 oz (90 g) tomato, sliced

chopped fresh parsley or chives to garnish

Heat milk in small saucepan. Add cheese; stir until cheese melts. Pour over macaroni. Serve with tomato slices and garnish with parsley or chives.
Makes 1 midday or evening meal serving.

Fun Fondue

2 oz (60 g) non-fat dry milk, mixed with 6 fl oz (180 ml) water

4 oz (120 g) hard cheese, grated

3 teaspoons cornflour

4 teaspoons white wine

pinch each dry mustard and ground red pepper

9 oz (270 g) crisp raw vegetables (carrot, cucumber, celery or fennel sticks)

Heat milk in small saucepan. Add cheese and heat gently; mix wine with cornflour and add to pan with seasonings. Stir until cheese melts. Serve warm and use as a dip with vegetables.
Makes 2 midday or evening meal servings.

Hearty Welsh Rarebit

1 slice (1 oz/30 g) bread

1 teaspoon dried onion flakes or ½ oz (15 g) fresh onion, chopped

5 fl oz (150 ml) skim milk

1 tablespoon plain flour

1 pinch dry mustard

2 oz (60 g) hard cheese, grated

3 oz (90 g) potato, mashed

salt and pepper to taste

3 oz (90 g) tomato, sliced

parsley sprigs to garnish

Toast the bread. Soak onions in milk for 5 minutes in saucepan; carefully stir in the flour and bring to the boil, stirring continuously. Simmer for 2 minutes. Remove from heat and add mustard, cheese, mashed potato, salt and pepper and mix well. Spread mixture onto toast, top with sliced tomatoes and place under grill until browned. Garnish with parsley.
Makes 1 midday or evening meal serving.

Orange 'Coeur à la Creme'

1 tablespoon unflavoured gelatine

4 fl oz (120 ml) cold water

4 fl oz (120 ml) boiling water

10 oz (300 g) cottage cheese

2 teaspoons sugar

½ teaspoon orange flavouring

½ teaspoon vanilla flavouring

½ teaspoon coconut flavouring

1 medium orange, peeled and sectioned

Sprinkle gelatine over cold water in blender container to soften. Add boiling water; blend until gelatine is dissolved. Add remaining ingredients, except orange; blend until smooth. Pour into small bowl. Chill until the consistency of unbeaten egg whites. Dice all but two of the orange sections and fold diced sections into gelatine mixture. Divide evenly into 2 small moulds and chill until set. Turn out and garnish each serving with one reserved orange section.
Makes 2 midday or evening meal servings.

Fun Fondue

PROTEIN FOODS—CHEESE

Baked Egg and Cheese Aubergine Slices

1 egg, slightly beaten

1 teaspoon mayonnaise

salt and pepper to taste

1 slice (1 oz/30 g) white bread, made into crumbs

1 oz (30 g) Parmesan cheese, grated

¼ teaspoon oregano

4 oz (120 g) aubergine, cut into ¼-inch (5-mm) thick slices

In small bowl combine egg, mayonnaise, salt and pepper. In separate bowl mix together breadcrumbs, cheese and oregano. Dip each slice of aubergine in egg mixture, then dip into crumb mixture to coat each side evenly. Place in shallow baking dish. Sprinkle with any extra egg and crumb mixture. Bake at 450°F, 230°C, Gas Mark 8 for 15 minutes, or until crispy, turning once.
Makes 1 midday or evening meal serving.

Pan Haggerty

3 oz (90 g) peeled potato

3 oz (90 g) onion

2 oz (60 g) Cheddar cheese

salt and pepper to taste

Slice potatoes and pat dry. Peel and slice onion. Grate cheese. Spray non-stick saucepan with non-stick cooking spray. Place layers of potato, onion and cheese in saucepan, reserving a little cheese for the top. Begin and end layers with potato. Season each layer with salt and

pepper. Cover with lid and cook until vegetables are tender. Sprinkle remainder of cheese on top and brown under the grill.
Makes 1 midday or evening meal serving.

Super Special Cottage Cheese Salad

8 oz (240 g) canned crushed pineapple, no sugar added

2 fl oz (60 ml) white wine vinegar

2 tablespoons vegetable oil

¾ teaspoon dry mustard

½ teaspoon salt

¼ teaspoon tarragon leaves

¼ teaspoon basil leaves

1½ oz (45 g) sliced mushrooms

1 head shredded lettuce

6 oz (180 g) tomato, cut into 8 wedges

1 oz (30 g) cucumber, sliced

1 oz (30 g) spring onions, sliced

10 oz (300 g) cottage cheese

Combine first 7 ingredients; add mushrooms and chill. Combine next 4 ingredients in salad bowl; toss with mushroom mixture. Divide salad evenly; top each portion with 5 oz (150 g) cottage cheese.
Makes 2 midday or evening meal servings.

Blackberry Dream

5 oz (150 g) blackberries

2½ oz (75 g) cottage cheese

2½ fl oz (75 ml) natural unsweetened yogurt

¼ teaspoon blackberry colour flavouring or other fruit flavouring

artificial sweetener to taste

Wash and hull blackberries and put in dessert bowl. Press cottage cheese through a sieve into a small basin. Add yogurt, flavouring and sweetener; beat thoroughly until it is thick and creamy. Pour over blackberries and serve at once, or chill and serve. Add protein as required.
Makes 1 midday or evening meal serving.

Cheddar Cheese Pudding

1 slice (1 oz/30 g) white bread, cut in half diagonally

1 oz (30 g) Cheddar cheese, grated

1 egg, slightly beaten

5 fl oz (150 ml) skim milk

pinch dry mustard

pinch ground red pepper

Preheat oven to 375°F, 190°C, Gas Mark 5. Place bread in shallow ramekin or ovenproof dish. Sprinkle cheese evenly over bread. In small bowl combine remaining ingredients. Pour over bread; place dish in larger baking pan which contains about ½ inch (1 cm) water. Bake for 20 minutes.
Makes 1 midday or evening meal serving.

Festive Cheese Salad

¼ lettuce, shredded

1½ oz (45 g) tomato, sliced

1½ oz (45 g) cucumber, sliced

1 oz (30 g) cooked green peas

1 oz (30 g) cooked beetroot, cubed

1 oz (30 g) spring onions, sliced

1 slice canned pineapple with 1 tablespoon juice, no sugar added, chopped

1 oz (30 g) Cheddar cheese, grated

1 oz (30 g) Edam cheese, cut into thin strips

1 teaspoon finely chopped fresh mint

1 teaspoon finely chopped fresh parsley

2 teaspoons mayonnaise

Arrange lettuce on plate and top with tomato, cucumber, peas, beetroot, chopped pineapple (reserve juice). Sprinkle grated cheese over the top and arrange strips of Edam cheese over this. In small bowl combine reserved pineapple juice, mint, parsley and mayonnaise and mix thoroughly. Spoon over salad ingredients. Chill and serve.
Makes 1 midday or evening meal serving.

Cheese, Corn and Courgette Bake

4 oz (120 g) onions, finely chopped

4 teaspoons margarine

1 lb 4 oz (600 g) courgettes, sliced

12 oz (360 g) drained canned whole kernel corn

1 pint (600 ml) skim milk

8 oz (240 g) Cheddar cheese, grated

dash hot sauce

salt and pepper to taste

In non-stick saucepan, combine onion and margarine. Cook for 10 minutes or until onions are tender. Stir in remaining ingredients. Transfer vegetable-cheese mixture to a large casserole. Cover and bake at 375°F, 190°C, Gas Mark 5, for 30 minutes. Divide evenly.
Makes 4 midday or evening meal servings.

Cheesy Grill

2½ oz (75 g) cottage cheese

1 teaspoon sugar

½ teaspoon vanilla flavouring

pinch cinnamon

1 slice (1 oz/30 g) white bread, toasted

In small bowl combine cottage cheese with sugar, flavouring and cinnamon. Spread on toast and place under grill until hot and bubbly. Add protein as required.
Makes 1 midday or evening meal serving.

Strawberry-Cheese Yogurt

10 oz (300 g) very ripe strawberries

1½ teaspoons unflavoured gelatine

4 fl oz (120 ml) water

10 oz (300 g) cottage cheese

10 fl oz (300 ml) natural unsweetened yogurt

4 fl oz (120 ml) orange juice, no sugar added

1 teaspoon vanilla flavouring

Set aside 8 small strawberries for garnish; slice remaining strawberries and arrange in bottom of pie dish. In small saucepan soften gelatine in water. Heat, stirring until dissolved. Combine with remaining ingredients in blender container. Blend until smooth. Pour onto sliced strawberries in pie dish. Chill for several hours until firm. Garnish with reserved berries. Divide evenly.
Makes 4 midday or evening meal servings. Add protein as required.

Strawberries and 'Cream'

5 oz (150 g) strawberries

2½ oz (75 g) curd cheese

2 tablespoons skim milk

artificial sweetener to taste

Hull the strawberries and slice, or leave whole. Place in serving dish. Beat curd cheese, milk and sweetener together. Pour over strawberries.
Makes 1 midday or evening meal serving. Add protein as required.

POULTRY

Poultry lends itself to so many different dishes. It can be spicy in a curry or bland in a white sauce. It is good both hot and cold. It should be weighed after cooking if possible.

Remove skin before sauteeing, stir-frying or stewing, but if the chicken has been baked, grilled or roasted, remove the skin before it is served. If you choose smoked poultry, take the lower end of the serving size range given in the menu plan.

Jellied Chicken Mousse

1 tablespoon unflavoured gelatine

1 chicken stock cube

5 fl oz (150 ml) boiling water

salt and pepper to taste

8 oz (240 g) skinned and boned cooked chicken, cut into small pieces

lettuce and tomato for garnish

Dissolve gelatine and stock cube in boiling water; add salt and pepper to taste. Pour into blender container and add chicken. Blend for 30 seconds. Divide evenly between 2 individual moulds and refrigerate until set. Turn out onto plates and garnish with lettuce and tomato.
Makes 2 servings.

Chicken Stir-Fry

2 teaspoons vegetable oil

6 oz (180 g) skinned and boned chicken breast, cut into thin strips

1½ oz (45 g) onion, sliced

1½ oz (45 g) mushrooms, sliced

3 oz (90 g) beansprouts

2 teaspoons soy sauce

1 teaspoon arrowroot or cornflour

4 fl oz (120 ml) chicken stock made with ¼ stock cube

Heat oil in wok or deep frying pan. Add chicken and saute for 3 minutes. Add onion and mushrooms and saute for 2 to 3 minutes. Add bean sprouts and saute for a further minute. Sprinkle with soy sauce. Mix arrowroot with the stock. Pour this over and stir well. Cover and simmer for a further 10 minutes. Serve at once.
Makes 1 midday or evening meal serving.

Paella

1½ teaspoons salt

1 teaspoon oregano

1 teaspoon lemon juice

¼ teaspoon freshly ground pepper

1 garlic clove, crushed

3 tablespoons vegetable oil

1 lb 2 oz (540 g) skinned and boned chicken breast, cut into 1-inch (2.5-cm) cubes

6 oz (180 g) onion, chopped

6 oz (180 g) green pepper, seeded and chopped

1 lb 2 oz (540 g) cooked rice

9 oz (270 g) fresh peas or frozen small peas, thawed

8 fl oz (240 ml) boiling water

4 tablespoons tomato puree, mixed with 4 fl oz (120 ml) water

¾ teaspoon capers

½ teaspoon ground coriander

½ teaspoon saffron or turmeric

6 oz (180 g) shelled cooked prawns

6 oz (180 g) drained canned, mussels

shredded canned pimientos to garnish

In small cup combine salt, oregano, lemon juice, pepper and garlic to make a paste. Heat oil in large, heavy non-stick saucepan; saute chicken, onion and pepper. Stir in seasoned paste. Add rice, peas, boiling water, tomato puree mixed with water, capers, coriander and saffron or turmeric; heat thoroughly. Stir in prawns and mussels. Bring to the boil, then reduce heat and simmer for 10 minutes. Garnish with pimientos. Serve hot. Divide evenly.
Makes 6 midday or evening meal servings.

Paella

PROTEIN FOODS—POULTRY, VEAL AND GAME

Roast Chicken with Spiced Cherry Sauce

12 oz (360 g) frozen, stoned, sweet cherries, no sugar added

3 lb (1 kg 440 g) chicken *

salt, white pepper, garlic powder and paprika to taste

6 fl oz (180 ml) chicken stock made with ½ stock cube

6 fl oz (180 ml) low-calorie carbonated orange drink

1 teaspoon sugar

¼ cinnamon stick

¼ teaspoon lemon juice

1 clove

1 tablespoon cornflour, mixed with 1 tablespoon water

Set cherries aside to thaw. Sprinkle chicken with salt, pepper, garlic powder and paprika. Place on a rack in roasting tin and roast at 350°F, 180°C, Gas Mark 4, for 1½ hours or until done. Baste occasionally with stock. While chicken is roasting, combine juice from cherries, orange drink, sugar, cinnamon, lemon juice and clove in a medium saucepan. Add cornflour and stir. Place over medium heat; cook, stirring constantly, until mixture thickens. Add cherries; stir until coated with sauce and thoroughly heated. To serve, slice chicken and remove skin. Serve 4 oz (120 g) sliced chicken per portion; to each portion add ¼ of the sauce.
Makes 4 midday or evening meal servings.
★A 3 lb (1 kg 440 g) chicken will yield about 1 lb (480 g) cooked meat.

Chicken in White Sauce

4 teaspoons margarine

4 teaspoons plain flour

10 fl oz (300 ml) skim milk

salt and pepper to taste

6 oz (180 g) mushrooms, sliced

6 oz (180 g) cooked peas

1 lb (480 g) skinned and boned cooked chicken, cut into bite-sized pieces

8 oz (240 g) cooked rice

Melt margarine in non-stick saucepan. Stir in flour. Gradually add milk and cook until sauce thickens. Season to taste. Add mushrooms, peas and chicken pieces. Cover and simmer very gently for 10 to 15 minutes. Divide evenly and serve each portion with 2 oz (60 g) rice.
Makes 4 midday or evening meal servings.

Chicken Pilaf

12 fl oz (360 ml) chicken stock made with 1 stock cube

2 oz (60 g) cooked brown rice

8 oz (240 g) canned pineapple tidbits, no sugar added

3 oz (90 g) peeled potato, cut into ½-inch (1 cm) dice

pinch cinnamon

pinch cumin

8 oz (240 g) diced poached chicken

In medium saucepan combine all ingredients except chicken. Cover and simmer for 30 minutes or until potato is tender. Add chicken and heat until chicken is thoroughly hot. Divide evenly.
Makes 2 midday or evening meal servings.

Chicken Breasts with Tarragon

1 teaspoon vegetable oil

1 x 8 oz (240 g) chicken breast, skinned

pinch tarragon leaves

1 oz (30 g) onion, chopped

1 oz (30 g) carrot, chopped

2 tablespoons dry white wine with 2 tablespoons water

1 tablespoon chopped fresh parsley

Heat oil in non-stick frying pan. Add chicken breast and saute until browned on both sides, ending with bone side down. Sprinkle chicken evenly with tarragon, then onion and carrot. Pour wine and water over and around the chicken; cover and reduce heat. Simmer for 25 to 30 minutes or until chicken is tender. Remove chicken to serving platter and keep warm. Add 2 teaspoons parsley to pan and cook, stirring, until liquid is slightly reduced. Pour liquid over chicken, top with remaining parsley.
Makes 1 midday or evening meal serving.

PROTEIN FOODS—POULTRY, VEAL AND GAME

Chicken Cacciatore

2 tablespoons vegetable oil

1½ lbs (720 g) skinned and boned chicken breasts

6 oz (180 g) green pepper, seeded and cut into strips

2 oz (60 g) onion, sliced

1 garlic clove, crushed

8 fl oz (240 ml) water

8 tablespoons tomato puree

1 teaspoon oregano

½ teaspoon salt

Heat oil in non-stick saucepan and saute chicken for 2 to 3 minutes. Add green pepper, onion and garlic; saute for 4 minutes. Add remaining ingredients; cover and simmer, stirring occasionally, for 40 minutes or until done. Divide evenly.
Makes 4 midday or evening meal servings.

Grilled Chicken

3 lbs (1 kg 440 g) chicken portions, quarters or pieces*

salt and pepper to taste

Sprinkle chicken with salt and pepper. Place skin side down on rack in grill pan. Grill 3 to 6 inches (8 to 15 cm) from source of heat. Grill for 20 to 25 minutes, turn and grill for 15 to 20 minutes or until fork-tender. Remove skin. Divide evenly.
Makes 4 midday or evening meal servings.
*3 lbs (1 kg 440 g) chicken portions will yield about 1 lb (480 g) cooked meat.

Herbed Chicken and Noodles

8 oz (240 g) skinned and boned cooked chicken, diced

¼-½ teaspoon fennel seeds

1 teaspoon oregano

1 teaspoon sage

1 teaspoon seasoning salt

⅛ teaspoon chilli powder

12 oz (360 g) cooked lentils

3 garlic cloves, crushed

3 tablespoons soy sauce

2 bay leaves

1 chicken stock cube

2 pints (1 litre 200 ml) water (approximately)

8 oz (240 g) hot cooked egg noodles

Put all ingredients except noodles into a large saucepan. Bring to the boil and simmer until mixture thickens. Remove bay leaves. Divide into four equal portions and serve each portion with 2 oz (60 g) noodles.
Makes 4 midday or evening meal servings.

Chicken Hotpot

1½ teaspoons margarine

12 oz (360 g) chicken portions, skinned*

¼ chicken stock cube, dissolved in 6 fl oz (180 ml) boiling water

3 oz (90 g) tomato, seeded and diced

1½ oz (45 g) onion, thinly sliced

1 teaspoon dry white wine

1 garlic clove, crushed

½ teaspoon sugar

3 oz (90 g) drained canned whole kernel corn

Melt margarine in thick based or non-stick saucepan. Add chicken portions and brown on all sides. Add remainng ingredients, except corn. Cover and cook for about 35 minutes or until chicken is tender. Add corn and cook for about 8 to 10 minutes more, or until heated through, adding a little more water if contents of pan become too dry.
Makes 1 midday or evening meal serving.
*12 oz (360 g) chicken portions will yield about 4 oz (120 g) cooked meat.

Chinese Stir-Cooked Chicken

1 teaspoon marmalade

1½ teaspoons soy sauce

1½ teaspoons lemon juice

½ teaspoon cornflour

⅛ teaspoon crushed red chilies

pinch garlic powder

pinch ginger powder

6 oz (180 g) skinned and boned chicken breast, cut into 1-inch (2.5 cm) pieces

½ medium orange, sliced

1 oz (30 g) cooked peas

In bowl combine marmalade, soy sauce, lemon juice, cornflour, crushed chilies, garlic and ginger powder. Add chicken and toss to coat all pieces with marinade. Let stand for 1 hour, stirring occasionally. Cut each orange slice in half; reserve. Heat medium non-stick saucepan; transfer chicken and marinade to saucepan and cook for 5 minutes, stirring often. Add peas; cook for 5 minutes longer or until peas are hot. Serve garnished with halved orange slices.
Makes 1 midday or evening meal serving.

Chicken and Sardine Mexican Style

1 oz (30 g) onion, diced

1 small garlic clove, crushed

3 oz (90 g) tomato, chopped

2 fl oz (60 ml) chicken stock, made with ½ stock cube

1 teaspoon chopped fresh parsley

2 oz (60 g) skinned and boned cooked chicken, diced

2 oz (60 g) flaked drained canned sardines

½ hot chili pepper, seeded and minced or dash chili powder

pepper to taste

shredded lettuce to garnish

Brown onion and garlic in non-stick frying pan. Add tomato, stock and parsley and cook for 10 minutes. Add chicken, sardines and chili pepper. Simmer, uncovered, for 15 minutes, or until chicken is well heated through. Season with pepper. Serve garnished with lettuce.
Makes 1 midday or evening meal serving.

Shredded Chicken with Peanut Sauce

3 teaspoons vegetable oil

6 oz (180 g) partially frozen, skinless and boneless chicken breast, cut into thin strips

2 oz (60 g) onion, finely diced

2 garlic cloves, crushed

3 tablespoons crunchy peanut butter

2 tablespoons each lemon juice and soy sauce

artificial sweetener to taste

dash hot sauce

6 oz (180 g) broccoli florets, steamed until tender crisp

Heat vegetable oil in wok or non-stick frying pan until hot. Stir-fry strips of chicken for 1 to 2 minutes or until firm to the touch. With a slotted spoon, remove chicken and reserve. Add onion to wok or non-stick frying pan and stir-fry for 2 minutes or until onion becomes translucent. Add garlic and continue to stir-fry until garlic becomes golden. Remove wok or non-stick frying pan from heat, stir in remaining ingredients, except broccoli florets. Add chicken to wok or non-stick frying pan and cook until heated through. Divide evenly. To serve, top with steamed broccoli.
Makes 2 midday or evening meal servings.

Shredded Chicken with Peanut Sauce

PROTEIN FOODS—POULTRY, VEAL AND GAME

Coq Au Vin

3 lbs (1 kg 440 g) chicken portions, skinned*

8 fl oz (240 ml) red wine

12 fl oz (360 ml) chicken stock, made with 1 stock cube

12 oz (360 g) tomato, skinned and finely diced

2 garlic cloves, finely chopped

1 teaspoon dried thyme

6 oz (180 g) mushrooms, quartered

4 oz (120 g) small onions or shallots

1 bay leaf

salt and pepper to taste

Place chicken on rack in grill pan and grill 5 inches (12 cm) from source of heat for 8 minutes or until chicken is firm to the touch (turn at least once during cooking). Meanwhile place remainder of ingredients in a large saucepan and bring to the boil. Cook for 2 to 3 minutes. In a large ovenproof casserole, arrange chicken portions; pour over stock/vegetable mixture. Cover and bake in moderate oven, 350°F, 180°C, Gas Mark 4, for 1½ to 2 hours or until chicken is tender. Divide evenly.
Makes 4 midday or evening meal servings.
*3 lbs (1 kg 440 g) chicken portions will yield about 1 lb (480 g) cooked meat.

Chicken Soup with Vegetables

3½ pints (2 litres) water

2 chicken stock cubes

12 oz (360 g) skinned and boned chicken, diced*

4 oz (120 g) carrots, sliced

4 oz (120 g) celery, sliced

2 oz (60 g) onion, diced

3 parsley sprigs

1 bay leaf

¼ teaspoon thyme

salt and freshly ground pepper to taste

Combine all ingredients except salt and pepper in a saucepan. Simmer for 1 hour. Season with salt and pepper. Discard parsley and bay leaf. Divide evenly into large soup bowls.
Makes 2 midday or evening meal servings.
*12 oz (360 g) chicken portions will yield about 4 oz (120 g) cooked meat.

Oven Chicken with Vegetables

10 oz (300 g) carrots, diced

8 oz (240 g) celery, diced

4 oz (120 g) onions, diced

1 roasting chicken, 3 lbs (1 kg 440 g), skinned and cut into quarters*

salt, pepper, paprika and poultry seasoning to taste

4 tablespoons tomato ketchup

2 tablespoons prepared mustard

In large shallow casserole combine carrots, celery and onions. Season chicken pieces and place over vegetables. Combine ketchup and mustard and pour evenly over chicken. Bake at 375°F, 190°C, Gas Mark 5, for 1 hour or until chicken is tender. Divide chicken, vegetables and sauce evenly.
Makes 4 midday or evening meal servings.
*A 3 lb (1 kg 440 g) chicken will yield about 1 lb (480 g) cooked meat.

Chinese Chicken with Green Peppers and Mushrooms

12 oz (360 g) skinned and boned chicken, cut into bite-size pieces

2 teaspoons cornflour

4 tablespoons soy sauce

1 tablespoon vegetable oil

½ oz (15 g) dried mushrooms, reconstituted and quartered

6 oz (180 g) green pepper, seeded and cut into squares

2 oz (60 g) spring onions, chopped

2 tablespoons red wine vinegar

salt and pepper to taste

4 fl oz (120 ml) chicken stock, made with ½ stock cube

In bowl toss together chicken and cornflour; add soy sauce and mix well. Set aside to marinate for 20 to 30 minutes. Heat oil in non-stick frying pan; add chicken and marinade. Cook, stirring constantly, until chicken is well browned. Remove from frying pan and set aside. Add remaining ingredients to frying pan, except stock, and cook for 5 minutes. Add chicken and stock; cook, stirring constantly, until mixture boils. Reduce heat and simmer for 10 minutes. Divide evenly.

Makes 2 midday or evening meal servings.

Poached Chicken

Poaching is an excellent method for cooking skinned and boned chicken breasts and other skinned chicken portions. In wide shallow saucepan, bring to the boil enough water to cover chicken. Reduce heat. Add chicken in one layer. Cover and simmer until chicken is done, approximately 20 to 30 minutes, depending on size of chicken pieces. Remove chicken from liquid; serve or chill for later use. Poaching liquid may be chilled until fat congeals. Remove and discard fat. Liquid can be used in recipes calling for chicken stock.

Poached Chicken in Sauce

Sauce

| 2 tablespoons margarine |
| 2 tablespoons plain flour |
| 1/8 teaspoon salt |
| pinch white pepper |
| 10 fl oz (300 ml) skim milk |
| 1/8 teaspoon nutmeg |
| 1/8 teaspoon Worcester sauce |

| 1 lb (480 g) cooked broccoli florets |
| 8 oz (240 g) skinned and boned, poached chicken |
| 4 oz (120 g) Cheddar or other hard cheese, grated |

To Prepare Sauce: Melt marga-rine in non-stick saucepan. Add flour, salt and pepper and cook over moderate heat for about 2 minutes, stirring constantly. Gradually add milk. Cook, stir-ring constantly with a wire whisk until mixture thickens. Combine sauce, nutmeg and Worcester sauce; set aside. In ovenproof dish arrange broccoli and chicken. Pour sauce over chicken and top with cheese. Bake at 400°F, 200°C, Gas Mark 6, for approximately 15 minutes or until chicken and sauce are hot and cheese is melted and bubbly. Divide evenly.

Makes 4 midday or evening meal servings.

Chicken Pita

| 8 oz (240 g) onion, thinly sliced |
| juice of 1 small lemon |
| 1/2 teaspoon cinnamon |
| 1 white cardamom, split at the top |
| 4 x 8 oz (240 g) chicken breasts, skinned and boned |
| salt and pepper to taste |
| 8 teaspoons corn oil |
| 4 x 3 oz (90 g) pita bread |

| 3 lb (1 kg 440 g) chicken* |

| 1/2 hot chili pepper, seeded and minced or dash chili powder |

Dry-fry onion until translucent, adding a little of the lemon juice to prevent sticking. Add the cinnamon, cardamom and chicken. Brown chicken on both sides and add remaining lemon juice, salt and pepper to taste. Cook until chicken is cooked through—about 15 minutes.

Remove frying pan from heat and stir in the oil. Slit the pita bread to make a pocket and fill with one chicken portion and a quarter of the onion mixture. Place the filled pita bread on a baking tray and bake in a preheated oven, 350°F, 180°C, Gas Mark 4, for 10 minutes. Serve piping hot with a mixed salad.

Makes 4 midday or evening meal servings.

Basic Roast Chicken

| 6 fl oz (180 ml) chicken stock, made with 1 stock cube |
| 1 tablespoon finely chopped celery |
| 1 tablespoon dried onion flakes |
| 1 teaspoon dried sweet pepper flakes |
| salt and pepper to taste |
| 3 lbs (1 kg 440 g) chicken* |

In small saucepan combine first 5 ingredients and simmer for 15 minutes. Place chicken, breast-side up, on rack in shallow, un-covered roasting pan. Roast at 325°F, 160°C, Gas Mark 3, allowing about 20 minutes per lb (480 g). If meat thermometer is used, insert into centre of the inner thigh muscle. Cook to an internal temperature of 180 to 185°F (80° to 85°C). Baste fre-quently with stock mixture. Remove skin and divide evenly.

Makes 4 midday or evening meal servings.

*A 3 lb (1 kg 440 g) chicken will yield about 1 lb (480 g) cooked meat.

PROTEIN FOODS—POULTRY, VEAL AND GAME

Chicken and Egg Loaf

12 oz (360 g) cooked chicken meat

3 oz (90 g) carrot, sliced

1 egg, hard-boiled

1 oz (30 g) canned pimiento

3 slices 3 oz (90 g) white bread, made into crumbs

5 eggs, beaten

2 teaspoons lemon juice

½ teaspoon salt

¼ teaspoon hot sauce

⅛ teaspoon white pepper

Sauce

3 oz (90 g) green pepper, seeded and finely chopped

2 oz (60 g) onion, chopped

1 garlic clove, crushed

1 lb 6 oz (660 g) canned tomatoes, crushed

6 tablespoons tomato puree, mixed with 4 fl oz (120 ml) water

6 fl oz (180 ml) beef stock, made with 1 stock cube

1½ teaspoons basil

¾ teaspoon salt

½ teaspoon chopped fresh parsley

½ teaspoon oregano

⅛ teaspoon pepper

Put chicken, carrot, hard-boiled egg and pimiento through mincer. Stir in the breadcrumbs, beaten eggs, lemon juice, salt, hot sauce and pepper. Transfer to non-stick loaf tin. Bake at 350°F, 180°C, Gas Mark 4, for 30 minutes or until firm. To make sauce, combine green pepper, onion and garlic in medium saucepan. Cook for 2 to 3 minutes. Add remaining ingredients; simmer for about 35 minutes, or until sauce reaches desired consistency, stirring often. Slice Chicken & Egg Loaf and pour sauce over portions. Divide evenly.
Makes 6 midday or evening meal servings.

Yogurt-Baked Chicken

3 lbs (1 kg 440 g) chicken pieces, skinned*

1 garlic clove, cut

10 fl oz (300 ml) natural unsweetened yogurt

4 oz (120 g) onion, finely chopped

2 tablespoons chopped fresh parsley

1 tablespoon water

¼ teaspoon sage

¼ teaspoon tarragon

Dry chicken pieces and rub with cut garlic clove. Place in shallow baking tin. Bake at 350°F, 180°C, Gas Mark 4, for 40 minutes or until tender. Combine remaining ingredients in small bowl; spoon over chicken. Bake at 275°F, 140°C, Gas Mark 1, for 25 minutes or until sauce is hot and bubbly and onion tender. Divide evenly.
Makes 4 midday or evening meal servings.
*3 lb (1 kg 440 g) chicken portions will yield about 1 lb (480 g) cooked meat.

Paprika Chicken with Noodles

4 tablespoons low-fat spread

3 oz (90 g) onion, thinly sliced

2 tablespoons plain flour

2 tablespoons paprika

1 teaspoon dried basil

½ teaspoon dried tarragon

½ teaspoon salt

pinch pepper

12 fl oz (360 ml) chicken stock, made with 1 stock cube

10 fl oz (300 ml) natural unsweetened yogurt

8 teaspoons dry white wine

1 lb (480 g) skinned and boned cooked chicken breast, shredded

8 oz (240 g) cooked noodles

3 oz (90 g) mushrooms, sliced

1 tablespoon chopped fresh parsley

Heat low-fat spread in a large saucepan. Add onion and saute over medium heat until beginning to soften. Stir in flour, paprika, basil, tarragon, salt and pepper. Stir in chicken stock and cook over moderate heat, stirring well, for about 3 minutes or until mixture thickens. Remove from heat; add yogurt, wine, chicken, noodles and mushrooms. Heat gently for 10 minutes. Sprinkle with parsley. Divide evenly.
Makes 4 midday or evening meal servings.

Paprika Chicken with Noodles

PROTEIN FOODS—POULTRY, VEAL AND GAME

Chicken Korma

2 tablespoons vegetable oil

1½ lbs (720 g) skinned and boned chicken breasts

4 oz (120 g) onion, chopped

1 garlic clove, crushed

1 oz (30 g) hot chili pepper, chopped

½ teaspoon paprika

¼ teaspoon cardamom

¼ teaspoon coriander

¼ teaspoon cumin

5 fl oz (150 ml) water

2 tablespoons tomato puree

Heat oil in non-stick saucepan and saute chicken for 2 to 3 minutes. Add remaining ingredients in order given. Cover and simmer, stirring occasionally, for 40 minutes or until chicken is tender. Divide evenly.
Makes 4 midday or evening meal servings.

Easy Chicken Mould

1 tablespoon unflavoured gelatine

4 fl oz (120 ml) water

5 fl oz (180 ml) chicken stock made with 1 stock cube

4 tablespoons mayonnaise

1 tablespoon lemon juice

¼ teaspoon white pepper

salt to taste

10 fl oz (300 ml) natural unsweetened yogurt

1 lb (480 g) skinned and boned cooked chicken, diced

2 oz (60 g) celery, diced

6 oz (180 g) cooked asparagus spears, chilled

4 oz (120 g) drained canned pimientoes, cut into strips

In saucepan sprinkle gelatine over water to soften. Heat, stirring constantly until gelatine is dissolved. In bowl combine stock, mayonnaise, lemon juice, pepper and salt; stir in gelatine mixture and yogurt; refrigerate until consistency of unbeaten egg whites, about 15 minutes. Fold in chicken and celery. Pour into large ring mould. Chill until firm. Turn out on serving plate. Fill centre with asparagus. Garnish with pimientos. Divide evenly.
Makes 4 midday or evening meal servings.

Mushroom-Chicken Salad

6 oz (180 g) mushrooms

1 teaspoon lemon juice

1 lb (480 g) skinned and boned cooked chicken, cut into thin strips

4 slices 4 oz (120 g) white bread, toasted and cut into cubes

4 oz (120 g) cucumber, peeled and cubed

4 oz (120 g) chicory, thickly sliced

5 fl oz (150 ml) natural unsweetened yogurt

4 tablespoons mayonnaise

1 tablespoon white wine vinegar

¼ teaspoon each dried tarragon and marjoram

¼ teaspoon salt or to taste

8 olives, stoned and chopped

1 tablespoon chopped fresh chives

1 tablespoon chopped fresh parsley

Slice mushrooms thinly and sprinkle with lemon juice. Mix together the mushrooms, chicken, bread cubes, cucumber and chicory. To make the dressing, combine the remaining ingredients and mix well. Toss the chicken-mushroom mixture in the dressing and divide evenly between 4 salad plates. Sprinkle with chives and parsley.
Makes 4 midday or evening meal servings.

Orange Chicken Salad

8 oz (240 g) skinned and boned cooked chicken, diced

10 oz (300 g) cottage cheese

2 medium oranges, peeled and diced

2 oz (60 g) celery, diced

2 tablespoons mayonnaise

1 tablespoon grated fresh orange rind

½ teaspoon salt

⅛ teaspoon white pepper

lettuce leaves

In bowl combine all ingredients except lettuce. Shred lettuce and arrange on 4 plates. Divide chicken mixture evenly over lettuce.
Makes 4 midday or evening meal servings.

Foil-Baked Chicken Rolls

2 boned and skinned chicken breasts, 6 oz (180 g) each

salt and freshly ground pepper to taste

2 teaspoons prepared mustard

2 teaspoons low-fat spread

2 teaspoons chopped chives

2 teaspoons chopped fresh parsley

2 teaspoons lemon juice

½ teaspoon garlic powder

Pound chicken breasts until they are about ¼ inch (5 mm) thick. Season with salt and pepper. Place each breast on a 12 x 12-inch (30 x 30 cm) piece of aluminium foil. Combine remaining ingredients in small bowl. Divide evenly and spread over each chicken breast. Roll chicken breast, tucking ends in. Seal rolls in foil. Place in baking pan. Bake at 375°F, 190°C, Gas Mark 5, for 30 minutes. Serve 1 foil packet per portion and open them at the table.
Makes 2 midday or evening meal servings.

Lemon Baked Chicken

6 oz (180 g) skinned and boned chicken breast

2½ fl oz (75 ml) natural unsweetened yogurt

2 teaspoons lemon juice

pinch paprika

½ teaspoon soy sauce

⅛ teaspoon each thyme, marjoram, pepper and ginger

½ garlic clove, finely chopped

1½ teaspoons sesame seeds, toasted

Cut several small slits in chicken with tip of a knife. Place chicken breast in a small baking dish. To prepare marinade: combine remaining ingredients, except sesame seeds, in a small bowl. Pour marinade evenly over chicken. Cover and marinate in refrigerator, turning chicken once, for several hours, or overnight. Sprinkle chicken evenly with sesame seeds. Bake with marinade at 375°F, 190°C, Gas Mark 5, for about 30 minutes or until chicken is tender.
Makes 1 midday or evening meal serving.

Hot Savoury Chicken

4 oz (120 g) skinned and boned cooked chicken

2 oz (60 g) celery

2 oz (60 g) onion

2 oz (60 g) mushrooms

2 teaspoons soy sauce

1 fl oz (30 ml) orange juice, no sugar added

1 tablespoon vinegar

artificial liquid sweetener to taste

salt and pepper to taste

pinch ground nutmeg (optional)

2 oz (60 g) peas

3 oz (90 g) drained canned whole kernel corn

2 oz (60 g) boiled rice

Dice chicken, celery, onion and mushrooms. Mix soy sauce, orange juice, vinegar, sweetener, salt, pepper, and nutmeg in a large basin. Add chicken, onion, celery and mushrooms and marinate for at least 1 hour. Cook this mixture in non-stick saucepan for 10 minutes. Add peas, corn and rice and cook for a further 2 to 3 minutes.
Makes 1 midday or evening meal serving.

Rabbit Stew

12 fl oz (360 ml) cider vinegar

12 fl oz (360 ml) water

4 oz (120 g) onions, sliced

1 teaspoon salt

1 teaspoon ground cloves

3 bay leaves

¼ teaspoon crushed peppercorns, or more to taste

⅛ teaspoon allspice

2 lbs (960 g) rabbit, cut into pieces

6 fl oz (180 ml) chicken stock, made with ½ stock cube

¼ teaspoon gravy browning

2 teaspoons cornflour, dissolved in 2 teaspoons water

In large bowl combine first 8 ingredients. Add rabbit; cover and refrigerate for 1 to 2 days, turning occasionally. Remove rabbit; reserve marinade. Grill rabbit 4 inches (10 cm) from source of heat, turning once, for 12 minutes or until brown. Transfer rabbit and reserved marinade to large saucepan; cover and simmer for 1 hour or until tender. Remove rabbit and keep warm. Add stock and gravy browning to marinade. Stir in cornflour and cook, stirring constantly, until thickened. Strain sauce through double-layered muslin. Discard solids. Serve sauce with rabbit. Divide evenly.
Makes 4 midday or evening meal servings.

Rabbit Moutardes

2 oz (60 g) onion, diced

2 oz (60 g) carrot, diced

2 oz (60 g) swede, diced

1 stick celery, diced

2 x 8 oz (240 g) rabbit back portions

1 Bouquet Garni (see page 179)

10 fl oz (300 ml) chicken stock, made with ½ stock cube

salt and pepper to taste

½ teaspoon Dijon-style mustard

½ teaspoon English mustard

5 fl oz (150 ml) natural, unsweetened yogurt

Place all ingredients except mustard and yogurt in a casserole and cook over low heat until rabbit is tender, approximately 1 hour. Remove Bouquet Garni. Remove rabbit portions to warm serving plate. Whisk mustard and yogurt together and add to rabbit liquor. Do not bring back to the boil. Pour over rabbit and serve immediately. Divide evenly.
Makes 2 midday or evening meal servings.

Italian Veal and Peppers

1 tablespoon vegetable oil

12 oz (360 g) stewing veal, cut into 1-inch (2.5-cm) cubes

4 tablespoons tomato puree

4 fl oz (120 ml) water

4 oz (120 g) onions, sliced

1 chicken stock cube

1 garlic clove, crushed

½ teaspoon basil

½ teaspoon oregano

freshly ground pepper to taste

8 oz (240 g) green peppers, seeded and cut into ½-inch (1-cm) strips

6 oz (180 g) broccoli spears

Heat oil in thick-based or non-stick frying pan; add veal and saute for 3 to 4 minutes. Add all remaining ingredients except green peppers. Cover and cook over low heat for 45 minutes. Add peppers and continue cooking for 10 minutes longer or until veal and peppers are tender. Divide evenly. Serve with broccoli.
Makes 2 midday or evening meal servings.

Italian Veal and Peppers

PROTEIN FOODS—POULTRY, VEAL AND GAME

Spicy Veal Casserole

1½ lbs (720 g) boneless veal, cut into 2-inch (5-cm) cubes, lightly grilled on a rack

12 oz (360 g) small onions or shallots

3 fl oz (90 ml) water

4 tablespoons tomato puree

3 tablespoons red wine vinegar

8 teaspoons dry red wine

2 garlic cloves, crushed

1 teaspoon brown sugar

1 teaspoon salt

1 teaspoon pickling spice, tied in muslin

3 oz (90 g) button mushrooms

3 oz (90 g) frozen peas

2 tablespoons chopped fresh parsley

Place veal and onions in medium casserole. Mix together water, tomato puree, vinegar, wine and seasonings and pour into casserole, stirring to distribute ingredients. Cover casserole and simmer for about 1 hour or until veal is almost tender. Add mushrooms and peas and cook for a further 10 to 15 minutes. Sprinkle with parsley. Divide evenly.
Makes 4 midday or evening meal servings.

Sweet-and-Sour Veal Balls in Cabbage

1½ lbs (720 g) minced veal

1 oz (30 g) onion, grated

½ teaspoon salt

¼ teaspoon garlic powder

⅛ teaspoon pepper

12 oz (360 g) cabbage, shredded

3 oz (90 g) onion, sliced

4 fl oz (120 ml) orange juice, no sugar added

1 tablespoon lemon juice

In bowl combine veal, grated onion, salt, garlic powder and pepper. Mix well and shape into balls 1 inch (2.5 cm) in diameter. Place on rack in baking tin; bake at 350°F, 180°C, Gas Mark 4, turning as necessary to brown all sides. Place the shredded cabbage and sliced onion in medium saucepan. Add orange juice, lemon juice and enough water to cover. Bring to the boil. Add veal balls, cover and simmer for 20 minutes or until cabbage is soft. Divide evenly.
Makes 4 midday or evening meal servings.

Veal Balls in Tomato Sauce

Sauce

3 oz (90 g) green pepper, seeded and finely chopped

2 oz (60 g) onion, chopped

1 garlic clove, crushed

1 lb 6 oz (660 g) canned tomatoes, crushed

11 tablespoons tomato puree mixed with 4 fl oz (120 ml) water

6 fl oz (180 ml) beef stock, made with ½ stock cube

1½ teaspoons basil

¾ teaspoon salt

½ teaspoon chopped fresh parsley

½ teaspoon oregano

⅛ teaspoon pepper

1½ lbs (720 g) minced veal

2 slices (2 oz/60 g) white bread, made into crumbs

4 fl oz (120 ml) skim milk

¼ teaspoon garlic powder

⅛ teaspoon thyme

pinch salt and pepper

To Prepare Sauce: In medium saucepan combine green pepper, onion and garlic. Cook for 2 to 3 minutes. Add remaining ingredients; simmer for about 35 minutes or until sauce reaches desired consistency, stirring often.
To Prepare Veal Balls: In a bowl combine all ingredients for making veal balls. Shape into balls 1½ inches (4 cm) in diameter. Place on a rack and bake at 375°F, 190°C, Gas Mark 5, for

40 minutes or until browned. Divide evenly. Serve with sauce. *Makes 4 midday or evening meal servings.*

Simple Veal Marengo

1 tablespoon margarine

2 oz (60 g) onion, diced

½ garlic clove, crushed

1 tablespoon plain flour

6 fl oz (180 ml) chicken stock, made with ½ stock cube

2 tablespoons tomato puree

8 oz (240 g) diced cooked veal

3 oz (90 g) mushrooms, sliced

¼ teaspoon thyme

¼ teaspoon tarragon

⅛ teaspoon grated orange rind

pinch pepper

4 oz (120 g) hot cooked noodles

Melt margarine in large non-stick saucepan. Add onion and garlic. Cook until onion is soft. Stir in flour and cook until blended. Add stock and tomato puree. Cook, stirring constantly, until smooth and thickened. Stir in remaining ingredients, simmer for 10 minutes. Divide evenly. Serve with hot cooked noodles.
Makes 2 midday or evening meal servings.

Italian Summer Salad

3 oz (90 g) drained canned tuna

1 oz (30 g) drained canned anchovies

6 teaspoons mayonnaise

1 teaspoon lemon juice

½ teaspoon capers

pinch celery seed

4 oz (120 g) sliced cooked veal

freshly ground pepper to taste

lemon slices to garnish

In bowl combine tuna, anchovies, mayonnaise, lemon juice, capers and celery seed. Mash finely. Place veal in shallow container. Spread tuna mixture over veal and refrigerate for several hours or overnight. Sprinkle with pepper. Garnish top with slices of lemon. Divide evenly.
Makes 2 midday or evening meal servings.

Sweet and Sour Veal with Rice

12 oz (360 g) stewing veal, cut into 1-inch (2.5-cm) cubes

12 fl oz (360 ml) beef stock, made with 1½ stock cubes

1 tablespoon chopped fresh parsley

¼ teaspoon dill seed

salt and pepper to taste

½ small pineapple, peeled, cored and diced

3 oz (90 g) mushrooms, sliced

1 tablespoon cornflour, dissolved in 1 tablespoon water

4 oz (120 g) cooked rice

Brown veal cubes in preheated non-stick frying pan. Transfer to medium saucepan. Add stock, parsley, dill seed, salt and pepper. Cover and simmer over low heat for 40 minutes or until veal is very tender. Add water if necessary to keep veal barely covered. Add pineapple and mushrooms; cover and simmer for 5 minutes or until mushrooms are cooked. Add cornflour and cook, stirring constantly, until thickened. Serve over rice. Divide evenly.
Makes 2 midday or evening meal servings.

Sweet and Spicy Curried Veal

1 x 6 oz (180 g) boneless veal steak

½ medium apple, chopped

2 oz (60 g) onion, chopped

4 fl oz (120 ml) chicken stock, made with ½ stock cube

1½ teaspoons cornflour

1 teaspoon curry powder

salt and pepper to taste

2½ fl oz (75 ml) natural unsweetened yogurt

2 oz (60 g) hot cooked rice

Preheat oven to 350°F, 180°C, Gas Mark 4. Lay veal in shallow ovenproof dish. Place apple and onion in a little of the stock and cook until tender, about 5 minutes. Add cornflour, curry powder and seasoning slowly, then rest of stock, and simmer until it thickens. Add the yogurt to the mixture and blend. Pour over the veal and cook in oven for 1 hour. Serve with rice.

Makes 1 midday or evening meal serving.

Veal-Stuffed Cannelloni

12 oz (360 g) minced veal, shaped into 4 patties

4 tablespoons tomato puree

4 fl oz (120 ml) water

2 teaspoons basil

1 teaspoon oregano

½ teaspoon garlic powder

salt and pepper to taste

6 oz (180 g) cooked spinach, chopped

4 fl oz (120 ml) chicken stock, made with 1 stock cube

1 tablespoon chopped fresh parsley

pinch nutmeg

4 oz (120 g) cooked cannelloni shells (approximately 4)

Cook veal patties in preheated non-stick frying pan until done. In small bowl crumble one patty and add tomato puree mixed with water, basil, oregano, ¼ teaspoon garlic powder, salt and pepper. Mix well. Set aside. Crumble remaining patties into medium bowl. Add all remaining ingredients except cannelloni shells; mix well. Divide mixture evenly and fill cannelloni shells. Place in an 8 x 8-inch (20 x 20 cm) baking dish. Top with veal sauce mixture. Cover. Bake at 350°F, 180°C, Gas Mark 4, for 30 minutes. Divide evenly.

Makes 2 midday or evening meal servings.

Chicken in Lemon and Orange Sauce

4 x 12 oz (360 g) chicken joints, skinned*

8 fl oz (240 ml) orange juice, no sugar added

4 teaspoons cornflour

artificial sweetener to taste

1 lemon

watercress to garnish

Place chicken joints under hot grill and cook briskly for 5 minutes, turning once. Meanwhile put orange juice, cornflour, artificial sweetener, grated rind and juice of 1 lemon into a saucepan. Bring to the boil, stirring all the time. Place chicken joints in ovenproof casserole and pour over sauce. Cover with lid or foil and put in hot oven, 425°F, 220°C, Gas Mark 7, for 20 minutes. Garnish with watercress. Divide evenly.

Makes 4 midday or evening meal servings.

*One 12 oz (360 g) chicken joint will yield about 4 oz (120 g) cooked meat.

Chicken in Lemon and Orange Sauce

PROTEIN FOODS—POULTRY, VEAL AND GAME

Veal Paprika

1 tablespoon vegetable oil

1½ lbs (720 g) stewing veal, cut into ½-inch (1-cm) cubes

4 oz (120 g) onion, chopped

4 tablespoons tomato puree

4 fl oz (120 ml) water

1 teaspoon paprika

¼ teaspoon salt

⅛ teaspoon garlic powder

⅛ teaspoon white pepper

2½ fl oz (75 ml) natural unsweetened yogurt

Heat oil in thick-based or non-stick frying pan. Saute veal. Transfer to medium saucepan. Add onion and cook, stirring occasionally until onion is browned. Add tomato puree, water, paprika, salt, garlic powder and white pepper. Cover and simmer for 30 minutes or until veal is tender. Remove from heat; fold in yogurt. Divide evenly.

Makes 4 midday or evening meal servings.

Veal Chops with Herbs

2 veal chops, 8 oz (240 g) each, 1 inch (2.5 cm) thick

2 teaspoons plain flour

2 teaspoons margarine

pinch each salt and pepper

4 fl oz (120 ml) white wine

2 tablespoons chopped fresh parsley

2 tablespoons chopped fresh basil or 1 teaspoon dried basil

Grill veal chops on rack in grill pan until rare. Sprinkle evenly on all sides with flour. Melt margarine in a non-stick frying pan; brown chops over medium high heat. Season to taste. Reduce heat and add half of the wine; cover and simmer for 15 to 20 minutes or until chops are barely tender. Add herbs and remaining wine; continue to cook for about 5 minutes, turning chops twice. Serve each chop with half the pan juices. Divide evenly.

Makes 2 midday or evening meal servings.

Piquant Tripe

1½ lbs (720 g) tripe, cut into strips

1¼ (720 ml) pints water

2 beef stock cubes

1 lemon, cut into slices

12 oz (360 g) green beans, halved

6 oz (180 g) carrots, sliced

3 oz (90 g) celery sticks, cut into 2-inch (5-cm) lengths

8 teaspoons cornflour

2 tablespoons water

Combine tripe, water, stock cubes and lemon slices in a large saucepan. Cook covered, over low heat, for 1 hour. Add green beans, carrots and celery. Cook for about 20 minutes or until vegetables are tender. Mix cornflour with water, add to tripe, bring to the boil and cook for 2 minutes. Divide evenly.

Makes 4 midday or evening meal servings.

Roast Turkey

Place turkey on a rack in a shallow roasting tin, breast side up. Roast at 325°F, 160°C, Gas Mark 3. Allow about 20 minutes per lb (480 g) for a bird under 12 lbs (5 kg 760 g) and about 15 minutes per lb (480 g) if larger. If a meat thermometer is used, insert into the centre of inner thigh muscle, not touching bone. When thermometer registers 180° to 185°F (80° to 85°C), turkey is done. Baste every half hour with mixture of dried onion flakes, dried pepper flakes, and chopped celery cooked in 12 fl oz (360 ml) chicken stock made with 1 stock cube. Remove skin and weigh portions (3 to 4 oz [90 to 120 g] servings).

Turkey and Spaghetti Casserole

Sauce

2 tablespoons margarine

1 oz (30 g) onion, diced

1 oz (30 g) mushrooms, sliced

2 tablespoons plain flour

⅛ teaspoon salt

pinch white pepper

10 fl oz (300 ml) skim milk

dash Worcester sauce

Turkey and Spaghetti

8 tablespoons tomato puree

6 fl oz (180 ml) water

6 oz (180 g) green pepper, seeded and diced

4 oz (120 g) celery diced

1 chicken stock cube

1 garlic clove, crushed

½ teaspoon basil

1 teaspoon sugar

12 oz (360 g) cooked thin spaghetti

1½ lbs (720 g) skinned and boned cooked turkey, cubed

To Prepare Sauce: Melt margarine in small saucepan. Add onion and mushrooms and cook gently until tender. Add flour, salt and pepper and cook over moderate heat for about 2 minutes, stirring constantly. Gradually add milk. Cook, stirring constantly with a wire whisk until mixture thickens. When mixture thickens, add Worcester sauce.

To Prepare Casserole: In medium saucepan combine tomato puree, water, green pepper, celery, stock cube, garlic, basil and sugar. Simmer for 15 to 20 minutes or until vegetables are tender. In large shallow casserole, spread half of the sauce. Add half the spaghetti, turkey and tomato mixture. Repeat layers. Bake at 350°F, 180°C, Gas Mark 4, for 30 minutes or until piping hot. Divide evenly.
Makes 6 midday or evening meal servings.

Turkey Casserole

12 oz (360 g) green peppers, seeded and diced

6 oz (180 g) onions, finely chopped

6 oz (180 g) mushrooms, sliced

1 garlic clove, crushed

¾ teaspoon paprika

½ teaspoon Worcester sauce

¼ teaspoon dry mustard

8 oz (240 g) skinned and boned cooked turkey, shredded

8 oz (240 g) cooked elbow macaroni

4 oz (120 g) Cheddar cheese, grated

paprika to garnish

In non-stick frying pan combine green peppers, onion, mushrooms, garlic, paprika, Worcester sauce and dry mustard; cook until vegetables are soft. Add turkey and cook for 5 minutes longer. Place macaroni in large casserole. Pour turkey mixture over macaroni; sprinkle with cheese and paprika. Bake at 400°F, 200°C, Gas Mark 6, for 25 minutes or until thoroughly heated. Divide evenly.
Makes 4 midday or evening meal servings.

Curried Turkey

1½ teaspoons margarine

1 oz (30 g) diced onion

1½ teaspoons flour

¾ teaspoon curry powder

dash salt

pinch ginger

2½ fl oz (75 ml) skim milk

4 oz (120 g) skinned and boned cooked turkey, diced

1 oz (30 g) canned apple slices, no sugar added

1 oz (30 g) cooked diced celery

2 oz (60 g) cooked noodles, hot

Melt margarine in non-stick saucepan. Add onion and cook for 10 minutes. Blend in flour and seasonings and cook for 5 minutes. Gradually add milk, stirring constantly. Cook until thickened. Stir in remaining ingredients, except noodles. Place in ovenproof dish and bake at 375°F, 190°C, Gas Mark 5, for 15 to 20 minutes, or until thoroughly heated. Serve over hot noodles.
Makes 1 midday or evening meal serving.

FISH

We can have fresh, canned or frozen fish, and in such variety that there is little risk of getting bored with it. Choosing fish presents few problems; just remember to check weights, particularly with canned or frozen fish, and to drain all the liquid from canned fish before use. When buying fresh fish be sure that it is firm, with a good colour and shining scales. Be adventurous, try some of the less familiar items on the fishmonger's slab—you don't know what you're missing! If you choose smoked fish, take the lower end of the serving range.

Fish is an excellent source of protein and is usually low in calories. Weigh it after cooking whenever possible, or allow 2 oz (60 g) for skin and bone, and 2 oz (60 g) for shrinkage in cooking.

Lemon and fish have a special affinity, and a sprinkling of juice or wedges used in garnishing add a delicious zest to your dishes.

Piquant Lemon Sole

1 teaspoon margarine, softened

1 teaspoon plain flour

1 teaspoon sweet mustard pickle relish

1 teaspoon lemon juice

¼ teaspoon Worcester sauce

1 x 6 oz (180 g) fillet lemon sole

Combine first 5 ingredients into a chunky paste and spread on lemon sole fillet. Place fish in baking dish and bake at 450°F, 230°C, Gas Mark 8, for 12 to 16 minutes or until fish is opaque and flakes easily when tested with a fork. Serve with accumulated pan juices.
Makes 1 midday or evening meal serving.

Chinese Prawns with Rice

2 tablespoons vegetable oil

8 oz (240 g) celery, diagonally cut into thin slices

4 oz (120 g) onions, sliced

16 oz (480 g) peeled prawns

6 oz (180 g) spinach leaves, chopped

4 oz (120 g) Chinese pea pods (mange tout)

4 oz (120 g) drained canned water chestnuts, sliced

3 oz (90 g) drained canned bamboo shoots, sliced

12 fl oz (360 ml) chicken stock, made with 1 stock cube

2 fl oz (60 ml) soy sauce

2 tablespoons cornflour, dissolved in 2 tablespoons water

¼ teaspoon pepper

8 oz (240 g) cooked rice

Heat oil in large non-stick frying pan. Saute celery and onion; add prawns, spinach, Chinese pea pods (mange tout), water chestnuts and bamboo shoots. Cover and cook for 1 minute. In small bowl combine stock, soy sauce, cornflour and pepper. Stir into prawn-vegetable mixture. Cook, stirring, for 2 minutes or until sauce is thickened. Serve over hot rice. Divide evenly.
Makes 4 midday or evening meal servings.

Baked Prawns Thermidor

4 tablespoons margarine

3 oz (90 g) mushrooms, sliced

4 tablespoons plain flour

1 teaspoon salt

½ teaspoon dry mustard

pinch ground red pepper

10 fl oz (300 ml) skim milk

8 oz (240 g) peeled prawns

2 slices (2 oz/60 g) white bread, made into crumbs

2 oz (60 g) Parmesan cheese, grated

2 oz (60 g) Cheddar cheese, finely diced

½ teaspoon paprika

parsley sprigs to garnish

Melt margarine in non-stick saucepan; add mushrooms. Cook for 5 minutes. Blend in flour, salt, mustard and pepper. Slowly add milk, stirring constantly; cook until thick. Add prawns; stir to combine. Transfer mixture to 3-pint (1 litre 800 ml) casserole. In a medium bowl, combine breadcrumbs, Parmesan cheese, Cheddar cheese and paprika. Sprinkle over prawn mixture. Bake at 400°F, 200°C, Gas Mark 6, for 20 minutes or until top is brown and bubbly. Garnish with parsley sprigs. Divide evenly.
Makes 4 midday or evening meal servings.

Baked Prawns Thermidor

PROTEIN FOODS—FISH

Baked Scampi

1½ lbs (720 g) large peeled scampi

2 tablespoons lemon juice

4 tablespoons margarine, melted

4 tablespoons finely chopped fresh parsley

2 garlic cloves, crushed

2 slices (2 oz/60 g) white bread, made into crumbs

1 teaspoon paprika

4 lemon wedges

Make scampi butterflies by cutting lengthwise along the back, being careful not to cut all the way through; spread and flatten to form the butterfly shape. Place 6 oz (180 g) scampi in each of 4 individual baking dishes. Sprinkle each with 1½ teaspoons lemon juice. In small bowl, combine margarine, 3 tablespoons parsley, and garlic; dot each portion of scampi with quarter of the margarine mixture. In another bowl, combine breadcrumbs, remaining parsley and paprika. Sprinkle a quarter of the breadcrumb mixture over each serving. Bake at 400°F, 200°C, Gas Mark 6, for 15 minutes or until scampi are pink and crumbs are golden brown. Garnish each serving with 1 lemon wedge.
Makes 4 midday or evening meal servings.

Cornish Chowder

2 tablespoons vegetable oil

4 oz (120 g) leeks, chopped

4 oz (120 g) onion, sliced

2 garlic cloves, crushed

8 oz (240 g) tomatoes

1 pint (600 ml) chicken stock, made with 1 stock cube

dash turmeric (optional)

1 bay leaf

12 oz (360 g) skinned cod fillet, cut into 1-inch (2.5-cm) cubes

8 oz (240 g) shelled cooked mussels

dash salt and ground red pepper

1 tablespoon cornflour, mixed to a paste with 2 tablespoons water

Heat oil in a large non-stick saucepan; saute leeks, onion and garlic. Add tomatoes, stock, turmeric and bay leaf. Bring to the boil, add fish and mussels; cook for 10 to 15 minutes. Add salt, pepper and cornflour. Remove the bay leaf and cook for a further 5 minutes. Divide evenly.
Makes 4 midday or evening meal servings.

Sauteed Haddock

1 x 6 oz (180 g) haddock fillet

2 teaspoons plain flour

salt and pepper to taste

2 teaspoons vegetable oil

Wash and pat fish dry with paper towel. Season flour with salt and pepper, coating fish on both sides with the mixture. Heat oil in non-stick frying pan and cook fish on both sides until golden brown, approximately 10 minutes.
Makes 1 midday or evening meal serving.

Curried Haddock Salad

1 small head lettuce

4 oz (120 g) cooked boned cod or haddock

1 medium eating apple, cored and grated

2 slices canned pineapple with 2 tablespoons juice, no sugar added

2 oz (60 g) onion, finely chopped

1 teaspoon curry powder, or to taste

salt and pepper to taste

1 tablespoon mayonnaise

2 oz (60 g) cooked peas

3 oz (90 g) tomato

Wash the lettuce and arrange round the edge of a plate. Flake the fish and arrange on the lettuce leaves. Chop pineapple slices. Combine grated apple, chopped pineapple and juice, chopped onion, curry powder, seasoning and mayonnaise. Spoon the mixture over the fish. Garnish with peas and sliced tomato and serve.
Makes 1 midday or evening meal serving.

Haddock Pie

1½ oz (45 g) cooked smoked haddock fillet

5 fl oz (150 ml) skim milk

1 teaspoon cornflour

2 teaspoons parsley flakes

salt and pepper to taste

3 oz (90 g) cooked potato, mashed

1 oz (30 g) Cheddar cheese, grated

3 oz (90 g) tomato, sliced

Flake fish and put to one side. Make sauce; place milk, cornflour, parsley and seasoning to taste in medium sized saucepan. Bring to the boil, stirring to prevent burning and lumps forming. Cook for 1 minute; add flaked fish, potato and half the cheese. Mix to combine ingredients. Spoon into a shallow ovenproof dish, arrange sliced tomato over the top and sprinkle on remaining cheese. Place under hot grill and cook until top is golden and crisp.
Makes 1 midday or evening meal serving.

Smoked Haddock and Butter Bean Salad

3 oz (90 g) cooked butter beans

1½ oz (45 g) flaked cooked smoked haddock

1 tablespoon lemon juice

2 teaspoons vegetable oil

3 oz (90 g) tomato, skinned and diced

salt and pepper to taste

Combine all ingredients in small bowl and toss to mix thoroughly. Chill and serve.
Makes 1 midday or evening meal serving.

Baked Whiting and Vegetables

4 oz (120 g) leeks, sliced

3 oz (90 g) mushrooms, sliced

6 oz (180 g) skinned whiting fillet

6 fl oz (180 ml) chicken stock, made with 1 stock cube

pepper to taste

Spread half the vegetables on the base of an ovenproof casserole. Cover with fish and top with the rest of the vegetables. Pour over chicken stock and add pepper to taste. Cover with lid or foil and bake in oven, 375°F, 190°C, Gas Mark 5, for 30 to 40 minutes, or until vegetables are tender crisp and fish flakes easily with a fork.
Makes 1 midday or evening meal serving.

Halibut Souffle Ring

4 eggs, separated

12 oz (360 g) halibut fillets, minced

½ oz (15 g) non-fat dry milk

2 fl oz (60 ml) water

½ teaspoon salt

¼ teaspoon pepper

9 oz (270 g) cooked whole green beans

4 tablespoons tomato puree mixed with 4 fl oz (120 ml) water, heated

Preheat oven to 375°F, 190°C, Gas Mark 5. In large bowl beat egg yolks slightly. Add fish, milk, water, salt and pepper; mix thoroughly. In separate bowl, beat egg whites until stiff and fold into fish mixture. Pour into 2-pint (1 litre 200 ml) non-stick cake ring tin; set in pan containing 1 inch (2.5 cm) water; bake for 30 to 40 minutes. Turn out onto serving dish. Garnish with green beans and serve with tomato puree. Divide evenly.
Makes 4 midday or evening meal servings.

Curried Cod

pepper to taste

1 teaspoon lemon juice

2 fl oz (60 ml) chicken stock, made with ¼ stock cube

1 x 6 oz (180 g) skinned cod fillet

2 teaspoons dried onion flakes

2 fl oz (60 ml) tomato juice

½ teaspoon curry powder

salt and pepper to taste

dash Worcester sauce

2 oz (60 g) cooked rice

Add pepper and lemon juice to stock. Place fish in an ovenproof dish and pour stock over. Cover with foil and bake in moderately slow oven, 325°F, 160°C, Gas Mark 4, for about 10 minutes. Drain off the cooking liquid; soak the onion flakes in water until soft. Drain and mix with tomato juice, curry powder, salt, pepper and Worcester sauce in a saucepan. Bring to the boil and cook for 1 to 2 minutes. Pour over fish. Serve with rice.
Makes 1 midday or evening meal serving.

PROTEIN FOODS—FISH

Cod and Tomato Bake

2 x 3 oz (90 g) tomatoes

1 slice (1 oz/30 g) bread, made into crumbs

1 teaspoon chopped fresh parsley

½ teaspoon grated lemon rind

½ teaspoon thyme

½ teaspoon salt and pepper

5 fl oz (150 ml) skim milk

2 tablespoons low-fat spread, melted

12 oz (360 g) boneless cod steaks

Slice top off tomatoes and scrape seeds out into a bowl. Mix together breadcrumbs, parsley, lemon rind, thyme, salt and pepper with half the skim milk and half the low-fat spread. Roll this stuffing mixture into small balls and place on top of cod steaks. Roll up and secure with a toothpick. Reserve a little of the stuffing mix; put into tomato cases and replace lids. Put the other half of the skim milk in the bottom of the cooking dish and spread the remainder of the low-fat spread on top of the fish. Add tomatoes to dish and place in centre of oven, 350°F, 180°C, Gas Mark 4, for approximately 25 minutes. When cooked, serve fish, sprinkled with a little parsley. Divide fish and stuffed tomatoes evenly and serve with mixed salad.
Makes 2 midday or evening meal servings.

Cod Kebabs

12 oz (360 g) cod fillets, cut into large cubes

4 oz (120 g) small onions

3 oz (90 g) green pepper, seeded and cut into 1-inch (2.5-cm) cubes

4 oz (120 g) tomatoes, cut into quarters

4 button mushrooms

4 small bay leaves

lemon juice to taste

salt and freshly ground pepper to taste

¼ teaspoon paprika

chopped fresh parsley to garnish

Cook fish, onions and green pepper in saucepan, with water to cover, for 5 minutes; drain. Divide fish and vegetables into 4 equal portions of each. Thread 1 portion of each and 1 bay leaf onto a skewer, alternating ingredients; repeat with remaining portions and 3 more skewers. Brush with lemon juice and season with salt and pepper. Sprinkle with paprika and grill for about 8 minutes. Turn, brush with lemon juice and season. Sprinkle with parsley.
Makes 2 midday or evening meal servings, 2 skewers each.

Bouillabaisse For One

2 oz (60 g) onion or leek, diced

1 garlic clove, crushed

1 parsley sprig

1 small bay leaf

pinch saffron or turmeric

pinch thyme

pinch paprika

salt and pepper to taste

16 fl oz (480 ml) water

3 oz (90 g) tomato, diced

3 oz (90 g) peeled potato, diced

6 oz (180 g) skinned fish fillets

In small non-stick saucepan saute onion and garlic for 2 minutes. Add parsley and seasonings; cook for 1 minute longer. Add all remaining ingredients except fish. Cover; simmer for 5 minutes. Add fish; simmer for about 7 minutes or until fish flakes easily at touch of a fork. Serve in soup bowl.
Makes 1 midday or evening meal serving.

Taramasalata

Serve with celery, carrot and mushrooms.

1½ slices (1½ oz/45 g) white bread

2 to 3 tablespoons water

3 oz (90 g) smoked cod roe (must be fresh and soft)

2 tablespoons lemon juice

2 tablespoons olive oil

dash hot sauce

Dice bread; place in dish and add 2 to 3 tablespoons of water. Leave until water has been absorbed, then squeeze out excess. Place in blender container with rest of ingredients and puree until smooth. Pour into dish. Chill well before serving. Divide evenly.
Makes 2 midday or evening meal servings. Add protein as required.

Taramasalata

116

PROTEIN FOODS—FISH

Coquilles St Jacques

6 oz (180 g) fresh or frozen scallops

3 oz (90 g) button mushrooms, sliced

8 fl oz (240 g) skim milk

1 tablespoon chopped fresh parsley

pinch garlic powder

salt and pepper to taste

1 tablespoon cornflour

2 oz (60 g) grated hard cheese

6 oz (180 g) hot peeled cooked potato

4 teaspoons margarine

Preheat oven to 400°F, 200°C, Gas Mark 6. Slice scallops and place in saucepan with mushrooms, 6 fl oz (180 ml) skim milk, parsley, garlic powder and seasoning to taste. Bring to the boil over medium heat and simmer gently for 5 minutes. Mix cornflour to a paste with a little water; add to scallop mixture and cook until thickened. Stir in half the cheese; beat potato with 2 fl oz (60 ml) skim milk, margarine and seasoning. Divide potato evenly and make a border round 2 scallop shells or small oven-proof dishes. Divide scallop mixture evenly between the shells. Sprinkle each with half the remaining cheese and bake for approximately 20 minutes.
Makes 2 midday or evening meal servings.

Curried Kedgeree

4 oz (120 g) cooked rice

3 oz (90 g) cooked peas

4 oz (120 g) cooked diced onions

6 oz (180 g) tomatoes, chopped

8 oz (240 g) drained canned tuna

1 to 2 teaspoons curry powder

8 fl oz (240 ml) tomato juice

salt and pepper to taste

In a large saucepan combine rice, peas, onions, tomatoes and tuna with 1 to 2 teaspoons curry powder, or to taste. Add tomato juice, salt and pepper and cook slowly for 10 minutes. Divide evenly.
Makes 2 midday or evening meal servings.

Curried Fish Scramble

2 oz (60 g) drained canned tuna

1 egg

2 tablespoons skim milk

1 teaspoon curry powder

salt and pepper to taste

Mash tuna; beat egg in small basin with milk, curry powder and seasoning. Add tuna and mix. Pour into non-stick saucepan and cook, stirring occasionally to prevent burning, about 5 minutes. Serve hot or cold.
Makes 1 midday or evening meal serving.

Sardine Platter

Salad

2 oz (60 g) canned button mushrooms

2 oz (60 g) cooked cauliflower florets

2 oz (60 g) small tomatoes

2 oz (60 g) drained canned sardines

1 oz (30 g) celery, diagonally cut into thin slices

1 oz (30 g) cooked beetroot, sliced

1 egg, hard-boiled and cut into quarters

2 oz (60 g) canned pimiento, sliced

Dressing

1 tablespoon vegetable oil

1 tablespoon red wine vinegar or tarragon vinegar

pinch each white pepper, salt and crushed fresh garlic

To Prepare Salad: Arrange the first 7 ingredients on large plate. Top with dressing. Garnish with pimientos.
To Prepare Dressing: Combine all ingredients in a jar with tight-fitting cover. Cover and shake vigorously before using.
Makes 1 midday or evening meal serving.

Sardine Surprise

4 oz (120 g) drained canned sardines

2½ fl oz (75 ml) natural unsweetened yogurt

1 tablespoon tomato puree

½ to 1 teaspoon curry powder

1 teaspoon onion flakes

salt and pepper to taste

3 oz (90 g) celery, diced

lettuce leaves

Mash sardines thoroughly and add yogurt, puree, curry powder, onion flakes, salt and pepper. Mix well. Fold in diced celery and serve on a bed of crisp lettuce.
Makes 1 midday or evening meal serving.

Fish Souffle

2 eggs, separated

salt and pepper to taste

1 tablespoon lemon juice

1 teaspoon Worcester sauce or to taste

2 slices (2 oz/60 g) white bread, made into crumbs

4 oz (120 g) onions, minced

6 oz (180 g) minced raw fish, (without skin or bone)

4 slices lemon for garnish

Preheat oven to 375°F, 190°C, Gas Mark 5. Beat egg yolks with salt, pepper, lemon juice and Worcester sauce. Gradually add the breadcrumbs and onion. Beat whites until stiff. Gently fold the minced fish and yolk mixture into the beaten whites.

Turn into a souffle dish or casserole and bake for 1 hour. Serve garnished with lemon. Divide evenly.
Makes 2 midday or evening meal servings.

Gefilte Fish

12 oz (360 g) boned white fish, chopped

12 oz (360 g) boned pike, chopped

4 oz (120 g) onions, chopped

1 oz (30 g) celery, chopped

2 teaspoons salt

¼ teaspoon garlic powder

¼ teaspoon pepper

2 fl oz (30 ml) skim milk

1 tablespoon unflavoured gelatine

16 fl oz (480 ml) water

1 teaspoon chicken stock powder

6 oz (180 g) cooked carrots, sliced

Put fish, onion and celery through the mincer twice. In bowl combine fish mixture with salt, garlic powder and pepper. Gradually add milk and combine. Shape into 4 equal, oval patties. Poach in simmering, salted water for 15 minutes. Remove patties with a slotted spoon and place on serving dish. Allow to cool, cover and refrigerate. In another saucepan, sprinkle gelatine over water and allow to soften. Add stock powder and heat, stirring to dissolve. Chill until slightly firm. Dice and arrange jelly and carrots around poached fish. Divide evenly.
Makes 4 midday or evening meal servings.

Fish Pie

12 oz (360 g) peeled cooked potatoes

5 fl oz (150 ml) skim milk

4 teaspoons margarine

2 eggs, hard-boiled

8 oz (240 g) flaked cooked fish

4 oz (120 g) boiled onions, diced

2 eggs

1 tablespoon tomato puree

2 tablespoons water

1 tablespoon chopped fresh parsley

1 teaspoon Worcester sauce

salt and pepper to taste

In medium bowl mash potatoes with milk and margarine until blended. Set aside. Chop hard-boiled eggs and place in separate bowl; add fish, onions, 1 egg, tomato puree mixed with water, parsley, Worcester sauce, salt, pepper and about a quarter of the potato mixture; mix well. Spoon into 8 x 8 x 2-inch (20 x 20 x 5 cm) baking dish. Spread with remain potato mixture. Beat remaining egg and pour over potato. Bake at 400°F, 200°C, Gas Mark 6, for 20 to 30 minutes or until top is golden brown. Divide evenly.
Makes 4 midday or evening meal servings.

PROTEIN FOODS—FISH

Tuna Mac Salad

4 oz (120 g) cooked macaroni

8 oz (240 g) drained canned tuna

2 tablespoons mayonnaise

2 teaspoons chopped fresh parsley

3 oz (90 g) cucumber, finely chopped

2 oz (60 g) onion, chopped

salt and pepper to taste

seasoning salt (optional)

¼ teaspoon celery seed

2 teaspoons lemon juice

lettuce and sliced tomatoes

Chop macaroni and add flaked tuna. Add all remaining ingredients and mix well. Transfer to bowl; cover and chill in refrigerator for 2 to 3 hours. Divide evenly and serve with lettuce and tomatoes.
Makes 2 midday or evening meal servings.

Spicy Stuffed Herring

1 x 6 oz (180 g) filleted herring

1 slice (1 oz/30 g) bread, made into crumbs

2 teaspoons dry mustard

½ teaspoon dried dill

1 tablespoon chopped fresh parsley

2 tablespoons skim milk

salt and pepper to taste

2 fl oz (60 ml) cider vinegar

2 fl oz (60 ml) water

Lay herring flat on a board. Mix together bread, mustard, dill, parsley, skim milk, salt and pepper into a paste and spread over fillet. Roll fillet up and

secure with orange stick. Place in ovenproof casserole and pour over vinegar and water. Cover and bake in slow oven, 300°F, 150°C, Gas Mark 2, for 1 to 1½ hours. Serve hot or cold.
Makes 1 midday or evening meal serving.

Tomato Tuna Sauce with Spaghetti

6 fl oz (180 ml) tomato juice

1 tablespoon tomato puree

salt and pepper to taste

1 tablespoon chopped fresh parsley

dash garlic granules

dash onion salt

½ teaspoon dried oregano

½ teaspoon dried basil

4 oz (120 g) drained canned tuna

2 oz (60 g) hot cooked spaghetti

Combine first 9 ingredients in saucepan and simmer for 10 minutes. Pour over hot spaghetti and serve at once.
Makes 1 midday or evening meal serving.

Tuna Surprise

1 tablespoon margarine

1 tablespoon cornflour

5 fl oz (150 ml) skim milk

salt and pepper to taste

pinch dry mustard

1 oz (30 g) grated hard cheese

2 oz (60 g) cooked rice

2 oz (60 g) cooked peas

3 oz (90 g) cooked diced carrots

2 oz (60 g) drained canned tuna

1 slice (1 oz/30 g) white bread, made into crumbs

Preheat oven to 400°F, 200°C, Gas Mark 6. Melt margarine in saucepan; stir in cornflour. Blend in milk and cook, stirring, until sauce thickens. Add salt and pepper to taste. Remove saucepan from heat; stir in mustard and cheese. Add rice, vegetables and tuna and mix well. Pour into ovenproof dish and top with breadcrumbs. Bake in oven for 25 minutes until cooked through and brown.
Makes 1 midday or evening meal serving.

Stir-Fry Tuna

4 teaspoons vegetable oil

2 medium red apples, peeled, cored and diced

4 oz (120 g) onions, thinly sliced and separated into rings

1 lb (480 g) drained canned tuna, broken into chunks

1 tablespoon curry powder

¼ teaspoon dry mustard

6 oz (180 g) frozen peas

4 tablespoons raisins

8 tablespoons dry white wine

Put oil in thick based non-stick frying pan. Add apples and onions and saute for about 1 minute. Add remaining ingredients and cook for about 5 minutes or until mixture is hot and well blended. Divide evenly.
Makes 4 midday or evening meal servings.

Stir-Fry Tuna

PROTEIN FOODS—FISH

Tuna, Lentils and Macaroni

6 oz (180 g) canned tomatoes

2 teaspoon dried onion flakes

1½ oz (45 g) sliced mushrooms

½ teaspoon each marjoram and oregano

3 oz (90 g) cooked lentils

2 oz (60 g) drained canned tuna

2 teaspoons vegetable oil

salt and pepper to taste

2 oz (60 g) hot cooked small tube macaroni

Place tomatoes, onion flakes, mushrooms and herbs in saucepan. Bring to the boil and cook until onion is soft. Add lentils, tuna, oil and seasoning to taste. Reheat and simmer for 6 minutes, or until all contents are heated. Pour over macaroni and serve at once.
Makes 1 midday or evening meal serving.

Tuna and Haricot Bean Salad

1 teaspoon wine vinegar

2 teaspoons vegetable oil

¼ teaspoon Dijon-style mustard

salt and pepper to taste

3 oz (90 g) drained canned haricot beans

2 oz (60 g) drained canned tuna

1 oz sliced onion rings

1 tablespoon chopped fresh parsley

Mix together wine vinegar, oil, mustard, salt and pepper to taste. Pour over drained beans.

Flake tuna and mix with the beans. Place on a serving plate; arrange onion rings over the top and scatter with chopped parsley.
Makes 1 midday or evening meal serving.

Shrimped Egg on Toast

1 oz (30 g) onion, chopped

3 oz (90 g) mushrooms

3 fl oz (90 ml) chicken stock, made with ¼ stock cube

dash soy sauce

salt and pepper to taste

½ teaspoon celery salt

1 teaspoon plain flour

2 oz (60 g) drained canned shrimps

1 egg, hard-boiled and cut into large chunks

3 oz (90 g) cooked peas

1 slice (1 oz/30 g) bread, toasted

Brown onion and mushrooms in non-stick saucepan over low heat. Add stock, soy sauce, salt and pepper to taste and celery salt. Simmer until mushrooms are tender. Remove from heat and thicken with flour. Add shrimps, egg and peas and reheat, stirring carefully so as not to break the egg. Serve immediately on toast.
Makes 1 midday or evening meal serving.

Kipper Kedgeree

3 oz (90 g) kipper fillets

2½ fl oz (75 ml) natural unsweetened yogurt

1 teaspoon lemon juice

4 oz (120 g) hot cooked rice

salt and pepper to taste

2 eggs, hard-boiled

chopped fresh parsley for garnish

Place kipper in a shallow saucepan of water; bring to the boil and poach gently for 2 minutes. Drain fish and flake, removing any skin. Mix with yogurt, lemon juice, rice and seasonings and transfer to serving dish. Finely chop eggs and sprinkle over the kipper mixture. Garnish with finely chopped parsley. Divide evenly.
Makes 2 midday or evening meal servings.

Kipper Cocktail

6 oz (180 g) skinned drained canned kipper fillets

4 fl oz (120 ml) orange juice, no sugar added

2 sticks celery, chopped

pepper to taste

1 small lettuce, shredded

1 lemon, sliced

Cut kippers into slices. Mix them with orange juice and celery. Season well with pepper and divide mixture evenly between two individual sundae glasses on a bed of shredded lettuce. Garnish with lemon slices.
Makes 2 midday or evening meal servings.

Kipper Pate

6 oz (180 g) drained canned kipper fillets

1 oz (30 g) non-fat dry milk

2 tablespoons water

4 teaspoons margarine

ground red pepper to taste

1 tablespoon lemon juice

¼ teaspoon powdered mace (optional)

lemon and cucumber slices for garnish

Place all ingredients except garnish in a bowl and mash or pound well until they form a paste. Transfer to a small dish; garnish with lemon and cucumber. Chill well Divide evenly.
Makes 2 servings.

Lemon Grilled Trout

1 x 8-oz (240-g) cleaned trout

2 fl oz (60 ml) lemon juice

2 teaspoons chopped fresh parsley

1 teaspoon margarine

parsley sprigs and lemon wedges to garnish

Cut trout in half lengthwise. Place skin side up on foil-lined grill pan. Sprinkle with 2 tablespoons lemon juice. Grill, 4 inches (10 cm) from source of heat, for 3 minutes. Turn trout over and sprinkle with remaining lemon juice. Grill for 3 to 5 minutes until fish flakes easily at the touch of a fork. Dot with margarine and grill for 1 minute longer. Garnish with parsley and lemon wedges.
Makes 1 midday or evening meal serving.

Savoury Prawns with Rice

4 fl oz (120 ml) chicken stock, made with ½ stock cube

6 oz (180 g) green pepper, seeded and chopped

4 oz (120 g) onions, chopped

12 oz (360 g) tomatoes, chopped

1 teaspoon oregano

1 teaspoon salt

½ teaspoon rosemary

½ teaspoon pepper

dash hot sauce

1 lb (480 g) peeled prawns

8 oz (240 g) cooked rice

In medium saucepan, combine chicken stock, green pepper and onions. Simmer until tender, for 5 minutes. Add tomatoes and seasonings; simmer gently for 10 minutes. Add prawns and heat thoroughly. Divide evenly into 4 portions and serve each over 2 oz (60 g) hot rice.
Makes 4 midday or evening meal servings.

Fish Mayonnaise

12 oz (360 g) skinned cod fillets

salt and pepper to taste

8 oz (240 g) peeled prawns

1 lb (480 g) cucumber, peeled and diced

4 tablespoons mayonnaise

chopped chives for garnish

Poach cod in water seasoned with salt and pepper. When fish flakes easily with a fork, lift out carefully with a fish slice. Flake fish into bowl; add prawns and cucumber. Add mayonnaise and mix carefully. Divide evenly and serve garnished with chives.
Makes 4 midday or evening meal servings.

Stuffed Fish Fillets

3 oz (90 g) tomato, peeled and diced

1 oz (30 g) mushrooms, chopped

1 oz (30 g) onion, finely chopped

3 tablespoons water

2 tablespoons chopped fresh parsley

1 garlic clove, crushed

4 oz (120 g) Cheddar cheese, diced

¾ oz (23 g) dried bread crumbs

4 fish fillets, 3 oz (150 g) each

salt, pepper and garlic powder to taste

lemon slices and parsley sprigs to garnish

In non-stick frying pan combine tomato, mushrooms, onion, water, parsley and garlic. Cook over medium heat, stirring occasionally until onion is soft. Remove from heat. Stir in cheese and breadcrumbs; set aside. Sprinkle fish with salt, pepper and garlic powder. Place each fillet in small individual oven-proof casserole. Spoon equal amounts of stuffing mixture over each fillet. Bake at 350°F, 180°C, Gas Mark 4 for 20 minutes or until fish flakes easily at the touch of a fork. Garnish each serving with lemon slices and parsley sprigs.
Makes 4 midday or evening meal servings.

PROTEIN FOODS—FISH

Seafood Chef's Salad

3 oz (90 g) cooked macaroni twists

2 oz (60 g) boned cooked seafood, cut into 1-inch (2.5-cm) cubes

1½ oz (45 g) green pepper, seeded and diced

1 oz (30 g) celery, diced

½ oz (15 g) spring onion, chopped

1 tablespoon mayonnaise

1 tablespoon water

1 tablespoon chili sauce

salt and pepper to taste

lettuce leaves

1 egg, hard-boiled and quartered

In bowl combine macaroni, seafood, green pepper, celery and spring onion. In separate bowl combine mayonnaise, water and chili sauce. Pour over salad; toss to combine. Season with salt and pepper. Serve on lettuce leaves surrounded with egg quarters.
Makes 1 midday or evening meal serving.

Seafood Salad

½ medium red apple, cored and diced

1 tablespoon lemon juice

4 oz (120 g) boned cooked seafood, cut into 1-inch (2.5-cm) cubes

2 oz (60 g) pickled cucumber, chopped

1½ oz (45 g) cucumber, peeled and diced

1 tablespoon mayonnaise, mixed with 1 tablespoon water

½ oz (15 g) drained canned pimiento, chopped

lettuce leaves

Place apple in medium bowl; sprinkle with lemon juice and toss. Add all remaining ingredients except lettuce. Chill. Serve on bed of lettuce leaves.
Makes 1 midday or evening meal serving.

Mussels with Noodles

12 fl oz (360 ml) chicken stock made with 1½ stock cubes

2 tablespoons chopped fresh parsley

1 garlic clove, crushed

1 bay leaf

¼ teaspoon salt

⅛ teaspoon white pepper

1 lb (480 g) drained canned mussels, minced

8 oz (240 g) hot cooked noodles

Combine all ingredients except mussels and noodles in small saucepan. Bring to the boil; reduce heat and simmer for 5 minutes. Add mussels; heat thoroughly. Remove bay leaf. Divide evenly and serve over pasta.
Makes 4 midday or evening meal servings.

Mussels Vinaigrette

4 tablespoons vegetable oil

2 fl oz (60 ml) red wine vinegar or tarragon vinegar

¼ teaspoon salt

pinch white pepper

1 lb (480 g) drained canned mussels

2 oz (60 g) onion, sliced

6 oz (180 g) lettuce, shredded

Combine first 4 ingredients in jar with tight-fitting cover. Cover and shake vigorously before using. Combine mussels, dressing and onion in bowl and refrigerate for 1 hour. Serve on lettuce. Divide evenly.
Makes 4 midday or evening meal servings.

Mussel Soup

1¼ (750 ml) pints water

6 oz (180 g) peeled potato, sliced

4 oz (120 g) onions, sliced

1½ chicken stock cubes

1 garlic clove, crushed

pinch thyme

1 lb (480 g) cleaned shelled cooked mussels

4 oz (120 g) cooked rice

1 teaspoon chopped fresh parsley

In large saucepan combine water, potato, onions, stock cubes, garlic and thyme. Bring to the boil; reduce heat and cover. Simmer for 15 minutes or until potato is tender. Add mussels and rice; cook for 5 minutes or until mussels are tender. Sprinkle with parsley. Divide evenly.
Makes 4 midday or evening meal servings.

Mussel Soup

Portuguese Fish

1½ lbs (720 g) skinned haddock fillet

salt and pepper to taste

1 tablespoon lemon juice

8 oz (240 g) diced onions

1 garlic clove, chopped, optional

8 oz (240 g) sliced tomatoes, skinned

4 tablespoons tomato puree

4 teaspoons margarine

Cut haddock into 4 x 6 oz (180 g) portions. Place in an ovenproof dish. Sprinkle with salt, pepper and lemon juice. Place onions in saucepan with a little water and cook until just tender. Add chopped garlic if desired, tomatoes and tomato puree; cook on a low heat for 10 minutes. Pour sauce over fish, dot with margarine. Cover and bake in hot oven, 425°F, 220°C, Gas Mark 7, for 20 to 25 minutes. Divide evenly.
Makes 4 midday or evening meal servings.

Mackerel in Mustard Sauce

4 x 8 oz (240 g) cleaned mackerel

2 fl oz (60 ml) lemon juice

1½ teaspoons salt

5 teaspoons Dijon-style mustard

2 teaspoons chopped fresh parsley

2 garlic cloves, crushed

freshly ground pepper to taste

Cover fish with water in bowl. Add 2 tablespoons lemon juice and 1 teaspoon salt; let stand for 15 minutes. Drain and dry fish. In small bowl, combine remaining ingredients. Spread over fish. Loosely wrap fish in foil; place on baking sheet. Bake at 350°F, 180°C, Gas Mark 4, for about 30 minutes or until fish flakes easily at the touch of a fork. Divide evenly.
Makes 4 midday or evening meal servings.

Peppery Prawns

2 lbs (960 g) peeled prawns

12 fl oz (360 ml) chicken stock, made with 2 stock cubes

4 fl oz (120 ml) red wine

4 oz (120 g) onions, sliced

2 teaspoons dry mustard

1 teaspoon hot sauce

½ teaspoon thyme

lemon slices to garnish

parsley sprigs to garnish

In saucepan combine all ingredients except lemon and parsley. Bring to the boil; reduce heat and simmer for about 4 minutes or until shrimps turn pink. Remove from heat. Allow to cool. Chill shrimps in liquid. Drain and discard liquid. Garnish shrimps and onions with lemon slices and parsley sprigs. Divide evenly.
Makes 8 midday or evening meal servings.

Pickled Fish

6 oz (180 g) skinned coley fillet

2 oz (60 g) onion

4 tablespoons cider vinegar

2 tablespoons water

1 teaspoon curry powder

salt and pepper to taste

artificial sweetener (optional)

Grill fish, skin side up, for 3 to 4 minutes, according to thickness. Turn and grill a further 3 to 4 minutes. Transfer to a shallow dish. Meanwhile, slice onion into a small saucepan, add vinegar, water, curry powder, seasoning and sweetener if desired. Bring to the boil and cook until soft but still crisp, about 5 to 6 minutes. Pour onion mixture over the fish. Chill well and serve with mixed salad.
Makes 1 serving.

Shrimp Chow Mein

12 fl oz (360 ml) tomato juice

6 oz (180 g) green pepper, seeded and finely sliced

3 oz (90 g) button mushrooms, finely sliced (optional)

2 oz (60 g) celery, diagonally sliced

1 tablespoon soy sauce

2 teaspoons dried onion flakes

1 teaspoon lemon juice

salt and pepper to taste

8 oz (240 g) drained canned shrimps

7 oz (210 g) drained canned bean sprouts

Combine all ingredients, except shrimps and bean sprouts, in saucepan. Bring to the boil;

cover and reduce heat and simmer for 10 minutes. Add shrimps and bean sprouts; cook for about 3 minutes or until heated through. Divide evenly.
Makes 2 midday or evening meal servings.

Salmon, Pilchard & Cucumber Mousse

2 oz (60 g) canned drained pilchards

2 oz (60 g) canned drained salmon

1 slice (1 oz/30 g) bread, made into crumbs

½ oz (15 g) non-fat dry milk

2 teaspoons mayonnaise

1 teaspoon lemon juice

2 teaspoons parsley flakes

1 teaspoon chopped chives

1 tablespoon unflavoured gelatine dissolved in 5 fl oz (150 ml) hot water

¼ teaspoon onion or garlic salt

pinch black pepper

3 oz (90 g) cucumber, grated

3 oz (90 g) tomato, sliced

shredded lettuce

Combine all ingredients except tomato and lettuce in a large basin and beat together thoroughly, or put into liquidiser and blend until smooth. Pour into a mould and place in refrigerator until set. Turn out onto a bed of shredded lettuce, surrounded by sliced tomato.
Makes 1 midday or evening meal serving.

Salmon Loaf

3 slices (3 oz/90 g) white bread, made into crumbs

1 oz (30 g) non-fat dry milk, mixed with 8 fl oz (240 ml) water

12 oz (360 g) drained canned salmon, flaked

1 tablespoon margarine, melted

1 tablespoon dried onion flakes, reconstituted in 1 tablespoon water

1 teaspoon lemon juice

2 eggs, beaten

4 eggs, hard-boiled

In large bowl, combine breadcrumbs and dissolved milk. Let stand for 10 minutes. In medium bowl combine salmon, margarine, onion flakes, lemon juice and beaten eggs. Add to bread mixture; mix thoroughly. Spoon half the mixture into a 9 x 5 x 3-inch (23 x 12 x 8-cm) non-stick loaf tin. Shell the hard-boiled eggs and arrange in a row through the centre of the salmon mixture. Cover with remaining salmon mixture. Bake at 350°F, 180°C, Gas Mark 4, for 45 to 50 minutes or until loaf is firm and browned. Divide evenly.
Makes 6 midday or evening meal servings.

Salmon Salad with Garlic Dressing

Salad

5 fl oz (150 ml) natural unsweetened yogurt

1 tablespoon prepared mustard

1 teaspoon seasoned salt

1 lb (480 g) drained canned salmon, flaked

8 oz (240 g) cooked peas

4 oz (120 g) celery, thinly sliced

2 oz (60 g) pickled cucumber, diced

lettuce leaves

Garlic French Dressing

4 tablespoons vegetable oil

2 fl oz (60 ml) red wine vinegar or tarragon vinegar

¼ teaspoon salt

pinch white pepper

1 garlic clove, crushed

To Prepare Salad: Combine dressing, yogurt, mustard and seasoned salt. Add salmon, peas, celery and pickle. Toss to combine. Chill. Divide evenly and serve on lettuce leaves.

To Prepare Dressing: Combine all ingredients in a jar with tight-fitting cover. Cover and shake vigorously.

Makes 4 midday or evening meal servings.

PROTEIN FOODS—FISH

Spinach and Plaice Salad

6 oz (180 g) spinach

rosemary sprig

2 teaspoons chopped fresh parsley

2 teaspoons chopped chives

2 teaspoons margarine

6 oz (180 g) skinned plaice fillet

2 teaspoons vinegar

1 bay leaf

salt and pepper to taste

10 fl oz (300 ml) water

2½ fl oz (75 ml) natural unsweetened yogurt

lettuce for garnish

Wash and chop spinach roughly. Place in saucepan of boiling water; add rosemary, parsley, chives and margarine. Cook until spinach is soft. Put to one side to cool. Put plaice in a shallow saucepan and add vinegar, bay leaf, salt, pepper and water. Bring just to boiling point and allow fish to cook with water simmering for about 6 minutes. Lift fish out of water and put to one side to cool. Place spinach in basin and chop finely. Add cooled and flaked fish. Add yogurt and mix thoroughly. Serve piled onto lettuce leaves.
Makes 1 serving.

Baked Fish Delight

6 oz (180 g) white fish fillet

lemon juice

4 oz (120 g) peeled shrimps

2 teaspoons finely chopped chives

2 teaspoons finely chopped parsley

6 oz (180 g) tomatoes

salt and pepper to taste

2 tablespoons skim milk

Preheat oven to 375°F, 190°C, Gas Mark 5. Place fish in small ovenproof dish lined with foil. Sprinkle with lemon juice. Put peeled shrimps on top and sprinkle with chives and parsley. Cut tomatoes and place round edges. Season to taste. Pour skim milk over fish. Draw foil together and bake in oven for 20 minutes. Serve with salad. Divide evenly.
Makes 2 midday or evening meal servings.

Baked Cod Steaks

2 tablespoons lemon juice

½ teaspoon salt

½ teaspoon paprika

4 x 6 oz (180 g) boneless cod steaks

4 oz (120 g) onions, chopped

6 oz (180 g) green pepper, cut into strips

1 lemon, cut into wedges

Preheat oven to 425°F, 220°C, Gas Mark 7. Combine lemon juice, salt and paprika. Pour into a shallow ovenproof dish. Add fish and leave to marinate for 1 hour, turning once. Cook onions in non-stick pan with a little water until soft. Drain. Arrange strips of green pepper over cod steaks; sprinkle onions over fish. Bake uncovered in oven for 15 minutes or until fish flakes. Serve with lemon wedges. Divide evenly.
Makes 4 midday or evening meal servings.

Baked Fish and Vegetables

6 oz (180 g) green pepper, seeded and sliced

4 oz (120 g) tomato, sliced

4 oz (120 g) onions, sliced

12 oz (360 g) skinned fish fillets

¼ teaspoon salt

⅛ teaspoon pepper

2 fl oz (60 ml) water

1 tablespoon margarine

⅛ teaspoon paprika

6 oz (180 g) whole green beans

Place 3 oz (90 g) green pepper, 2 oz (60 g) tomato and 2 oz (60 g) onions in baking dish. Season fish with salt and pepper and arrange on top of vegetables. Cover with remaining vegetables. Add water, dot with margarine and sprinkle with paprika. Bake at 350°F, 180°C, Gas Mark 4, for 20 to 25 minutes or until fish is cooked. Divide evenly and serve with beans.
Makes 2 midday or evening meal servings.

Baked Fish and Vegetables

MEAT

Meat makes a meal hearty, and the range of recipes is endless. You can be lavish and extravagant with a piece of steak or economical and cunning with a hot pot or meat loaf.

We use only lean meat—cut off the fat before you cook it—and it should be grilled, roasted or baked on a rack, or boiled. We select up to a total of 3 meat meals weekly (if desirable) and allow 2 oz (60 g) for shrinkage on cooking and 2 oz (60 g) for the bone when buying it raw.

Meat is not only a delicious part of our meals, it represents sound nutrition.

Quick-and-Easy Cassoulet

12 oz (360 g) drained canned dried kidney or white beans, plus 4 fl oz (120 ml) liquid

6 oz (180 g) frankfurters, cut into 1-inch (2.5-cm) thick slices

9 oz (270 g) cooked carrots, sliced

4 tablespoons tomato puree

4 fl oz (120 ml) water

2 teaspoons chopped fresh parsley

1 small garlic clove, crushed

Combine all ingredients in large saucepan. Cover; bring to the boil. Reduce heat and simmer for 15 minutes. Remove cover and continue cooking until thickened, stirring occasionally. Divide evenly.
Makes 4 midday or evening meal servings.

Pork Chop with Apricot Sauce

1 x 8 oz (240 g) pork chop

pinch each salt, pepper and paprika

4 canned apricot halves, with 2 tablespoons juice, no sugar added

2 fl oz (60 ml) water

artificial sweetener to taste

¼ teaspoon cinnamon

1 clove

2 teaspoons cornflour, dissolved in 1 tablespoon water

Season chop with salt, pepper and paprika. Place on rack and grill for 30 minutes, turning once after 15 minutes. Meanwhile place apricots, juice and water in blender container and blend until pureed. Transfer to saucepan; add sweetener, cinnamon and clove. Simmer for 5 minutes. Stir in dissolved cornflour and cook, stirring constantly until thickened. Remove clove. Serve over chop.
Makes 1 midday or evening meal serving.

Grilled Beef with Wine and Herbs

4 fl oz (120 ml) red wine

3 oz (90 g) chopped onion

1 teaspoon Worcester sauce

1 garlic clove, crushed

¼ teaspoon dried tarragon

1 teaspoon chopped fresh parsley

12 oz (360 g) boneless top rump of beef

Combine the wine, onion, Worcester sauce, garlic and herbs in a basin. Place the beef in the mixture and turn the meat several times. Cover the basin closely with cling film and refrigerate for at least 4 hours or overnight. When ready to cook, drain the meat thoroughly and reserve the marinade. Grill the beef on a rack under moderate heat, turning once, for about 25 minutes or until done to taste. While the meat is cooking, heat the marinade in a small saucepan. Carve the cooked beef into long, thin slices (cutting across the grain). Divide evenly and serve each portion with half the marinade.
Makes 2 midday or evening meal servings.

Crockpot Hot Pot

4 oz (120 g) carrots, sliced

4 oz (120 g) onions, sliced

15 fl oz (450 ml) beef stock, made with 1 stock cube and 1 tablespoon cornflour

1 teaspoon basil flakes

8 oz (240 g) cooked sliced beef

6 oz (180 g) peeled cooked potato, sliced

salt and pepper to taste

Place carrots, onions, stock and basil in saucepan. Bring to the boil and simmer for 15 to 20 minutes, or until vegetables are tender. Meanwhile heat 'Crockpot'. When vegetables are cooked, strain liquid from them and reserve it. In crockpot place layers of meat, carrots and onions, alternately. Cover the top with sliced potato; sprinkle with salt and pepper to taste. Pour in cooking liquid until just below potatoes and cover with lid. This meal can cook indefin-

itely in the crockpot, but can also be cooked in a casserole dish and placed in oven, 375°F, 190°C, Gas Mark 5, for about 45 to 60 minutes, until potato is nicely browned. Divide evenly.
Makes 2 midday or evening meal servings.

Suffolk Hot Pot

4 oz (120 g) leeks, sliced

8 oz (240 g) carrots

4 oz (120 g) swede

¼ teaspoon cinnamon

½ level teaspoon mixed herbs

8 oz (240 g) cooked boneless lean lamb, minced

salt and pepper to taste

1 beef stock cube

6 oz (180 g) peeled potatoes

chopped fresh parsley to garnish

Spray a non-stick frying pan with non-stick cooking spray. Dry-fry leeks until golden. Thinly slice carrots and swede. Add cinnamon and herbs to meat and mix well. Layer vegetables, leeks and meat in a 2-pint (1 litre 200 ml) casserole dish, ending with a layer of meat. Lightly season each layer. Make up stock cube with 15 fl oz (450 ml) water and pour over contents of casserole to just cover. Thinly slice potatoes and drop into boiling, salted water for 3 minutes to prevent them going brown. Cover dish with potato slices and place in hot oven, 375°F, 190°C, Gas Mark 5, for 1 hour or until vegetables are cooked and potatoes

brown. Divide evenly and serve sprinkled with parsley.
Makes 2 midday or evening meal servings.

Polynesian Beef

1 lb 2 oz (540 g) chuck steak, cut into 1-inch (2.5-cm) cubes

12 fl oz (360 ml) beef stock, made with 1 stock cube

12 oz (360 g) canned pineapple chunks, no sugar added, drained (reserve liquid)

3 oz (90 g) onion, grated

1 tablespoon soy sauce

1 tablespoon cider vinegar

1 garlic clove, crushed

½-inch (1-cm) slice fresh ginger root, mashed

¼ teaspoon salt

¼ teaspoon dry mustard

2 teaspoons cornflour, dissolved in 2 tablespoons water

6 oz (180 g) cooked rice

1 tablespoon chopped fresh parsley

Grill beef on rack for 5 to 8 minutes, turning to brown all sides. In bowl combine stock, pineapple juice, onion, soy sauce, vinegar, garlic, ginger, salt and mustard. Add beef. Cover; refrigerate overnight. Transfer beef and marinade to saucepan and simmer for 30 minutes or until beef is tender. Stir in cornflour and simmer until thickened. Add pineapple; cook for 3 minutes. Divide evenly into 3 portions. Serve each portion over 2 oz (60 g) hot rice. Sprinkle with parsley.
Makes 3 midday or evening meal servings.

Savoury Lamb and Bean Stew

6 oz (180 g) cooked dried butter beans

4 oz (120 g) diced cooked lamb

8 fl oz (240 ml) chicken stock, made with 1 stock cube

3 oz (90 g) canned tomatoes, chopped

3 oz (90 g) peeled potato, diced

3 oz (90 g) drained canned whole kernel corn

2 oz (60 g) onion, diced

¾ teaspoon salt

¼ teaspoon thyme

Combine all ingredients in medium saucepan. Cover and cook for 1 hour or until sauce is very thick. Divide evenly.
Makes 2 midday or evening meal servings.

Ham and Rice Salad

2 oz (60 g) cooked white rice

½ teaspoon cider vinegar

salt and pepper to taste

1 tablespoon mayonnaise

2 oz (60 g) cooked peas

1½ oz (45 g) diced cooked ham

1 oz (30 g) Cheddar cheese, grated

½ oz (15 g) pickled cucumber, chopped

1 teaspoon chives

In bowl combine rice, vinegar, salt and pepper. Stir in mayonnaise. Add remaining ingredients; toss. Chill.
Makes 1 midday or evening meal serving.

PROTEIN FOODS—MEAT

Mushroom Kidneys

6 oz (180 g) trimmed lamb's kidneys

2½ fl oz (75 ml) chicken stock made with ½ stock cube

2 fl oz (60 ml) tomato juice

1 oz (30 g) onion, chopped

1½ oz (45 g) mushrooms, sliced

¼ teaspoon salt

⅛ teaspoon white pepper

1 bay leaf

Simmer kidneys in chicken stock until tender, about 15 to 20 minutes. Drain. Combine tomato juice, chopped onion and mushrooms in a saucepan and season with salt, pepper and bay leaf. Simmer for 20 minutes. Place the kidneys in a serving dish and pour sauce over them.
Makes 1 midday or evening meal serving.

Toad in the Hole

2 x 1 oz (30 g) grilled beef sausages

1 egg

1 tablespoon plain flour

3 tablespoons skim milk

salt and pepper to taste

Cut grilled sausages into ½-inch (1-cm) lengths. Place them in a small ovenproof dish. Beat egg with the flour; gradually add milk and beat. Add salt and pepper to taste. Pour batter over the sausages and place in preheated oven, 350°F, 180°C, Gas Mark 4, for 20 to 25 minutes.
Makes 1 midday or evening meal serving.

Steak and Tomato Casserole

6 oz (180 g) skirt steak

2 oz (60 g) onion, sliced

3 oz (90 g) tomato, skinned

4 fl oz (120 ml) tomato juice

Dry-fry onion, put meat on rack under hot grill and cook for 10 minutes on each side. Put in casserole with onion slices and rest of the ingredients. Cover and bake in oven, 350°F, 180°C, Gas Mark 4, for ½ to ¾ hour or until meat is tender.
Makes 1 midday or evening meal serving.

Veal and Pork Hot Pot

1½ lbs (720 g) boned pork, cut into 1-inch (2.5-cm) cubes

1½ lbs (720 g) boned veal shoulder, cut into 1-inch (2.5-cm) cubes

1 pint 5 fl oz (750 ml) chicken stock, made with 2 stock cubes

1½ lbs (720 g) peeled potatoes, cut into 1-inch (2.5-cm) cubes

12 oz (360 g) carrots, cut into 2-inch (5-cm) thick slices

8 oz (240 g) cabbage, shredded

4 oz (120 g) peeled white turnips, cut into 2-inch (5-cm) thick slices

4 oz (120 g) onion, diced

Bouquet Garni (2 cloves, 2 thyme sprigs, 1 bay leaf, tied in muslin) (optional)

¼ teaspoon pepper

salt to taste

Grill pork and veal on rack until well browned on all sides. Transfer to heavy saucepan. Add remaining ingredients. Bring to the boil; reduce heat. Cover and simmer for 1½ to 2 hours, or until meat is very tender. Remove cover for the last hour if desired to reduce liquid. Discard bouquet garni if used. Divide evenly.
Makes 8 midday or evening meal servings.

Hot Minted Lamb Bap

1 x 2 oz (60 g) bap

4 oz (120 g) cooked boneless lean lamb, minced

1 oz (30 g) spring onions, chopped

1 teaspoon finely chopped fresh mint

1 teaspoon lemon juice

1 teaspoon vegetable oil

dash garlic powder

salt and pepper to taste

cucumber, tomato and celery

5 fl oz (150 ml) skim milk

Cut bap in half and scoop out middle; crumble and add to minced lamb, onions, mint, lemon juice, vegetable oil, garlic and seasonings. Mix thoroughly together. Pile mixture back into each half, place on baking sheet and bake in hot oven, 375°F, 190°C, Gas Mark 5, for 10 to 15 minutes. Serve piping hot with cucumber, tomato, celery and glass of milk.
Makes 1 midday or evening meal serving.

Hot Minted Lamb Bap

Lamb Stew

6 oz (180 g) fillet of lamb, cubed

1 teaspoon olive oil

1 oz (30 g) onion, chopped

1 teaspoon plain flour

¼ beef stock cube, dissolved in 3 fl oz (90 ml) boiling water

1 oz (30 g) carrot, sliced

1 oz (30 g) celery, sliced

1 garlic clove, peeled

½ bay leaf, crumbled

pinch thyme leaves

2 oz (60 g) cooked barley

1 tablespoon chopped fresh parsley

Grill lamb cubes on a rack in a grill pan, 4 inches (10 cm) from source of heat, until cooked through. Heat oil in a non-stick saucepan and add onion; stir and cook until golden. Sprinkle with flour and continue to cook, stirring until onions are browned. Add lamb cubes and remaining ingredients except chopped parsley; cover and simmer for about 25 minutes, or until lamb is tender. Garnish with chopped parsley.

Makes 1 midday or evening meal serving.

Quick-and-Easy Lamb Chops

2 x 8 oz (240 g) lamb chump chops

1 tablespoon dried onion flakes

1 teaspoon salt

½ teaspoon garlic powder

⅛ teaspoon pepper

2 tomatoes, 4 oz (120 g) each, cut in half

Grill chops on rack 3 to 4 inches (8 to 10 cm) from source of heat for 6 to 7 minutes or until browned. In a small cup combine onion flakes, salt, garlic powder, and pepper. Turn chops and arrange tomato halves, cut side up, on grill rack. Sprinkle onion flake mixture over chops and tomatoes; grill for 5 to 6 minutes or until chops are done. Divide evenly.

Makes 2 midday or evening meal servings.

Lancashire Hot Pot

8 oz (240 g) trimmed lamb chops

2 oz (60 g) onion, sliced

2 oz (60 g) carrot, sliced

2 oz (60 g) frozen garden peas

3 oz (60 g) sliced peeled potatoes

5 fl oz (150 ml) stock, made with 1 stock cube

Grill chops until well done. Place in bottom of ovenproof dish. Layer onion, carrot and peas over chops. Overlap potato slices on top and pour stock over. Cover and cook in oven, 350°F, 180°C, Gas Mark 4, for 1 hour. Remove cover for the last 15 minutes to brown top. Serve with red cabbage, finely shredded and tossed in vinegar.

Makes 1 midday or evening meal serving.

Frankfurters in Tomato Sauce

12 fl oz (360 ml) tomato juice

6 oz (180 g) green pepper, seeded and cut into 1-inch (2.5-cm) strips

1 tablespoon dried onion flakes

½ teaspoon mixed herbs

pinch each garlic powder, celery salt, parsley flakes and thyme

salt and pepper to taste

6 oz (180 g) frankfurters, cut into 1-inch (2.5-cm) pieces

2 oz (60 g) peas

1 oz (30 g) sliced carrot

parsley sprigs to garnish

In saucepan combine water, onion, tomato ketchup, vinegar, dry mustard, paprika and pepper; bring to the boil. Reduce heat; simmer for 5 minutes. Arrange frankfurters side by side in shallow 9 x 9-inch (23 x 23 cm) baking tin. Cover with onion-tomato ketchup mixture and bake at 350°F, 180°C, Gas Mark 4, for 30 to 40 minutes. Divide evenly.

Makes 3 midday or evening meal servings.

Chinese Pepper Steak with Mushrooms

1½ lbs (720 g) skirt steak

2 lbs (960 g) green peppers, seeded and sliced

6 oz (180 g) mushrooms, sliced

4 oz (120 g) onions, sliced

1 garlic clove, crushed

1½ teaspoons salt

½ teaspoon ginger

¼ teaspoon pepper

12 fl oz (360 ml) beef stock made with 1 stock cube

3 tablespoons soy sauce

2 tablespoons cornflour

Grill steak on rack for 12 minutes or until rare, turning once to brown both sides. In preheated non-stick frying pan or wok combine green peppers, mushrooms, onions and garlic; cook for 3 minutes, stirring constantly. Add salt, ginger and pepper. In small bowl combine stock, soy sauce and cornflour; stir to dissolve cornflour. Add to saucepan. Bring to the boil, stirring constantly until sauce is thickened and clear. Remove from heat. Slice steak; place equal amounts of steak on each of 4 plates and top each portion with quarter of the vegetable mixture.
Makes 4 midday or evening meal servings.

Beef Pate

2 teaspoons low-fat spread

4 oz (120 g) finely minced cooked beef

1 tablespoon chopped fresh parsley

1½ teaspoons lemon juice

¼ teaspoon celery seeds

salt and pepper to taste

1 slice (1 oz/30 g) bread, toasted

Melt low-fat spread in non-stick saucepan; add rest of ingredients except toast and beat thoroughly until mixture is smooth. Put in small dish and chill in refrigerator. Serve with hot toast cut into triangles.
Makes 1 midday or evening meal serving.

Meatballs

6 oz (180 g) minced beef

2 eggs

2 slices (2 oz/60 g) white bread, made into crumbs

½ garlic clove, crushed (optional)

¼ teaspoon oregano (optional)

salt and freshly ground pepper to taste

2½ pints (1 litre 500 ml) water

Combine all ingredients except water in bowl. Form into 10 meatballs of equal size. Place in saucepan with water. Simmer for 12 to 15 minutes or until meatballs are done to taste. Drain. Divide meatballs evenly.
Makes 2 midday or evening meal servings.

Orange Lamb with Rosemary

6 oz (180 g) boneless lamb, cubed

1½ oz (45 g) spring onions, chopped

1 teaspoon vegetable oil

½ chicken stock cube, dissolved in 6 fl oz (180 ml) hot water

2 oz (60 g) cooked pearl barley

1 medium orange, peeled and thinly sliced

1 tablespoon lemon juice

½ teaspoon crushed rosemary leaves

pinch each salt and pepper

On rack in a grill pan, cook lamb until rare, about 10 minutes. In a non-stick saucepan, saute spring onions in oil until lightly browned. Add lamb and all remaining ingredients; stir to combine. Cover and cook for 45 to 50 minutes or until lamb is tender. Allow dish to stand for 15 minutes before serving.
Makes 1 midday or evening meal serving.

PROTEIN FOODS—MEAT

Steak and Kidney Casserole

12 oz (360 g) cooked beef kidneys (see note)

12 oz (360 g) boned cooked beef, cut into ¾-inch (2-cm) cubes

10 teaspoons plain flour

1 beef stock cube, crumbled

1 teaspoon salt

⅛ teaspoon pepper

12 fl oz (360 ml) water

8 oz (240 g) onions, sliced

2 tablespoons Worcester sauce

¼ teaspoon thyme

6 x 3 oz (90 g) potatoes, baked

In saucepan sprinkle kidneys and beef with flour, crumbled stock cube, salt and pepper. Add 12 fl oz (360 ml) water, onions, Worcester sauce and thyme. Bring to the boil, reduce heat and simmer, stirring often, until thickened. Place beef-kidney mixture in 3-pint (1 litre 800 ml) casserole. Bake at 325°F, 160°C, Gas Mark 3, for 45 minutes. Divide evenly and serve with jacket potato.

Makes 6 midday or evening meal servings.

Note: Wash beef kidneys; remove excess fat and sinew. Cut into ¾-inch (2-cm) slices. Place in covered saucepan with water to cover and simmer for 1 hour or until tender. Drain and weigh.

Beef Chop Suey

1½ lbs (720 g) skirt steak

2 tablespoons soy sauce

4 fl oz (120 ml) water

4 oz (120 g) onions, sliced

3 oz (90 g) mushrooms, sliced

1½ oz (45 g) carrot, sliced

1½ oz (45 g) celery, sliced

1 beef stock cube

½ teaspoon sugar

salt to taste

2 oz (60 g) fresh or rinsed canned bean sprouts

1½ oz (45 g) canned bamboo shoots, sliced

1 tablespoon cornflour, dissolved in 2 tablespoons water

4 oz (120 g) tomato, cut into wedges

Preheat grill. Score steak and marinate in soy sauce for 10 minutes, turning once. Reserve marinade. Grill steak on a rack for 6 minutes; turn, grill for 4 minutes longer or until rare. Cool. Cut into strips. Set aside beef and juices from slicing. In non-stick frying pan over high heat combine water, onions, mushrooms, carrot, celery and stock cube. Cook for 2 minutes, stirring occasionally. Add reserved marinade, sugar and salt; mix well. When vegetables are tender-crisp, add steak slices and juices, bean sprouts and bamboo shoots. Stir-cook for 2 minutes. Add cornflour; stir until mixture thickens. Add tomato wedges; mix well. Cook for 1 minute longer. Divide evenly.

Makes 4 midday or evening meal servings.

Boiled Beef

2¼ lbs (1 kg 80 g) boned beef topside

3 pints (1 litre 800 ml) water

1 to 2 teaspoons salt

Bouquet Garni (4 cloves, 2 thyme sprigs, 1 bay leaf, tied in muslin)

1 lb 2 oz (540 g) cabbage, cut in wedges

1 lb 2 oz (540 g) peeled potatoes, diced

12 oz (360 g) small white onions

9 oz (270 g) white turnips, peeled and diced

9 oz (270 g) carrots, sliced

3 oz (90 g) celery with leaves, sliced

In large, strong saucepan combine beef, water, salt and bouquet garni; cover and simmer for 2 to 3 hours or until beef is tender. Add more water if necessary. Drain and refrigerate liquid. Discard bouquet garni. Cool beef and refrigerate. Remove and discard congealed fat from liquid. In large saucepan combine 1 pint 16 fl oz (1 litre 80 ml) liquid, beef and remaining ingredients. Simmer for 45 minutes or until vegetables are tender. Remove beef and vegetables from liquid; slice beef. Place on serving dish surrounded by vegetables. Divide beef and vegetables evenly. Divide liquid evenly into soup bowls.

Makes 6 midday or evening meal servings.

Beef Chop Suey

PROTEIN FOODS—MEAT

Shepherd's Pie

4 oz (120 g) minced cooked lamb

1 tablespoon tomato puree

4 fl oz (120 ml) beef stock, made with ½ stock cube

4 oz (120 g) cooked chopped onions

3 oz (90 g) cooked chopped carrot

salt and pepper to taste

1 teaspoon dried mixed herbs

3 oz (90 g) peeled cooked potato

paprika to garnish

Preheat oven to 400°F, 200°C, Gas Mark 6. Place the lamb in a saucepan with the tomato puree, stock, vegetables, salt, pepper and mixed herbs. Bring to the boil, stirring. Cover saucepan and simmer for 15 minutes. Spoon the meat mixture into an ovenproof dish. Mash the cooked potato and place on top of the meat. Sprinkle with a little paprika. Bake in oven for 15 minutes, or until top is golden brown.
Makes 1 midday or evening meal serving.

Sausage Surprise

6 oz (180 g) beef sausages

2 oz (60 g) canned tomatoes

2 oz (60 g) mushrooms

3 oz (90 g) peeled cooked potato

2½ fl oz (75 ml) skim milk

2 teaspoons low-fat spread

Place sausages in saucepan, cover with salted water and bring to the boil. Simmer for 10 minutes. Drain, cool and skin sau-sages. Cut into pieces and place in ovenproof casserole. Cover with tomatoes and mushrooms. Beat potato with milk and spread over sausage mixture. Dot the top with low-fat spread and place in hot oven, 375°F, 190°C, Gas Mark 5, for 15 to 20 minutes, or until top is golden brown.
Makes 1 midday or evening meal serving.

Frankfurters in Spicy Tomato Sauce

4 fl oz (120 ml) cold water

3 oz (90 g) onion, chopped, or 2 tablespoons dried onion flakes

6 tablespoons tomato ketchup

3 tablespoons cider vinegar

¾ teaspoon dry mustard

¾ teaspoon paprika

freshly ground pepper to taste

9 oz (270 g) frankfurters cut in half, lengthwise

Combine all ingredients, except frankfurters, peas, carrots and parsley sprigs in frying pan; simmer for 20 minutes. Grill frankfurters until golden brown. Add frankfurters, peas and carrots to tomato juice mixture; simmer for 5 minutes. Garnish with parsley. Divide evenly.
Makes 2 midday or evening meal servings.

Meat Loaf

1 tablespoon unflavoured gelatine

6 fl oz (180 ml) beef stock, made with ½ stock cube

6 oz (180 g) cooked carrots, mashed

4 oz (120 g) onions, grated

1 teaspoon salt

⅛ teaspoon dry mustard

pinch white pepper

12 oz (360 g) minced beef

1 teaspoon sugar, optional

½ teaspoon oregano

pinch garlic powder

freshly ground pepper to taste

In small saucepan sprinkle gela-tine over stock to soften. Place over low heat and simmer, stir-ring constantly, until gelatine is dissolved. Remove from heat; set aside. In small bowl combine carrots, 2 oz (60 g) onion, ½ tea-spoon salt, dry mustard and white pepper. Set aside. In large bowl combine minced beef, sugar if desired, oregano, garlic powder, pepper, remaining 2 oz (60 g) onion, ½ teaspoon salt and 2 fl oz (60 ml) stock mixture. On sheet of greaseproof paper, form beef mixture into rectangle about ½ inch (1 cm) thick. Spread with carrot mixture to within 1 inch (2.5 cm) of edges. Roll up from narrow end. Slide off grease-proof paper seam side down, onto rack in roasting tin. Brush remaining stock mixture over beef roll. Bake at 350°F, 180°C, Gas Mark 4, for 1 hour or until beef is done to taste. Divide evenly.
Makes 2 midday or evening meal servings.

Spicy Meatballs and Sauce

6 oz (180 g) minced beef

2 oz (60 g) onion, finely diced

3 oz (90 g) celery, diced

¾ teaspoon Worcester sauce

¾ teaspoon garlic salt

¼ teaspoon pepper

3 oz (90 g) courgettes, sliced

3 oz (90 g) canned crushed tomatoes

2½ fl oz (75 ml) beef stock, made with ½ stock cube

¼ teaspoon oregano

¼ teaspoon basil

2 oz (60 g) cooked rice

In a bowl combine minced beef, onion, celery, Worcester sauce, garlic salt and pepper. Divide evenly into 4 portions and form each into a ball. Bake on a rack at 375°F, 190°C, Gas Mark 5, for 20 minutes. Meanwhile in a sauce-pan, combine courgettes, toma-toes, stock, oregano and basil. Simmer for 15 minutes; add cooked meatballs and simmer for a further 15 minutes. Serve over hot rice.
Makes 1 midday or evening meal serving.

Coriander Lamb

1 large garlic clove

2 tablespoons coriander seeds

salt and pepper to taste

4 x 8 oz (240 g) lamb chump chops

parsley sprigs to garnish

Crush garlic with coriander seeds and mix thoroughly with salt and pepper. Press mixture into both sides of lamb chops and set aside, in a cool place, for at least 1 hour. Grill lamb on rack, turning once. Allow approximately 6 minutes each side, or grill until meat is cooked through and both sides are crisp and brown. Transfer to serving plate; garnish with parsley.
Makes 4 midday or evening meal servings.

Fidgety Pie

6 oz (180 g) cooked diced ham

6 oz (180 g) peeled potatoes, fairly thinly sliced

4 oz (120 g) onions, thinly sliced

2 medium sweet apples, cored and thinly sliced

salt and pepper to taste

½ chicken stock cube, made up to 10 fl oz (300 ml) with hot water

1 teaspoon sage

2 slices (2 oz/60 g) bread, made into crumbs

2 teaspoons margarine

Place alternate layers of ham, potatoes, onions and apple in ovenproof casserole. Season to taste. Pour over the stock to which the sage has been added. Cover with breadcrumbs and dot margarine on top. Place in fairly hot oven, 375°F, 190°C, Gas Mark 5, for 1 to 1½ hours. For the first half hour place at top of oven, and then remove to lower shelf for the rest of the cooking time. Divide evenly.
Makes 2 midday or evening meal servings.

Beef Pot Roast

1½ lbs (720 g) boned topside of beef

12 oz (360 g) drained canned whole potatoes

16 fl oz (480 ml) tomato juice

8 oz (240 g) onions, sliced

6 oz (180 g) green pepper, seeded and diced

3½ oz (105 g) carrot, grated

2½ oz (75 g) celery, diced

10 peppercorns, crushed

4 bay leaves

1 tablespoon sugar

2 teaspoons salt

½ teaspoon paprika

Roast beef on a rack at 375°F, 190°C, Gas Mark 5, for 45 minutes or until done. Place in large, strong saucepan with re-maining ingredients. Cover and simmer for 1 to 1½ hours, or until meat is very tender. Re-move beef and potatoes; slice beef. Transfer 4 fl oz (120 ml) remaining mixture to blender container and blend until smooth. Return to saucepan and mix thoroughly. Divide beef evenly and place each portion on an individual serving plate with 3 oz (90 g) potatoes. Divide sauce evenly and pour over each ser-ving of beef and potatoes.
Makes 4 midday or evening meal servings.

Beef with Peppers and Tomatoes

1½ lbs (720 g) skirt steak

12 oz (360 g) green peppers, seeded and sliced

4 oz (120 g) onions, thinly sliced

2 garlic cloves, crushed

1 beef stock cube

1 teaspoon salt

½ teaspoon pepper

2 fl oz (60 ml) soy sauce

2 fl oz (60 ml) water

2 tablespoons red wine

2 teaspoons cornflour

8 oz (240 g) cut green beans

8 oz (240 g) tomatoes, cut into wedges

parsley sprigs to garnish

Grill steak on a rack about 4 inches (10 cm) from source of heat for 15 minutes or until rare, turning once. Cut into thin slices; set aside. In non-stick frying pan combine green peppers, onions, garlic, stock cube, salt and pepper; saute for 5 minutes, stirring occasionally. In small bowl combine soy sauce, water and wine. Add cornflour; stir to dissolve. Stir into vegetable mixture; cook until thickened. Add green beans. Cook until beans are tender-crisp. Place steak in serving dish. Top with vegetable mixture. Garnish with tomato wedges and parsley sprigs. Divide evenly.
Makes 4 midday or evening meal servings.

Scotch Broth

1½ pints (900 ml) beef stock, made with 2 stock cubes

6 oz (180 g) carrots, diced

4 oz (120 g) turnip

2 oz (60 g) onion

2 oz (60 g) leeks

4 oz (120 g) cooked barley

8 oz (240 g) diced lean cooked beef

6 oz (180 g) peeled potato, diced

salt and pepper to taste

2 teaspoons cornflour

chopped fresh parsley to garnish

Mix together all ingredients, except cornflour and parsley, in large saucepan and simmer gently until vegetables are tender. Mix the cornflour with a little water and add to broth. Divide evenly; garnish with parsley.
Makes 2 midday or evening meal servings.

Barbecued Pork Fillet

2 tablespoons low-calorie tomato ketchup

1½ teaspoons wine vinegar

1 teaspoon demerara sugar

dash salt

2 tablespoons water

2 x 6 oz (180 g) pork fillets

To prepare marinade, combine first 4 ingredients; add water and stir. Place pork fillets in large shallow pan; add marinade. Cover and refrigerate for 5 to 6 hours or overnight. Remove chops with tongs; place on grill 4 inches (10 cm) from source of heat; brush with marinade. Cook for about 15 minutes per side, brushing with marinade occasionally, or until meat is tender and well browned. Divide evenly.
Makes 2 midday or evening meal servings.

Super Sausages

12 oz (360 g) beef chipolata sausages

4 oz (120 g) onions, chopped

15 oz (450 g) canned tomatoes

1 teaspoon mixed herbs

salt and pepper to taste

6 oz (180 g) green pepper

4 oz (120 g) cooked pasta shells

Grill sausages on rack until cooked through. Place onions, tomatoes, mixed herbs, salt and pepper in saucepan and cook until onions are tender. Meanwhile, cut top off pepper and take out seeds. Cut pepper into rings and blanch in boiling water for 1 minute; drain and set aside. Add pasta to tomato mixture and cook for 3 to 5 minutes. Pile onto hot serving dish; arrange cooked sausages in wheel with the pepper rings on top of the sausages. Divide evenly and serve at once with green salad.
Makes 2 midday or evening meal servings.

Super Sausages

PROTEIN FOODS—MEAT

Chili Con Carne

12 oz (360 g) minced beef

1 pint 4 fl oz (720 ml) water

12 oz (360 g) green peppers, seeded and diced

4 oz (120 g) onions, chopped

2 oz (60 g) celery, diced

1 oz (30 g) chili pepper, seeded and diced

½ garlic clove, crushed

3 oz (90 g) canned tomatoes, chopped with liquid

4 tablespoons tomato puree

1 tablespoon chili powder, or to taste

½ teaspoon black pepper

¼ to ½ teaspoon ground red pepper or a few drops hot sauce, or to taste

⅛ teaspoon cumin

2 cloves

1 bay leaf

salt to taste

12 oz (360 g) drained canned dried red kidney beans

In saucepan combine beef and 1 pint (600 ml) water; simmer for 15 minutes or until beef loses its red colour. Strain and refrigerate liquid until fat congeals on top; remove fat and discard. Set aside 6 fl oz (180 ml) liquid. Freeze remaining liquid for later use. In saucepan combine the next 5 ingredients. Cook for 5 minutes. Add tomatoes, tomato puree, 4 fl oz (120 ml) water, seasonings, beans, reserved 6 fl oz (180 ml) liquid and beef. Simmer for 30 minutes. Divide evenly.
Makes 4 midday or evening meal servings.

Lasagne

1 lb 2 oz (540 g) minced beef

4 oz (120 g) onions, diced

4 tablespoons chopped fresh parsley

¾ teaspoon garlic powder

salt and white pepper to taste

8 tablespoons tomato puree

8 fl oz (240 ml) water

6 fl oz (180 ml) beef stock, made with ½ stock cube

2 teaspoons oregano

15 oz (450 g) curd cheese

1 lb 2 oz (540 g) cooked lasagne

In bowl combine beef, onions, 2 tablespoons parsley, ¼ teaspoon garlic powder, salt and pepper. Shape into large patties and place on rack in baking tin. Bake at 400°F, 200°C, Gas Mark 6, for 20 minutes or until firm. Cool and crumble. In saucepan combine beef, tomato puree, water, stock, oregano, ¼ teaspoon garlic powder, salt and pepper. Simmer for 25 minutes, stirring occasionally. Set aside. In separate bowl combine cheese, remaining 2 tablespoons parsley, ¼ teaspoon garlic powder, salt and pepper. Spread a thin layer of meat sauce in the bottom of an 8 x 8-inch (20 x 20 cm) baking tin. Arrange alternate layers of lasagne, cheese and meat sauce, ending with with a layer of meat sauce. Bake at 350°F, 180°C, Gas Mark 4, for 40 minutes. Allow to stand for 15 minutes before serving. Divide evenly.
Makes 6 midday or evening meal servings.

Tongue and Potato Salad

12 oz (360 g) peeled cooked potatoes, diced

8 oz (240 g) cooked peas

8 oz (240 g) cooked tongue, diced

9 oz (270 g) cooked cut green beans

3 oz (90 g) celery, diced

1½ oz (45 g) dill pickled cucumber, chopped

2½ fl oz (75 ml) natural unsweetened yogurt

2 tablespoons mayonnaise

1 tablespoon lemon juice

In bowl combine first 6 ingredients. In separate bowl combine remaining ingredients; pour over potato mixture and toss to combine. Chill. Divide evenly.
Makes 4 midday or evening meal servings. Add protein as required.

Barbecued Steak

1 oz (30 g) dried onion flakes

2 tablespoons Worcester sauce

2 tablespoons lemon juice

1 garlic clove, crushed

¾ teaspoon salt

2¼ lbs (1 kg 80 g) boned steak, cut into 1½-inch (4-cm) thick slices

1 tablespoon chopped fresh parsley

2 tablespoons margarine (optional)

In bowl combine first 5 ingredients; let stand for 10 minutes. Add beef. Cover and refrigerate for 2 to 6 hours. Remove steak from marinade and grill on a rack, basting with remaining marinade. Cook until done to taste. Sprinkle with parsley. Dot with margarine if desired. Divide evenly.

Makes 6 midday or evening meal servings.

Spicy Meat Sauce

1 lb (480 g) cooked minced beef, crumbled

1¼ (750 ml) pints water

2 oz (60 g) canned tomatoes, pureed in food mixer or blender

8 tablespoons tomato puree, mixed with 8 fl oz (240 ml) water

1 oz (30 g) dried onion flakes

1 oz (30 g) celery, finely chopped

3 tablespoons Worcester sauce

1 tablespoon chopped fresh parsley

2 teaspoons sugar (optional)

2 teaspoons garlic salt

2 teaspoons paprika

2 bay leaves

1 teaspoon chili powder, or to taste

½ teaspoon oregano

½ teaspoon salt

¼ teaspoon cinnamon

¼ teaspoon pepper

¼ teaspoon thyme

chopped fresh parsley to garnish

Combine all ingredients, except garnish, in large saucepan. Simmer sauce, uncovered, for 2 hours or until thick. Remove bay leaves. Garnish with parsley. Serve hot. Divide evenly.

Makes 4 midday or evening meal servings.

Moussaka

Sauce

1 tablespoon margarine

1 tablespoon plain flour

⅛ teaspoon salt

pinch white pepper

5 fl oz (150 ml) skim milk

Meat and Vegetables

8 oz (240 g) peeled aubergine, cut into ½-inch (1-cm) thick slices

8 oz (240 g) onions, diced

8 oz (240 g) canned tomatoes, chopped

4 fl oz (120 ml) water

3 tablespoons tomato puree

2 tablespoons chopped fresh parsley

pinch cinnamon

pinch allspice

salt and pepper to taste

8 oz (240 g) cooked minced lamb or beef, crumbled

To Prepare Sauce: Melt margarine in non-stick saucepan. Add flour, salt and pepper and cook over moderate heat for about 2 minutes, stirring constantly. Gradually add milk. Cook, stirring constantly with a wire whisk until mixture thickens.

To Prepare Moussaka: Brown aubergine slices on both sides in non-stick frying pan over high heat, pressing slices with back of spatula to release moisture. Set aside. In the same pan, brown the onions slightly. Add tomatoes, water, tomato puree, parsley, cinnamon, allspice, salt and pepper. Simmer for 5 minutes. Add crumbled meat

and cook for 10 more minutes. In non-stick casserole place half the aubergine slices and half meat mixture; repeat layers. Spoon Sauce on top. Bake at 375°F, 190°C, Gas Mark 5, for 35 minutes or until top begins to brown. Divide evenly.

Makes 2 midday or evening meal servings.

Ham and Tuna Mousse

2 teaspoons unflavoured gelatine

2½ fl oz (75 ml) hot water

5 fl oz (150 ml) skim milk

2 slices (2 oz/60 g) bread, torn into pieces

8 oz (240 g) drained canned tuna

6 oz (180 g) finely diced cooked ham

6 oz (180 g) cucumber, finely chopped

1 tablespoon chopped chives

2 teaspoons mayonnaise

1 teaspoon basil

salt and pepper to taste

6 oz (180 g) tomatoes, sliced

Sprinkle gelatine over water to soften and stir until dissolved. Place in blender container with skim milk and bread. Slowly add tuna, ham, cucumber, chives, mayonnaise, basil and seasoning to taste. Blend until smooth. Pour into wetted 2-pint (1 litre 200 ml) mould and chill in refrigerator. When set, turn out carefully onto a serving plate and decorate with sliced tomatoes. Divide evenly

Makes 4 midday or evening meal servings.

LIVER

If you've only had grilled or baked liver we think you're in for a treat once you discover our versatile range of flavourings and cooking methods. We've combined it with bread as in Faggots and with pineapple as in Sweet and Sour Liver. Do try these new ideas—you'll find that liver is really delicious. We can take it once a week.

When you're buying your liver make sure that it is fresh and avoid any which has a bluish tinge. Remember to allow 2 oz (60 g) for shrinkage in cooking. Don't over cook it—it's at its best while still pink in the centre.

Lemony Calf Liver

1½ lbs (720 g) calf liver

salt and freshly ground pepper to taste

2 tablespoons vegetable oil

1 tablespoon lemon juice

1 teaspoon finely chopped fresh parsley

Dry liver with paper towel; season with salt and pepper. Place in flameproof casserole, brush with oil and lemon juice and grill, 4 inches (10 cm) from source of heat, turning once, until done. Sprinkle with parsley and serve. Divide evenly.
Makes 4 midday or evening meal servings.

Chicken Liver Pate

12 oz (360 g) chicken livers

juice of 2 lemons

4 teaspoons Worcester sauce

½ teaspoon each salt and nutmeg

¼ teaspoon garlic powder

2 slices (2 oz/60 g) white bread, made into crumbs

2 medium apples, cored and sliced

lettuce leaves

1 lemon slice

parsley sprigs to garnish

Combine first 5 ingredients in saucepan; simmer for 10 minutes. Stir in breadcrumbs. Transfer to blender container and blend until smooth. Pour into dish and chill. Line a serving platter with lettuce leaves. Transfer pate to centre of platter. Surround with apple slices and garnish with lemon slice and parsley sprigs. Divide evenly.
Makes 2 midday or evening meal servings.

Breadcrumbed Liver

6 oz (180 g) calf liver, cut into ¼-inch (5-mm) slices

juice of ½ lemon

¾ oz (20 g) plain dried breadcrumbs

¼ teaspoon fennel seeds (optional)

pinch each salt and pepper

2 teaspoons olive oil

lemon slices to garnish

Marinate liver slices in lemon juice for ½ hour. Put breadcrumbs, fennel seeds, salt and pepper in blender and blend until the seeds are crushed. Spread crumb mixture in a shallow plate, press liver slices into crumbs to coat. Turn and repeat until all crumbs are used. In a non-stick frying pan, saute breaded liver strips in oil until golden on each side. Garnish with lemon slices.
Makes 1 midday or evening meal serving.

Chicken Livers in Orange Sauce

1½ lbs (720 g) chicken livers

salt and pepper to taste

4 medium oranges, peeled and sliced (reserve 2 slices)

8 fl oz (240 ml) orange juice, no sugar added

1 oz (30 g) onion, chopped

1 teaspoon soy sauce

½ teaspoon marjoram

1 teaspoon chopped fresh parsley

Cut each liver in half, sprinkle with salt and pepper and place in grill pan. Grill 3 inches (8 cm) from source of heat for 1 minute on each side. Do not overcook; inside should be pink. Combine remaining ingredients in large non-stick saucepan. Bring to the boil; reduce heat. Simmer for 7 minutes or until mixture is reduced by about one third. Add grilled livers, cook just long enough to heat livers. Divide evenly. Garnish with reserved orange slices and parsley.
Makes 4 midday or evening meal servings.

Chicken Livers in Orange Sauce

PROTEIN FOODS—LIVER

Chicken Liver Kebabs

6 oz (180 g) chicken livers

4 fl oz (120 ml) chicken stock, made with ½ stock cube

1 tablespoon dried onion flakes

1 teaspoon lemon juice

1 teaspoon Worcester sauce

½ teaspoon seasoned salt

½ teaspoon salt

⅛ teaspoon pepper

1 slice (1 oz/30 g) wholewheat bread, made into crumbs

6 oz (180 g) small fresh mushrooms

6 oz (180 g) tomatoes

1 teaspoon cornflour

Wash livers and pat dry with paper towel; set aside. In small saucepan, heat stock, onion flakes, lemon juice, Worcester sauce, salts and pepper. Bring to the boil and simmer for 5 minutes. Dip livers into stock mixture, then roll in breadcrumbs. Slice stem ends from mushrooms and wipe caps with damp paper towel. Thread livers, mushrooms and tomatoes alternately onto a skewer and grill 5 inches (12 cm) from source of heat for 3 to 5 minutes per side, turning to brown evenly. Bring stock mixture to the boil and thicken with cornflour. Serve with kebab.
Makes 1 midday or evening meal serving.

Liver with Spices

2 tablespoons vegetable oil

4 oz (120 g) spring onions, sliced

2 oz (60 g) celery, chopped

1 garlic clove, crushed

1½ lbs (720 g) ox liver, cut into 1-inch (2-cm) cubes

1 tablespoon plain flour

⅛ teaspoon ginger

⅛ teaspoon pepper

6 fl oz (180 ml) water

3 tablespoons soy sauce

Heat oil in large non-stick saucepan and saute spring onions, celery and garlic for 3 minutes; remove from saucepan and set aside. Add liver to saucepan and brown on all sides over high heat. Sprinkle with flour, ginger and pepper. Stir in water and soy sauce, and simmer for 3 minutes. Add vegetables and cook to heat vegetables. Divide evenly.
Makes 4 midday or evening meal servings.

Faggots with Gravy

6 oz (180 g) lamb's liver

1 slice (1 oz/30 g) bread, made into crumbs

1 teaspoon dried onion flakes

thyme, salt and pepper to taste

Gravy

½ beef stock cube

5 fl oz (150 ml) water

pinch mixed herbs

2 teaspoons cornflour

Preheat oven to 375°F, 190°C, Gas Mark 5. Blanch liver in boiling water for 2 minutes, drain and cool. Mince liver and mix with breadcrumbs, onion flakes and seasoning. Make into mounds on flat ovenproof dish or baking tin and bake for 20 minutes until firm. Place stock cube, water and herbs in saucepan. Bring to the boil. Mix cornflour with 1 tablespoon water, add to stock and cook, stirring, for 2 minutes. Serve with the faggots.
Makes 1 midday or evening meal serving.

'Sweet and Sour' Liver

1½ pints (900 ml) water

12 oz (360 g) chicken livers

12 oz (360 g) green peppers, seeded and sliced

3 oz (90 g) bean sprouts

6 fl oz (180 ml) chicken stock, made with ½ stock cube

2 oz (60 g) onion, diced

1 teaspoon salt

¼ teaspoon ginger

pepper to taste

8 oz (240 g) canned pineapple chunks, no sugar added

½ oz (15 g) dried mushrooms, reconstituted in warm water and diced

2 tablespoons cider vinegar

1 tablespoon cornflour, dissolved in 3 tablespoons water

Bring water to the boil in large frying pan; add livers and boil for 1 minute. Drain and discard liquid. Add peppers, bean sprouts, stock, onion, salt, ginger and pepper. Cover and simmer for 10 minutes. Add pine-

apple and mushrooms to frying pan. Stir in vinegar and cornflour; simmer, stirring constantly, until mixture is thickened. Divide evenly.
Makes 2 midday or evening meal servings.

Liver with Croutons

2 oz (60 g) onion, sliced

12 oz (360 g) chicken livers, halved

2 fl oz (60 ml) chicken stock made with ¼ stock cube

3 tablespoons red wine vinegar

1 teaspoon capers

1 garlic clove, crushed

¼ teaspoon salt

⅛ teaspoon pepper

6 oz (180 g) cooked cauliflower florets

2 slices (2 oz/60 g) white bread, cut into ½-inch (1-cm) cubes and sauteed in

1 tablespoon vegetable oil

In non-stick frying pan, cook onions over medium heat until lightly browned. Add liver; cook for 10 minutes. Add stock, vinegar, capers, garlic, salt and pepper. Simmer for 10 minutes. Spoon chicken liver mixture onto serving dish. Surround with cauliflower florets and top with croutons. Divide evenly.
Makes 2 midday or evening meal servings.

Quick and Easy Chicken Livers with Mushrooms

1 teaspoon vegetable oil

3 oz (90 g) green pepper, seeded and diced

1½ oz (45 g) mushrooms, diced

1 oz (30 g) onion, diced

6 oz (180 g) chicken livers, chopped

2 teaspoons plain flour

½ teaspoon salt

⅛ teaspoon paprika

4 fl oz (120 ml) chicken stock, made with ½ stock cube

2 oz (60 g) cooked rice

Heat oil in non-stick fryng pan; saute green pepper, mushrooms and onion. Add livers and sprinkle with flour, salt and paprika. Saute over moderate heat, stirring frequently, until liver loses pink colour. Add stock and bring to the boil. Reduce heat and simmer, stirring often, until thickened. Serve over rice.
Makes 1 midday or evening meal serving.

Liver with Onion and Tomato Sauce

6 oz (180 g) onions

3 oz (90 g) green or red pepper, seeded and chopped (optional)

12 oz (360 g) pig's liver

10 fl oz (300 ml) stock made with 1 stock cube, any flavour

6 oz (180 g) canned tomatoes, chopped

salt and pepper to taste

parsley sprigs to garnish

Dry-fry onions and pepper gently in non-stick frying pan until lightly browned. Add liver and seal. Mix stock with tomatoes and pour over liver and onions. Cover and simmer for approximately 15 minutes, stirring occasionlly. Season to taste. Turn heat up and cook for a further 10 to 15 minutes, stirring frequently until stock is reduced to a thick gravy. Garnish with parsley. Divide evenly and serve with vegetable of your choice.
Makes 2 midday or evening meal servings.

Liver with Vegetables and Soy Sauce

½ clove garlic

salt to taste

6 oz (180 g) lamb's liver

2 oz (60 g) onion, sliced

3 oz (90 g) white cabbage, shredded

1½ oz (45 g) carrot, grated

1 oz (30 g) mushrooms, sliced

1 tablespoon soy sauce

pepper to taste

Crush garlic with a little salt. Wash and cut liver into thin strips. Sprinkle deep, non-stick frying pan with a little salt to prevent food sticking. Add onion and garlic and cook until onion becomes soft. Add liver and cook for 3 minutes. Stir in cabbage, carrot and mushrooms. Add soy sauce and pepper. Cook until vegetables are soft but still crisp, stirring occasionally, for about 6 minutes. Serve piping hot.
Makes 1 serving.

PROTEIN FOODS—LIVER

Mustard Grilled Liver

12 oz (360 g) calf liver, cut into ½-inch (1-cm) thick slices

salt and pepper to taste

1 slice (1 oz/30 g) white bread, made into crumbs

1 tablespoon chopped fresh parsley

1 tablespoon Dijon mustard

1 teaspoon dried onion flakes, reconstituted in 1 teaspoon water

1 garlic clove, crushed

1 tablespoon margarine

Sprinkle liver with salt and pepper; grill 3 inches (8 cm) from source of heat, turning once. In bowl combine crumbs, parsley, mustard, onion flakes and garlic. Place liver in heatproof shallow casserole. Top with crumb mixture. Dot with margarine. Place under grill for 1 minute. Divide evenly.
Makes 2 midday or evening meal servings.

Sauteed Liver and Onions with Rice

2 tablespoons vegetable oil

8 oz (240 g) onions, sliced

salt and pepper to taste

2 tablespoons plain flour

1½ lbs (720 g) lamb's liver, sliced

2 fl oz (60 ml) water

8 oz (240 g) hot cooked rice

Heat oil in large non-stick saucepan; add onions and saute for 4 to 5 minutes until tender but still crisp. Lift out and place on serving dish and keep warm. Add pepper and salt to flour and dip each slice of liver in flour until it is all used. Saute liver in saucepan for 3 to 5 minutes, turning once during cooking. Remove liver to serving dish; add water to saucepan and stir to combine all juices. Bring to the boil and pour over liver. Serve liver at once with rice. Divide evenly.
Makes 4 midday or evening meal servings.

Savoury Liver

6 oz (180 g) liver

1½ teaspoons plain flour, seasoned with salt and pepper

1 oz (30 g) onion

1 medium cooking apple, peeled

3 oz (90 g) peeled potato

½ teaspoon dried sage

5 fl oz (150 ml) water or stock made with ½ stock cube

seasoning salt and pepper to taste

chopped fresh parsley for garnish

Preheat oven to 350°F, 180°C, Gas Mark 4. Dip liver in seasoned flour and place in baking dish. Slice onion, apple and potato. Spread onion over the liver, followed by a layer of apple. Sprinkle with sage. Place a layer of potato over sage and apple. Add the water or stock with seasoning salt and pepper. Cover baking dish with lid or foil and bake for 40 minutes. Towards the end of cooking, uncover and allow potatoes to brown. Garnish with parsley.
Makes 1 midday or evening meal serving.

Liver Casserole

12 oz (360 g) calf or ox liver

4 oz (120 g) carrots, thinly sliced

6 oz (180 g) peeled potatoes, thinly sliced

4 oz (120 g) onion, sliced

8 fl oz (240 ml) beef stock, made with 1 stock cube

3 oz (90 g) canned tomatoes, chopped

½ teaspoon basil

1 bay leaf

salt and pepper to taste

6 oz (180 g) cooked Brussels sprouts

Cut liver into thin strips. Place in bowl and cover with boiling water; let stand for 3 minutes. Drain and dry with paper towels. In saucepan add carrots to boiling water, boil for 5 minutes; add potatoes and boil for 5 minutes longer. Drain. Layer liver, carrots, potatoes and onion in a large casserole. Combine remaining ingredients and add to casserole. Bake at 350°F, 180°C, Gas Mark 4, for 1 hour or until vegetables are tender. Serve with Brussels sprouts. Divide evenly.
Makes 2 midday or evening meal servings.

Liver Casserole

PEANUT BUTTER

A jar of peanut butter is a useful item to find on anyone's pantry shelf.

It's a valuable, versatile food, which is a marvellous source of protein. It mixes well with cheese, makes dips and creamy fillings, blends into a sauce which enhances chicken and makes a delicious accompaniment to a crisp salad. Try spreading it on bread with honey, too.

We can have 1 level tablespoonful at the morning meal and 3 level tablespoonfuls at the midday and evening meals. Don't forget that peanut butter replaces some fat servings. Check your menu plan (page 5) for the precise amounts.

Peanut Butter and Garlic Pate

5 oz (150 g) curd cheese (or sieved cottage cheese)

3 tablespoons crunchy peanut butter

1 garlic clove, crushed

2 drops hot sauce

salt and pepper to taste

1½ oz (45 g) melba toast or crispbread

Combine all ingredients except melba toast in a bowl and mix well. Let stand for half an hour. Divide evenly and serve with melba toast or crispbread.
Makes 2 midday or evening meal servings.

Macaroni with Cheese and Peanut Sauce

1 teaspoon low-fat spread

3 oz (90 g) button mushrooms, sliced

4½ teaspoons peanut butter

2½ oz (75 g) curd cheese

2 fl oz (60 ml) skim milk

salt and pepper to taste

2 oz (60 g) cooked macaroni

3 oz (90 g) cooked cauliflower

Melt low-fat spread in saucepan and saute mushrooms until tender. Blend peanut butter with curd cheese; mix in milk. Stir this mixture into mushrooms and bring to the boil, stirring. Season to taste and continue simmering for a further 2 to 3 minutes. If mixture is too thick, it may be thinned with a little skim milk (be sure to measure). Pour sauce over macaroni and cauliflower and stir briskly with a fork. Serve at once with mixed salad.
Makes 1 midday or evening meal serving.

Peanut Butter Pizza

1 x 1½ oz (45 g) muffin, split and lightly toasted

3 tablespoons peanut butter

2 teaspoons imitation bacon bits

Spread each muffin half with half of the peanut butter and top each half with 1 teaspoon of bacon bits. Grill for 2 to 3 minutes until peanut butter is bubbly.
Makes 1 midday or evening meal serving.

Noodle Salad with Peanut-Sesame Dressing

6 oz (180 g) skinned and boned cooked chicken, shredded

4 oz (120 g) cooked noodles

1½ oz (45 g) cucumber, peeled and cut into strips

1½ oz (45 g) bean sprouts, blanched

1½ oz (45 g) radishes, sliced

1½ oz (45 g) shredded lettuce

4½ teaspoons peanut butter

2 teaspoons warm water

1 tablespoon soy sauce

1 teaspoon vegetable oil

¼ teaspoon pepper

½ garlic clove, crushed

2 teaspoons sesame seeds, lightly toasted

Place chicken noodles and vegetables in a bowl. Mix peanut butter with warm water; add soy sauce, oil, pepper and garlic and stir well. Pour over salad and toss gently. Sprinkle with sesame seeds before serving. Divide evenly.
Makes 2 midday or evening meal servings.

PREPARED FOODS

You may be surprised to find fish cakes and bacon included in the Food Plan, but if you use them as part of your protein selection, exactly as indicated, you will find that they add variety to your menus and fit into today's life-style quite happily. (See page 71 for selections).

DRIED PEAS AND BEANS

These are an economical and low cost source of protein. Remember that they must be weighed after they have been cooked. We can use them fresh or canned. It's useful to know that 2 oz (60 g) of dried peas, beans or lentils will yield about 6 oz (180 g) when cooked.

You will note that we include commercial baked beans. They provide that popular quick-and-easy meal for us all—Beans on Toast!

Barbecued Baked Beans

7 to 8 oz (210 to 240 g) baked beans

3 oz (90 g) canned tomatoes, chopped

½ teaspoon barbecue spice

2 tablespoons low-calorie tomato ketchup

1 teaspoon Worcester sauce

Place baked beans in non-stick saucepan and add tomatoes, spice, ketchup and Worcester sauce. Heat thoroughly, stirring until heated through.
Makes 1 midday or evening meal serving.

Split Pea Minestrone

10 oz (300 g) courgettes, sliced

6 oz (180 g) onions, chopped

5 oz (150 g) mushrooms, sliced

2 oz (60 g) celery, diced

1 pint 4 fl oz (720 ml) ham or chicken stock, made with 2 stock cubes

12 oz (360 g) cooked dried split peas

½ teaspoon salt

½ teaspoon basil

pepper to taste

12 oz (360 g) peeled cooked potatoes, diced (optional)

In large non-stick saucepan combine courgettes, onions, mushrooms and celery. Cook for 5 minutes. Add all remaining ingredients except potatoes. Simmer, stirring occasionally, for 45 minutes or until soup thickens. Add water to adjust consistency, if necessary. Add potatoes if desired. Cook for 10 minutes. Divide evenly.
Makes 4 midday or evening meal servings. Add protein as required.

Kidney Baked Beans

1 oz (30 g) onion, chopped

½ chicken stock cube

½ medium apple, peeled, cored and grated

1 oz (30 g) carrot, grated

1 tablespoon tomato puree

1 tablespoon cider vinegar

¼ teaspoon dry mustard

⅛ teaspoon oregano

pinch cumin

salt and freshly ground pepper to taste

6 oz (180 g) drained canned kidney beans

In a 1-pint (600-ml) casserole combine onion and stock cube. Bake at 350°F, 180°C, Gas Mark 4, for about 10 minutes, stirring occasionally. Add apple and carrot and bake for 5 minutes, stirring once. In a bowl combine tomato puree, cider vinegar, mustard, oregano, cumin, salt and pepper. Stir in beans and combine with vegetables in casserole. Cover and bake for 45 minutes. Serve hot or cold.
Makes 1 midday or evening meal serving.

PROTEIN FOODS—DRIED PEAS AND BEANS

Beans in Leek Sauce

8 oz (240 g) leeks, sliced

1 vegetable stock cube dissolved in 10 fl oz (300 ml) water

2 teaspoons cornflour

10 fl oz (300 ml) skim milk

12 oz (360 g) cooked haricot beans

6 oz (180 g) garden peas, cooked

Cook sliced leeks in 10 fl oz (300 ml) water and stock cube for 10 minutes. Mix cornflour with milk and add to leeks and stock. Cook for a further 2 minutes. Add beans and peas. Heat thoroughly. Serve, evenly divided, in soup bowls.

Makes 2 midday or evening meal servings.

Curried Baked Beans

2 teaspoons vegetable oil

1½ oz (45 g) onion, finely diced

½ medium cooking apple, peeled and diced

½ to 1 teaspoon curry paste

7 to 8 oz (210 to 240 g) canned baked beans

1 tablespoon sultanas, soaked in 2 fl oz (60 ml) hot water

1 slice (1 oz/30 g) bread

Heat oil in non-stick saucepan. Add onion and apple and saute until they are tender, stirring all the time. Add curry paste and baked beans. Drain sultanas and add to beans. Cook, stirring, for a further minute. Serve at once with bread.

Makes 1 midday or evening meal serving.

Basil, Butter Bean and Vegetable Soup

8 oz (240 g) dried butter beans, soaked overnight

2 tablespoons vegetable oil

4 oz (120 g) onion, chopped

1 garlic clove, crushed

1 stick celery, chopped

8 oz (240 g) leeks, thinly sliced

1 lb (480 g) green cabbage, finely shredded

2 tablespoons chopped fresh basil, or ½ teaspoon dried basil

2 tablespoons tomato puree

sea salt to taste

freshly ground pepper to taste

2 tablespoons chopped parsley

Drain the beans and place in a saucepan. Add 3 pints (1 litre 800 ml) cold water and bring to the boil. Cover and simmer for about 2 hours or until tender. Shortly before the beans have finished cooking, heat the oil in a large saucepan; add the onion, garlic and celery and cook gently for 10 minutes, stirring frequently. Add the leeks, cabbage and basil and stir for 3 to 4 minutes. Drain the beans and add the cooking liquor to the vegetables, together with the tomato puree, salt and pepper to taste. Reserve the beans. Bring to the boil and simmer for about 30 minutes. Add the beans, with more water as necessary and continue simmering until all the vegetables are tender. Adjust the seasoning. Stir in the parsley and serve immediately.

Makes 4 midday or evening meal servings.

Soybean Stuffed Peppers

4 medium green peppers, 6 oz (180 g) each, halved and seeded

1½ lbs (720 g) cooked dried soybeans, mashed

12 oz (360 g) tomatoes, diced

4 oz (120 g) celery, diced

2 tablespoons water

2 teaspoons dried onion flakes

pinch garlic powder

salt and pepper to taste

2 slices (2 oz/60 g) white bread, made into crumbs

2 tablespoons low-fat spread, melted

In large saucepan cook pepper halves in boiling, salted water for 3 minutes or until tender-crisp. Drain; set aside to cool. In medium bowl combine next 7 ingredients; divide evenly into 8 portions and fill each pepper half. In small bowl combine breadcrumbs and low-fat spread. Sprinkle an equal amount of crumb mixture over each pepper half. Place peppers in large non-stick baking tin. Bake at 350°F, 180°C, Gas Mark 4, for 25 to 30 minutes or until peppers are soft.

Makes 4 midday or evening meal servings, 2 halves each.

Curried Baked Beans

PROTEIN FOODS—DRIED PEAS AND BEANS

Soybean and Vegetable Loaf

12 fl oz (360 ml) chicken stock made with 2 stock cubes

6 oz (180 g) green pepper, seeded and finely chopped

4 oz (120 g) celery, finely chopped

3 oz (90 g) mushrooms, sliced

3 oz (90 g) onion, finely chopped

1 garlic clove, crushed

1 lb 2 oz (540 g) cooked dried soybeans

8 oz (240 g) carrots, grated

4 tablespoons plain flour

4 tablespoons chopped fresh parsley

½ teaspoon oregano

½ teaspoon thyme

pinch ground cloves

6 eggs, slightly beaten

3 slices (3 oz/90 g) wholemeal bread, made into crumbs

In saucepan combine stock, green pepper, celery, mushrooms, onion and garlic. Cook for 5 minutes. Cool slightly. Stir in remaining ingredients in order given until well combined. Press mixture into large non-stick loaf tin. Bake at 350°F, 180°C, Gas Mark 4, for 40 minutes or until golden. Divide evenly.
Makes 6 midday or evening meal servings.

Soybean Cheese Casserole

8 fl oz (240 ml) chicken stock, made with 1 stock cube

6 oz (180 g) green pepper, seeded and chopped

4 oz (120 g) onion, chopped

1 garlic clove, crushed

4 oz (120 g) canned tomatoes, crushed

1 tablespoon tomato puree

1 teaspoon basil

¼ teaspoon oregano

salt and pepper to taste

12 oz (360 g) cooked dried soybeans

4 oz (120 g) sharp Cheddar cheese, grated

2 slices (2 oz/60 g) white bread, made into crumbs

In non-stick saucepan combine stock, green pepper, onion and garlic. Cook until vegetables are tender. Add tomatoes, tomato puree and seasonings. Simmer until slightly thickened; add soybeans. Transfer mixture to 3-pint (1 litre 800 ml) casserole. In small bowl combine cheese and crumbs. Sprinkle over tomato-bean mixture. Bake at 350°F, 180°C, Gas Mark 4, for 40 minutes or until golden. Divide evenly.
Makes 4 midday or evening meal servings.

Soybean Casserole

8 oz (240 g) celery, chopped

2 oz (60 g) onion, chopped

2 oz (60 g) green pepper, seeded and chopped

½ chicken stock cube, dissolved in 2 fl oz (60 ml) hot water

8 teaspoons plain flour

1 pint (600 ml) skim milk

1½ lbs (720 g) cooked dried soybeans

1 teaspoon salt

2 slices (2 oz/60 g) white bread, made into crumbs

4 teaspoons margarine

In saucepan cook celery, onion and green pepper for 3 minutes. Add dissolved stock cube; cook for 5 minutes. Blend in flour. Slowly add milk and cook, stirring constantly, until mixture thickens. Add beans and salt. Mix well. Pour into 2-pint (1 litre 200 ml) non-stick baking dish. Sprinkle evenly with breadcrumbs. Dot with margarine. Bake at 350°F, 180°C, Gas Mark 4, for 30 minutes or until golden brown. Divide evenly.
Makes 4 midday or evening meal servings.

Soyburgers

12 oz (360 g) minced beef

12 oz (360 g) cooked dried soybeans, mashed

1 tablespoon dried onion flakes

½ teaspoon salt

⅛ teaspoon pepper

Combine all ingredients in bowl. Divide into 4 equal patties. Place on rack and bake at 375°F, 190°C, Gas Mark 5, for 25 minutes or until done to taste. Serve hot.
Makes 4 midday or evening meal servings, 1 patty each.

Quick and Easy Bean Salad with Yogurt

12 oz (360 g) drained canned dried red kidney beans

3 oz (90 g) green pepper, seeded and diced

2 oz (60 g) celery, diced

2 oz (60 g) onion, diced

1 garlic clove, crushed

2½ fl oz (75 ml) natural unsweetened yogurt

1 tablespoon vegetable oil

1 tablespoon lemon juice

3 oz (90 g) mixed salad greens (endive, cos and round lettuce)

4 oz (120 g) tomato, sliced

1 tablespoon chopped chives

2 tablespoons chopped fresh parsley

salt and pepper to taste

In bowl combine beans, green pepper, celery, onion and garlic. In small cup combine yogurt, oil and lemon juice; pour over bean mixture. Chill until ready to use. Arrange greens on serving dish; top with bean mixture and surround with tomato slices. Sprinkle with chives, parsley, salt and pepper; serve at once. Divide evenly.
Makes 2 midday or evening meal servings.

Savoury Bean Salad

1 tablespoon vegetable oil

6 oz (180 g) peeled cooked potatoes, diced

6 oz (180 g) cooked carrots, diced

6 oz (180 g) tomatoes, diced

1 garlic clove, crushed

6 oz (180 g) cooked dried butter beans

2 fl oz (60 ml) water

½ oz (15 g) chopped fresh parsley

salt and freshly ground pepper to taste

6 oz (180 g) shredded lettuce

Heat oil in a non-stick frying pan; add potatoes, carrots, tomatoes and garlic. Saute for 3 minutes. Add beans and water. Simmer until most of the water is evaporated and beans are hot. Stir in parsley and season with salt and pepper. Remove from heat. Serve on lettuce. Divide evenly.
Makes 2 midday or evening meal servings. Add protein as required.

Split Pea Soup

4 oz (120 g) carrot, diced

3 oz (90 g) cooked onion, diced

12 oz (360 g) cooked dried split peas

16 fl oz (480 ml) water

2 chicken stock cubes, crumbled

½ bay leaf

In non-stick saucepan cook carrot and onion for 3 minutes. Add remaining ingredients. Cover and simmer, stirring often, for 25 to 30 minutes or until desired consistency. Divide evenly.
Makes 2 midday or evening meal servings.

Butter Bean Gratin

3 oz (90 g) hot cooked butter beans

2½ fl oz (75 ml) skim milk

1½ teaspoons cornflour

1 oz (30 g) hard cheese, grated

1 slice (1 oz/30 g) bread, made into crumbs

salt and pepper to taste

Put butter beans in ovenproof dish and keep warm. Put milk in saucepan, add cornflour and whisk thoroughly. Add half the cheese, salt and pepper and bring to the boil; cook for 1 minute, stirring. Pour sauce over beans; mix rest of cheese with breadcrumbs and sprinkle over the top. Brown under a hot grill. Serve at once.
Makes 1 midday or evening meal serving.

Three-Bean Soup

1½ lbs (720 g) cooked dried red kidney beans (reserve cooking liquid)

8 oz (240 g) cut green beans

1 to 2 garlic cloves, crushed

½ teaspoon basil

salt and pepper to taste

1½ lbs (720 g) cooked dried butter beans

12 oz (360 g) courgettes, diced

4 oz (120 g) canned tomatoes, chopped

1 lb (480 g) cooked noodles

In large saucepan combine reserved cooking liquid and enough water to make 3½ pints (2 litres) liquid. Add red kidney and green beans, garlic, basil, salt and pepper; bring to the boil, reduce heat and simmer for 45 minutes. Add butter beans, courgettes and tomatoes. Simmer for 30 minutes longer. Divide evenly into 8 soup bowls, each containing 2 oz (60 g) hot noodles.
Makes 8 midday or evening meal servings.

Cheese and Red Bean Dip

12 oz (360 g) drained canned dried red kidney beans (reserve 2 tablespoons liquid)

¼ teaspoon garlic powder

¼ teaspoon cumin seed, crushed

4 oz (120 g) Cheddar cheese, grated

4 tablespoons vegetable oil

In saucepan heat beans, mashing with a wooden spoon. Stir in garlic powder and cumin. Add reserved bean liquid. Stir in cheese until melted. Remove from heat; stir in oil. Divide evenly.
Makes 4 midday or evening meal servings.

Bean, Rice and Potato Soup

1½ lbs (720 g) cooked dried white beans (reserve cooking liquid)

3½ pints (2 litres) cooking liquid (or cooking liquid plus water to equal 3½ pints (2 litres)

12 oz (360 g) peeled potatoes, diced

8 oz (240 g) celery, chopped

4 oz (120 g) onions, diced

2 small garlic cloves, crushed

salt and white pepper to taste

8 oz (240 g) cooked brown rice

chopped fresh parsley to garnish

In a large saucepan combine beans, liquid, potatoes, celery, onion, garlic, salt and pepper. Bring to the boil. Reduce heat, cover and simmer for 30 minutes or until vegetables are tender. If desired, remove cover and cook until thickened, stirring occasionally. Adjust seasonings. Divide evenly into 4 soup bowls, each containing 2 oz (60 g) hot rice. Garnish each serving with chopped parsley.
Makes 4 midday or evening meal servings.

Sweet and Sour Beans with Frankfurters

12 oz (360 g) cooked dried haricot beans

1 medium apple, diced

6 oz (180 g) green pepper, seeded and diced

1 oz (30 g) onion or spring onion, finely diced

2 tablespoons tomato ketchup

1 teaspoon prepared mustard

few drops hot sauce

12 oz (360 g) canned tomatoes, crushed

6 oz (180 g) frankfurters, sliced diagonally

In shallow 4-pint (2 litres 250 ml) casserole combine first 8 ingredients. Top with tomatoes and frankfurters. Bake at 350°F, 180°C, Gas Mark 4, for 30 minutes. Divide evenly.
Makes 4 midday or evening meal servings.

Sweet and Sour Beans with Frankfurters

Butter Bean and Carrot Soup

12 oz (360 g) cooked dried butter beans

6 oz (180 g) carrots, sliced

4 oz (120 g) onions, sliced

2 tablespoons chopped fresh parsley

2 teaspoons Worcester sauce

½ teaspoon salt

white pepper to taste

1 oz (30 g) non-fat dry milk

6 fl oz (180 ml) water

chopped watercress to garnish

In large saucepan combine first 7 ingredients. Add water to cover. Bring to the boil; reduce heat and simmer for 20 minutes or until vegetables are tender. Pour bean mixture into blender container in two batches, if necessary; blend until pureed. Return to saucepan. Mix dry milk with water and stir in. Heat, but do not boil. Divide evenly and serve garnished with watercress.
Makes 2 midday or evening meal servings.

Spicy Lentils

1 tablespoon vegetable oil

4 oz (120 g) onions, finely diced (reserve 2 tablespoons)

4 oz (120 g) tomato, finely chopped

3 oz (90 g) green pepper, seeded and chopped

2 oz (60 g) canned pimiento, chopped

6 oz (180 g) cooked dried lentils

1 teaspoon chicken stock powder

½ teaspoon Worcester sauce

salt and pepper to taste

Heat oil in non-stick frying pan; add onions, tomato, green pepper and pimiento. Saute until tender-crisp. Add lentils, stock powder, Worcester sauce, salt and pepper. Cook, stirring occasionally, until thoroughly heated. Divide evenly: top each with 1 tablespoon reserved onion.
Makes 2 midday or evening meal servings. Add protein as required.

Quick Bean and Tuna Salad

2 tablespoons vegetable oil

2 teaspoon lemon juice or red wine vinegar

6 oz (180 g) drained canned butter beans

4 tablespoons chopped fresh parsley

½ oz (15 g) spring onion, chopped

salt and pepper to taste

4 oz (120 g) drained canned tuna

2 large lettuce leaves

In bowl combine oil and lemon juice or vinegar. Add beans, parsley, spring onion, salt and pepper. Toss to combine. Chill. Break tuna into chunks. Divide bean mixture evenly onto lettuce leaves. Top each with half the tuna.
Makes 2 midday or evening meal servings.

Lentil and Courgette Curry

1 tablespoon vegetable oil

3 oz (90 g) courgettes, sliced

2 oz (60 g) onion, diced

3 oz (90 g) mushrooms, sliced

¼ teaspoon curry powder

12 oz (360 g) cooked dried lentils

6 fl oz (180 ml) chicken stock, made with ½ stock cube

1 tablespoon chopped fresh parsley

½ teaspoon salt

½ teaspoon lemon juice

freshly ground pepper to taste

Heat oil in non-stick saucepan, add courgettes, onion, mushrooms and curry powder. Cook for 4 minutes. Add all remaining ingredients. Cover and simmer for 15 minutes or until vegetables are tender. Remove from heat. Divide evenly.
Makes 2 midday or evening meal servings.

PROTEIN FOODS—DRIED PEAS AND BEANS

Kidney Bean and Egg Salad

4 tablespoons mayonnaise

2 teaspoons prepared mustard

4 oz (120 g) onion, finely diced

4 oz (120 g) celery, diced

12 oz (360 g) drained canned dried red kidney beans

6 oz (180 g) cucumber, peeled and diced

4 lettuce leaves

4 eggs, hard-boiled and quartered

6 oz (180 g) cucumber, peeled and sliced

1 teaspoon capers

In bowl combine first 4 ingredients in order given. Add kidney beans and diced cucumber; chill. Divide evenly onto lettuce leaves; surround each with one egg and a quarter of the cucumber slices. Garnish with capers.
Makes 4 midday or evening meal servings.

Hot Chili Beans

1 tablespoon vegetable oil

4 oz (120 g) onion, chopped

12 oz (360 g) cooked dried red beans

4 oz (120 g) canned tomatoes, crushed

2 tablespoons chili sauce

1 teaspoon prepared mustard (optional)

½ teaspoon Worcester sauce

salt and ground red pepper to taste

4 oz (120 g) cooked brown rice

Heat oil in non-stick fryng pan; add onion and saute. Add all

remaining ingredients, except rice. Simmer, stirring occasionally, until hot. Serve over hot rice. Divide evenly.
Makes 2 midday or evening meal servings.

Lentils and Rice

4 oz (120 g) onions, finely chopped

½ teaspoon cumin

2 fl oz (60 ml) chicken stock, made with ¼ stock cube

12 oz (360 g) cooked dried red lentils (see note)

8 oz (240 g) cooked brown rice (see note)

½ teaspoon salt

4 teaspoons vegetable oil

In saucepan simmer onions and cumin in stock until liquid is evaporated. Add lentils, rice and salt. Cook until thoroughly heated. Remove from heat. Stir in oil. Serve hot or cold. Divide evenly.
Makes 4 midday or evening meal servings. Add protein as required.

Note: Cook lentils with 2 crushed garlic cloves. Discard garlic; drain and reserve liquid. Weigh lentils. Use reserved liquid for cooking the rice, adding more water if necessary. Measure rice.

Haricot Bean Soup

2¼ lbs (1 kg 80 g) cooked dried Haricot beans

16 fl oz (480 ml) water

8 oz (240 g) carrots, diced

8 oz (240 g) tomatoes, diced

6 oz (180 g) onions, diced

2 oz (60 g) celery, diced

2 garlic cloves, crushed

1 tablespoon chopped fresh parsley

1½ teaspoons salt

1 teaspoon cumin seed

½ teaspoon ground coriander

12 oz (360 g) cooked brown rice

6 lemon slices

In large saucepan combine all ingredients except rice and lemon. Cover and simmer for 1 hour or until beans are very soft; add more water to adjust consistency if desired. Divide evenly into deep bowls, each containing 2 oz (60 g) hot brown rice. Float a lemon slice on each serving.
Makes 6 midday or evening meal servings.

PROTEIN FOODS-DRIED PEAS AND BEANS

Bean and Meat Stew

8 oz (240 g) diced cooked lamb

4 oz (120 g) onion, chopped

2 garlic cloves, crushed

12 fl oz (360 ml) beef stock, made with 1 stock cube

1 tablespoon tomato puree

12 oz (360 g) cooked dried beans (such as haricot beans or butter beans)

3 tablespoons chopped fresh parsley

pinch thyme

In non-stick saucepan, combine lamb, onions and garlic; cook until onion is browned. Stir in stock and tomato puree. Add beans, parsley and thyme and cook until most of the liquid has evaporated. Divide evenly.
Makes 4 midday or evening meal servings.

Lentil Soup

10 fl oz (300 ml) water

6 oz (180 g) cooked dried lentils

1½ oz (45 g) tomato, chopped

1½ oz (45 g) carrot, diced

1 oz (30 g) peas

1 oz (30 g) celery, diced

1 chicken stock cube, crumbled

1 teaspoon chopped fresh parsley

½ teaspoon dill weed

salt and pepper to taste

Combine all ingredients in saucepan and simmer until vegetables are tender. Add more water to adjust consistency if desired.
Makes 1 midday or evening meal servings.

Chick Pea, Rice and Vegetable Stew

8 fl oz (240 ml) chicken stock, made with 1 stock cube

2 oz (60 g) carrot, sliced

2 oz (60 g) onion, chopped

1 bay leaf

1 garlic clove, crushed

12 oz (360 g) cooked dried chick peas

8 oz (240 g) canned tomatoes, chopped

6 oz (180 g) frozen broccoli, chopped

¼ teaspoon seasoned salt

⅛ teaspoon pepper

4 oz (120 g) cooked brown rice

In saucepan combine stock, carrot, onion, bay leaf and garlic. Simmer for 10 minutes. Add chick peas, tomatoes, broccoli, seasoned salt and pepper. Simmer for 15 minutes. Add rice. Cook over low heat for 4 minutes or until thoroughly heated; pour into serving dish. Divide evenly.
Makes 2 midday or evening meal servings.

Chick Pea, Rice and Vegetable Stew

PROTEIN FOODS—DRIED PEAS AND BEANS

Spicy Red Beans

2 teaspoons vegetable oil

½ chicken stock cube

1 oz (30 g) onion, diced

½ medium apple, peeled, cored and grated

1 oz (30 g) carrot, grated

1 tablespoon tomato puree, mixed with 1 tablespoon water

2 tablespoons cider vinegar

¼ teaspoon dry mustard

pinch oregano

pinch cumin

artificial sweetener to taste (optional)

salt and freshly ground pepper to taste

6 oz (180 g) drained, canned kidney beans

Preheat oven to 350°F, 180°C, Gas Mark 4. Heat oil in non-stick frying pan; add crumbled stock cube, onion, apple and carrot. Saute, stirring constantly for 5 minutes. Add tomato puree, cider vinegar, mustard, oregano, cumin, pepper and salt. Cover and simmer for 1 minute. Tip mixture into ovenproof casserole; add beans and stir to combine ingredients thoroughly. Cover with lid or foil and put in oven for 35 to 40 minutes. Serve hot or cold.

Makes 1 midday or evening meal serving.

Chick Pea and Vegetable Curry

1½ teaspoons coriander

1 teaspoon turmeric

½ teaspoon cumin

½ teaspoon ginger

½ teaspoon chili powder

1 tablespoon water

2 tablespoons onion flakes

4 teaspoons vegetable oil

1 medium cauliflower

1 lb (480 g) tomatoes, skinned

1 lb (480 g) carrots, diced

12 oz (360 g) broad beans, fresh or frozen

12 oz (360 g) peeled potatoes, diced

2 tablespoons lemon juice

1½ lbs (720 g) cooked chick peas

salt and pepper to taste

3 to 4 parsley sprigs

Make a paste with coriander, turmeric, cumin, ginger and chili powder and water. Gradually add enough boiling water to give a large cupful, stirring all the time. Soak onion flakes, drain and saute in oil in non-stick pan until brown. Cut cauliflower into florets and set aside. Add curry spices and tomatoes to onions in pan; bring to the boil. Add carrots, broad beans, potatoes, cauliflower, lemon juice, chick peas, salt and pepper with just enough water to cover the vegetables. Stir well and bring to the boil. Cover pan, simmer until vegetables are tender, shaking occasionally to prevent sticking.

Garnish with chopped parsley. Divide evenly.

Makes 4 midday or evening meal servings.

Persian Beans and Aubergine

6 oz (180 g) aubergine, cut into 1-inch (2.5-cm) cubes

2 oz (60 g) onion, chopped

¼ teaspoon minced fresh garlic

3 oz (90 g) drained canned tomatoes

¾ teaspoon coriander

⅛ teaspoon cumin

dash pepper

6 oz (180 g) drained canned chick peas

In a large non-stick saucepan cook aubergine over medium-high heat until lightly browned. Transfer aubergine to a 1-pint (600-ml) casserole. Add onion and garlic to the saucepan and cook for about 5 minutes or until onion is soft. Stir in the tomatoes and seasonings; bring the mixture to the simmer and transfer to the casserole. Add chick peas and stir to combine. Cover and bake at 375°F, 190°C, Gas Mark 5 for about 45 minutes, stirring occasionally, or until aubergine is tender and flavours are developed.

Makes 1 midday or evening meal serving.

TOFU

This is also called soybean curd. It is a high quality, low cost protein and provides the backbone of the diet for more than one billion people in East Asia. Here we find it in health food shops, and instructions for its use are printed on the package.

Take the serving size of Dried Peas/Beans and increase it by 2 oz (60 g). This gives us the correct serving of Tofu.

Tofu Omelette

2 eggs

2 tablespoons water

salt and pepper to taste

1 tablespoon vegetable oil

8 oz (240 g) tofu

2 teaspoons onion flakes, crushed

1 teaspoon curry powder

Beat eggs with water, salt and pepper. Heat oil in large non-stick pan. Pour in omelette mixture and cook briskly lifting the edges to allow the liquid egg to run onto base of pan and be cooked. Meanwhile mix tofu with onion flakes and curry powder, adding salt and pepper to taste—heat the tofu gently in a small non-stick pan and when omelette is cooked, spoon this mixture onto one half of the omelette, fold over uncovered half, divide into 2 equal portions and serve at once.
Makes 2 midday or evening meal servings.

Egg, Tofu and Alfalfa

8 oz tofu, cut into ¾-inch (2-cm) cubes

2 hard-boiled eggs

2 tablespoons mayonnaise

1 tablespoon Dijon-style mustard

1½ teaspoons lemon juice

1 tablespoon chopped fresh parsley

6 oz (180 g) alfalfa sprouts

Combine all ingredients except sprouts in a large bowl. Toss ingredients together until evenly coated. Place 3 oz (90 g) sprouts on each of 2 serving plates and mound half the tofu/egg mixture on each. Serve chilled.
Makes 2 midday or evening meal servings.

Tofu and Egg Salad

8 oz (240 g) canned pineapple chunks, no sugar added. Drain and reserve juice

2 teaspoons cider vinegar

2 teaspoons mayonnaise

8 oz (240 g) tofu, cut in small cubes

4 oz (120 g) cooked macaroni

6 oz (180 g) carrot, grated

4 oz (120 g) leeks, sliced

3 oz (90 g) tomato, sliced

Chinese leaves (cabbage), chopped

2 eggs, hard-boiled and quartered

Mix pineapple juice, vinegar and mayonnaise. Combine pineapple chunks with next 4 ingredients. Add juice mixture and toss. Divide between two plates; surround with chopped Chinese leaves and sliced tomato. Top each serving with an egg.
Makes 2 midday or evening meal servings.

Stir-Fried Vegetables with Tofu

3 oz (90 g) Chinese (leaves) cabbage, cut into 1-inch (2.5-cm) pieces

3 oz (90 g) broccoli flowerets

3 oz (90 g) carrots, sliced

2 fl oz (60 ml) water

3 oz (90 g) mange tout (Chinese pea pods)

2 teaspoons vegetable oil

1 lb (480 g) tofu, cut into pieces

3 oz (90 g) sliced courgettes

1½ oz (45 g) mushrooms

1½ oz (45 g) drained, canned water chestnuts

2 fl oz (60 ml) soy sauce (optional)

In a saucepan cook Chinese leaves, broccoli and carrots in water for 3 minutes. Add pea pods and cook for 1 minute more. Drain and reserve vegetables. In a wok, or saute pan, heat vegetable oil for 1 minute or until quite hot. Add cooked vegetables and remaining ingredients, except soy sauce. Stir and toss for 3 minutes or until vegetables are well heated. Sprinkle with soy sauce if desired. Divide evenly.
Makes 2 midday or evening meal servings.

PROTEIN FOODS—TOFU

Tofu and Peanut Butter Dip

8 oz (240 g) tofu

3 tablespoons peanut butter

5 fl oz (150 ml) natural unsweetened yogurt

Combine ingredients in blender container; blend until smooth. Divide evenly. Serve with crisp vegetables such as celery, cucumber and carrots cut into thin sticks.
Makes 2 midday or evening meal servings.

Creamy Tomato Tofu and Butter Bean Soup

2 teaspoons vegetable oil

1 oz (30 g) onion, finely diced

2 oz (60 g) tomato, skinned and diced

5 fl oz (150 ml) skim milk

½ teaspoon salt

pinch pepper

¼ teaspoon oregano

dash garlic granules

8 oz (240 g) tofu

6 oz (180 g) drained canned butter beans

2 tablespoons chopped fresh parsley

Put oil in a deep, non-stick saucepan, or thick-based saucepan and heat, add diced onion and saute until onion is translucent. Add tomato and saute for 2 to 3 minutes more. Add next 5 ingredients and cook, stirring constantly, for 1 minute. Remove from heat and leave to cool briefly. Add tofu and transfer to blender container and puree until smooth. Return mixture to saucepan and add butter beans and parsley. Bring to a gentle boil and cook until beans are heated thoroughly. Adjust seasoning and serve at once. Divide evenly.
Makes 2 midday or evening meal servings.

Bean Curd Balls with Tomato Sauce

12 oz (360 g) tofu, mashed

3 slices (3 oz/90 g) wholemeal bread, made into crumbs

2 garlic cloves, crushed

1½ oz (45 g) onion, chopped

3 eggs, lightly beaten

3 tablespoons grated Parmesan cheese

2 tablespoons prepared mustard

1 teaspoon Worcester sauce

1 tablespoon chopped fresh parsley

¼ teaspoon each dried basil, fennel seeds and dried marjoram

salt and pepper to taste

12 oz (360 g) tomatoes, pureed in blender

Combine all ingredients except pureed tomatoes in a large bowl and mix well. Shape into balls and brown over medium heat in a non-stick frying pan. Add pureed tomatoes and simmer for 10 to 15 minutes until sauce and tofu balls are well heated through. Divide evenly.
Makes 3 midday or evening meal servings.

Tofu and Peanut Butter Dip

164

FATS

Sauces and Salad Dressings

Women	....	3 servings daily
Men	....	3 servings daily
Teenagers	....	3 servings daily

	Serving
margarine (high in polyunsaturates)	................1 level tsp
low-fat spread	............................2 level tsps
mayonnaise	............................1 level tsp
mayonnaise (low-calorie)	................2 level tsps
salad cream	............................2 level tsps
vegetable oil	
safflower	............................1 level tsp
sunflower	............................1 level tsp
soybean	............................1 level tsp
corn	............................1 level tsp
cottonseed	............................1 level tsp
sesame	............................1 level tsp
olive oil	............................1 level tsp

Sauces and salad dressings, some with fats and others without, are combined in this section. We include hot and cold sauces, sweet and savoury, thick and thin. There are dressings to enliven salads as well as the conventional French dressings and mayonnaise,

You can use your servings of fat and oil at any time and you can cook with them. Non-stick cooking sprays are allowed, too, in an amount not exceeding 10 calories per day.

Red Pepper Sauce

2 to 3 garlic cloves, crushed

1 tablespoon dried onion flakes

2 tablespoons tomato puree, mixed with 2 fl oz (60 ml) water

1 stick celery

3 oz (90 g) red pepper

3 oz (90 g) mushrooms

salt and freshly ground pepper to taste

Bring the garlic, onion flakes and tomato puree and water to the boil in a saucepan and simmer for 10 minutes. Chop celery. Remove membranes and seeds from pepper and slice thinly. Wash mushrooms and cut into quarters. Add prepared vegetables to saucepan with salt and pepper. Cook for a further 10 minutes or until vegetables are cooked but still crisp. Serve with grilled steak.
Makes 1 serving.

Orange Sauce

2 fl oz (60 ml) cider vinegar

4 fl oz (120 ml) orange juice, no sugar added

1 tablespoon soy sauce

1½ teaspoons cornflour, dissolved in 2 teaspoons water

¾ teaspoon cherry flavouring

2 slices fresh ginger root

2 medium oranges, peeled and cut into sections

In small saucepan combine all ingredients except orange sections. Cook, stirring often, until thickened. Remove ginger root. Add orange sections. Divide evenly.
Makes 3 servings.

Sweet-and-Sour Sauce

2 fl oz (60 ml) cider vinegar

4 tablespoons tomato ketchup

2 fl oz (60 ml) water

2 to 3 tablespoons Worcester sauce

1 tablespoon lemon juice

½ teaspoon salt

1 tablespoon vegetable oil (optional)

2 teaspoons sugar

1 tablespoon cornflour, dissolved in 1 tablespoon water

In small saucepan combine vinegar, tomato ketchup, water, Worcester sauce, lemon juice, salt, oil and sugar. Bring to the boil; stir in cornflour. Cook, stirring constantly, until sauce thickens and clears. Divide evenly.
Makes 6 servings.

Mustard Sauce

8 teaspoons plain flour
2 tablespoons dry mustard
4 fl oz (120 ml) water
1 teaspoon chicken stock powder
1½ oz (45 g) shallots or spring onions, finely chopped
1 tablespoons lemon juice
1 tablespoon white wine vinegar
¼ teaspoon thyme
1 small bay leaf
15 fl oz (450 ml) skim milk
salt and white pepper to taste

In small bowl combine flour, mustard and 2 fl oz (60 ml) water to make a paste. Set aside. In medium saucepan combine remaining water and stock powder; add shallots or spring onions, lemon juice, vinegar, thyme and bay leaf. Simmer until most of liquid has evaporated. Remove and discard bay leaf. Add milk; heat gently. Using a wire whisk, beat mustard-flour mixture into milk mixture. Cook, stirring constantly, until thickened. Continue cooking for 5 minutes; do not boil. Season with salt and pepper. Divide evenly.
Makes 6 servings.

Mint Sauce

2 tablespoons chopped fresh mint
2 tablespoons lemon juice
2 tablespoons cider vinegar
artificial sweetener to taste

Combine all ingredients in a small bowl. Leave to stand for one hour. Divide evenly.
Makes 4 servings.

'Hollandaise'

1 tablespoon cornflour
4 fl oz (120 ml) water
1 chicken stock cube, crumbled
4 tablespoons low-fat spread
2 tablespoons mayonnaise
1 teaspoon lemon juice
dash hot sauce

In small saucepan dissolve cornflour in water. Add crumbled stock cube. Stir over medium heat until thickened. Remove from heat. Stir in low-fat spread until melted. Add mayonnaise; stir until blended. Add lemon juice and hot sauce; stir to combine. Divide evenly.
Makes 6 servings.

Tangy Yogurt Sauce

5 fl oz (150 ml) natural unsweetened yogurt
4 teaspoons tomato ketchup
1 tablespoon lemon juice
1 tablespoon mayonnaise
½ teaspoon grated fresh horseradish

Mix all ingredients together. Chill. Use for prawn cocktail or serve with tuna and other fish. Divide evenly.
Makes 2 servings.

Basic White Sauce

2 tablespoons margarine
2 tablespoons plain flour
⅛ teaspoon salt
pinch white pepper
10 fl oz (300 ml) skim milk

Melt margarine in non-stick saucepan. Add flour, salt and pepper and cook over moderate heat for about 2 minutes, stirring constantly. Gradually add milk. Cook, stirring constantly with a wire whisk, until mixture thickens. Divide evenly.
Makes 4 servings.

Caper White Sauce

To Basic White Sauce above, stir in 4½ teaspoons capers and ½ teaspoon sherry flavouring.

Curry Sauce

To Basic White Sauce above, add 1 teaspoon curry powder, or to taste, with the flour.

Dill Sauce

To Basic White Sauce above, add ¾ teaspoon dill weed and a pinch of nutmeg with salt and pepper in the basic recipe. Substitute fish stock for half the skim milk. Delicious with poached fish.

Herb Sauce

To Basic White Sauce recipe above, add 1 teaspoon chopped fresh parsley, ½ teaspoon chopped chives and ¼ teaspoon tarragon with the flour.

Horseradish/White Sauce

To Basic White Sauce recipe above, add 4½ teaspoons grated fresh horseradish and ½ teaspoon prepared mustard. Serve with chicken, beef, lamb or fish.

FATS

Mushroom White Sauce

To the Basic White Sauce recipe (see page 167), add 1 oz (30 g) diced onion and 1 oz (30 g) sliced mushrooms to margarine before adding flour. When sauce thickens, add a dash of Worcester sauce.

Basic French Dressing

This dressing can be varied in dozens of ways with a change of seasoning, vinegar and herbs, and the addition of finely diced vegetables.

4 tablespoons vegetable oil
2 fl oz (60 ml) red wine vinegar or tarragon vinegar
¼ teaspoon salt
pinch white pepper

Combine all ingredients in a jar with tight-fitting cover. Cover and shake vigorously before using. Divide evenly.
Makes 4 servings.

Garlic French Dressing

To above Basic French Dressing, add 1 crushed garlic clove. Refrigerate. Remove garlic before serving.

Garlic Italian Dressing

To above Basic French Dressing add 1 teaspoon Italian seasoning or ¼ teaspoon each of oregano, basil, thyme and rosemary. Two teaspoons prepared mustard may also be added.

Yogurt Cucumber Sauce

5 fl oz (150 ml) natural unsweetened yogurt
1½ oz (45 g) cucumber, peeled, seeded and diced
1 teaspoon lemon juice or cider vinegar
¼ teaspoon dill weed
⅛ teaspoon salt, or to taste
2 tablespoons mayonnaise (optional)
½ teaspoon aromatic bitters (optional)
¼ teaspoon paprika

In bowl combine yogurt and cucumber. Stir in lemon juice or cider vinegar, dill weed and salt. Blend in mayonnaise and aromatic bitters if desired. Sprinkle with paprika. Excellent with salmon or cold poached fish. Divide evenly.
Makes 4 servings.

Simple Salad Sauce

2 teaspoons lemon juice
2 teaspoons chopped chives
1 teaspoon chopped fresh mint or basil
1 teaspoon Dijon-style mustard
artificial sweetener to taste

Combine all ingredients in a small screw-top jar. Cover and shake vigorously and use when desired. Store in refrigerator.
Makes 1 serving.

Left: Basic French Dressing
Right: Mushroom White Sauce
Front: Yogurt Cucumber Sauce

FATS

Basic Brown Sauce

8 teaspoons margarine

8 teaspoons plain flour

1 tablespoon tomato puree, mixed with 2 tablespoons water

16 fl oz (480 ml) water

2 beef stock cubes, crumbled

2 teaspoons dried onion flakes, reconstituted in 2 teaspoons water

1½ teaspoons gravy browning

4 peppercorns

2 cloves

1 small bay leaf

pinch thyme

pinch garlic powder

Melt margarine in non-stick saucepan; using a wooden spoon or wire whisk, add flour and cook for 2 to 3 minutes, stirring frequently. Stir in tomato puree mixed with water. Slowly add remaining water, stirring constantly. Add all remaining ingredients. Cover and simmer for 30 minutes or until thickened, stirring often. Divide evenly.
Makes 4 servings.

Mustard Sauce

To Basic Brown Sauce above, add 2½ teaspoons dry mustard dissolved in 1 oz (30 g) non-fat dry milk, mixed with 4 fl oz (120 ml) water. Serve hot. Divide evenly.
Makes 4 servings.

Seafood Dressing

4 tablespoons mayonnaise

4 tablespoons chili sauce

¼ teaspoon chopped capers

pinch each basil, tarragon and savory

Combine all ingredients in small bowl. Chill before serving. Divide evenly.
Makes 4 servings, about 2 tablespoons each.

Pimiento Dressing

8 oz (240 g) canned pimientos

2 tablespoons cider vinegar

2 tablespoons prepared mustard

2 teaspoons sugar

Combine all ingredients in blender container and blend until smooth. Divide evenly.
Makes 4 servings.

Tomato Sauce

3 oz (90 g) green pepper, seeded and finely chopped

2 oz (60 g) onion, chopped

1 garlic clove, crushed

1 lb 6 oz (660 g) canned tomatoes, crushed

8 tablespoons tomato puree, mixed with 4 fl oz (120 ml) water

6 fl oz (180 ml) beef stock, made with ½ stock cube

1½ teaspoons basil

¾ teaspoon salt

½ teaspoon chopped fresh parsley

½ teaspoon oregano

⅛ teaspoon pepper

In medium saucepan combine green pepper, onion and garlic. Cook for 2 to 3 minutes. Add remaining ingredients; simmer for about 35 minutes or until sauce reaches desired consistency, stirring often. Divide evenly.
Makes 6 servings.

Gravy

10 fl oz (300 ml) water

1 beef or chicken stock cube

2 teaspoons cornflour, mixed with 1 tablespoon water

Put water and stock cube in saucepan. Bring to the boil, stirring until stock cube is dissolved. Mix cornflour with water and add to stock and cook, stirring, for 2 minutes.
Makes 2 servings.

Piquant Tomato Sauce

6 oz (180 g) canned tomatoes plus juice

3 oz (90 g) finely chopped onion

1 teaspoon basil flakes

1 tablespoon lemon juice

salt and pepper to taste

artificial sweetener to taste (optional)

Place all ingredients in saucepan. Bring to the boil; simmer until onion is tender. Cool, then put in blender container and blend until pureed. Delicious hot or cold. Use as desired. Divide evenly.
Makes 2 servings.

Fish Dressing

1 teaspoon mayonnaise

2 teaspoons tomato ketchup

½ teaspoon Dijon-style mustard

1 teaspoon low-calorie salad dressing

1 teaspoon dried dill weed

1 teaspoon lemon juice

Combine all ingredients in a small bowl. Beat thoroughly and place in the refrigerator for about 2 hours before using to blend flavours.
Makes 1 serving.

Fines Herbes Spread

Serve melted on fish or grilled meat.

8 tablespoons margarine

1 teaspoon chopped chives

1 teaspoon chopped fresh parsley

1 teaspoon tarragon

1 teaspoon marjoram

½ teaspoon grated lemon rind

pinch each salt and pepper

chopped fresh parsley and chives to garnish

In small bowl combine all ingredients, except garnish. Chill; form into a mound. Place in serving dish and garnish with parsley and chives. Divide evenly.
Makes 8 servings.

Lemon and Tarragon Sauce

1 tablespoon margarine

2 teaspoons plain flour

1 teaspoon chopped fresh tarragon or ¼ teaspoon dried tarragon

1 teaspoon grated lemon rind

5 fl oz (150 ml) skim milk

salt and pepper to taste

1 tablespoon lemon juice

In non-stick saucepan melt margarine. Add flour and mix until smooth. Add tarragon, lemon rind, milk, salt and pepper. Mix thoroughly and cook, stirring occasionally, until thickened. Beat in lemon juice and serve.
Makes 1 serving.

Cumberland Sauce

8 fl oz (240 ml) low-calorie ginger ale

2 teaspoons redcurrant jelly

2 teaspoons Dijon-style mustard

artificial sweetener to taste

¼ cinnamon stick

¼ teaspoon gravy browning

2 cloves

2 teaspoons cornflour, dissolved in 1 tablespoon water

Combine all ingredients except cornflour in a saucepan. Bring to the boil, lower heat and simmer for 2 to 3 minutes. Remove cinnamon stick and cloves; add cornflour and cook, stirring, until sauce thickens. Divide evenly. Serve with cold meat.
Makes 4 servings.

Yogurt Tomato Dressing

5 fl oz (150 ml) natural unsweetened yogurt

2 tablespoons tomato puree, mixed with 2 fl oz (60 ml) water

1 teaspoon chopped fresh basil

¼ teaspoon celery seed

Mix all ingredients together in bowl. Refrigerate for 1 hour before serving. Divide evenly.
Makes 4 servings.

Yogurt Dill Sauce

5 fl oz (150 ml) natural unsweetened yogurt

4 teaspoons mayonnaise

1½ teaspoons chopped fresh dill or ½ teaspoon dill seed

½ teaspoon grated fresh horseradish

pinch each salt, white pepper and hot sauce

Combine all ingredients in a bowl. Divide evenly.
Makes 4 servings.

Tartare Sauce

2 tablespoons mayonnaise

½ oz (15 g) pickled cucumber, chopped

½ teaspoon chopped fresh parsley

½ teaspoon prepared mustard

dash each Worcester Sauce, lemon juice and hot sauce

pinch salt

Combine all ingredients in small bowl. Divide evenly.
Makes 2 servings.

FATS

Hot Tartare Sauce

To the Basic White Sauce recipe (see page 167), add 1 oz (30 g) diced onion and 1½ oz (45 g) green pepper, seeded and diced, to margarine before adding flour. After sauce has thickened, stir in 2 tablespoons mayonnaise, 1½ teaspoons lemon juice, 1 oz (30 g) chopped pickled cucumber and 2 teaspoons chopped fresh parsley. Use for seafood, broccoli or asparagus.

Onion Sauce

6 oz (180 g) onions, chopped
2 tablespoons margarine
2 tablespoons plain flour
12 fl oz (360 ml) skim milk
salt and pepper to taste

Cook onions in water until soft. Drain and reserve cooking water. Melt margarine in small non-stick saucepan. Stir in flour, milk and seasoning. Cook over low heat until thickened. Stir in onion and add some of the cooking water if sauce is too thick. Cook for a further 2 minutes. Serve with roast lamb. Divide evenly.
Makes 6 servings.

Custard

2 pints (1 litre 200 ml) skim milk
4 tablespoons custard powder mixed with 2 fl oz (60 ml) water
artificial sweetener to taste

In medium saucepan combine milk, custard powder and sweetener. Heat, stirring constantly, until custard is thickened. Divide evenly. Serve with Rich Fruit Pudding (see page 12).
Makes 8 servings.

Sweet White Sauce

1 pint (600 ml) skim milk
4 tablespoons plain flour, mixed with 2 fl oz (60 ml) water
2 tablespoons caster sugar

In medium saucepan combine milk, flour and sugar. Heat, stirring constantly, until sauce is thickened. Divide evenly.
Makes 8 servings.

Creamy Cheese Sauce

2 tablespoons margarine
2 tablespoons plain flour
10 fl oz (300 ml) skim milk
2 oz (60 g) Cheddar cheese, grated
dash Worcester sauce, hot sauce or pinch nutmeg (optional)

Melt margarine in non-stick saucepan. blend in flour. Add milk; cook, stirring constantly, until thickened. Stir in cheese. Season with Worcester sauce, hot sauce, or nutmeg if desired. Divide evenly. Serve over hot vegetables.
Makes 2 midday or evening meal servings. Add protein as required.

Barbecue Fruit Sauce

3 oz (90 g) onion, finely chopped
3 tablespoons cider vinegar
1 tablespoon prepared mustard
2 teaspoons Worcester sauce
8 canned peach halves with 8 tablespoons juice, no sugar added
8 tablespoons tomato ketchup

In medium saucepan cook onion over medium heat for 1 to 2 minutes, stirring frequently. Add vinegar, mustard and Worcester sauce; cook, stirring constantly for about 3 minutes. Dice peach halves and add with peach juice and tomato ketchup. Reduce heat and simmer, stirring occasionally, for 15 to 20 minutes or until mixture thickens. Delicious served with ham, chicken and turkey. Divide evenly.
Makes 4 servings.

Mock Bearnaise Sauce

2 tablespoons low-fat spread
1 tablespoon mayonnaise
1 tablespoon tarragon vinegar
¼ teaspoon dried onion flakes, reconstituted in ¾ teaspoon water
⅛ teaspoon chopped fresh parsley
2 to 3 drops butter flavouring

Melt margarine in small non-stick saucepan. Stir in remaining ingredients. Cook, stirring constantly, until heated. Divide evenly.
Makes 2 servings.

Top: Creamy Cheese Sauce
Left: Barbecue Fruit Sauce
Right: Hot Tartare Sauce

OPTIONAL

Beverages
water, soda water, mineral or spring water

coffee, tea. Select in reasonable amounts

Condiments
Select in reasonable amounts

artificial sweetener	mustard
baking powder	pepper
bicarbonate of soda	rennet
curry powder	salt
dried vegetable flakes	seasonings
flavourings	soy sauce
gravy browning	spices
herbs	vinegar
horseradish, fresh	Worcester sauce
hot sauce (pepper sauce)	
lemon juice	
lime juice	

This section gives you the items which add a lift to your spirits—perhaps a glass of wine with your dinner or a tablespoonful in a casserole, or a Knickerbocker Glory as a dessert. You can give a lift to your cooking with herbs and spices and flavourings. We include such treats as honey and treacle, also a variety of delicious drinks, both hot and cold.

The speciality foods are outside our usual rule of 'no need to count calories' and they must be limited to a total of 20 calories per day.

These items are all optional of course. They are not part of the total nutrition 'package' but they make the difference between routine eating and a taste of adventure. They have been accounted for in the overall planning of the Food Plan.

The following recipes have been created using items from this optional section.

Extras
Select up to 3 servings daily if desired

	Serving
anchovy essence	1 level tsp
bacon bits, imitation	1 level tsp
bran	1 level tbsp
barbecue, chilli, steak sauce	2 level tsps

Chicken Consomme with Wine

12 fl oz (360 ml) chicken stock, made from 1 stock cube

6 oz (180 g) leeks, finely chopped

4 fl oz (120 ml) dry white wine

6 parsley sprigs

pinch basil

Combine ingredients in a saucepan; bring to the boil. Reduce heat and cook, partially covered, for 30 minutes. Pour liquid through a strainer; discard solids. Divide evenly.
Makes 2 servings.

Bacon and Onion Jacket Potato

1 oz (30 g) raw lean back bacon

1 oz (30 g) onion

few drops lemon juice

3 oz (90 g) hot, baked jacket potato

Grill and dice bacon. Peel, dice and grill onion on foil sprinkled with lemon juice. Cut jacket potato in half, scoop out potato into basin. Add cooked bacon and onion. Mix together and pile back into shells. Place under grill to heat through. Serve with salad.
Makes 1 serving.

Golden-Glazed Turnips

4 teaspoons margarine

4 teaspoons golden syrup

pinch nutmeg

pinch ginger

12 oz (360 g) peeled turnips, cooked

Melt margarine in non-stick frying pan. Stir in syrup, nutmeg and ginger. Add turnips and stir over low heat until lightly browned and well coated with the syrup. Divide evenly.
Makes 4 servings.

cheese, grated	1 level tsp	yeast concentrated extract	1 level tsp

cheese, grated ....1 level tsp
chocolate sauce, spread, syrup ....½ level tsp
cocoa or carob, unsweetened...........1 level tsp
coconut, shredded.............................1 level tsp
coffee whitener ....1 level tsp
curry paste ....½ level tsp
custard powder..................................1 level tsp
egg white ....½
flour, cornflour, arrowroot.................1 level tsp
gelatine, unflavoured....................1½ level tsps
honey ....½ level tsp
jam ....½ level tsp
ketchup...2 level tsps
marmalade ....½ level tsp
olives 2
relish, any type ....2 level tsps
sago ....1 level tsp
seeds—caraway, poppy, sesame ....½ level tsp
stock cube...½
stock powder.....................................1 level tsp
sugar ....½ level tsp
tapioca ....1 level tsp
tomato paste/puree ....1 level tbsp
treacle/syrup ....½ level tsp
wheatgerm ....1 level tsp
wine (for cooking).....................................2 tsps
yeast ....1 level tsp

yeast concentrated extract ....1 level tsp

Bonus

Select up to 3 servings weekly if desired

bacon, lean back, (grilled) ....1 oz (30 g) raw
beer ....½ pint (300 ml)
cider..½ pint (300 ml)
cream, single ....3 level tbsps
fruit..2 servings
ice-cream (commercial) ....2 oz (60 g)
jelly, fruit flavoured ....6 oz (180 g) (prepared)
sherry, dry/medium ....3 fl oz (90 ml)
spirits ....1½ fl oz (45 ml)
wine, red or white, champagne...4 fl oz (120 ml)

Speciality Foods

You need not be concerned about counting calories. However, if the following items are used, calories MUST be counted. Limit intake to a total of 20 calories per day.

beverage, carbonated	
fruit flavoured squash	
jams	
ketchup	All
salad dressings	low-calorie
soups	

Bacon and Egg Spaghetti

1 egg

1 garlic clove, crushed

1 teaspoon dill seed

salt and pepper to taste

2 oz (60 g) hot cooked spaghetti

1 oz (30 g) hard cheese, grated

1 oz (30 g) lean back bacon, grilled and chopped

mixed green salad

parsley sprigs for garnish

Heat a heatproof serving bowl until it is hot to the touch. Break the egg into the hot bowl and beat with the garlic, dill seed, salt and pepper. Fold the piping hot spaghetti into the egg mixture. This has the effect of cooking the egg. Sprinkle with grated cheese and chopped bacon, and serve with green salad. Garnish with parsley.
Makes 1 serving.

Soda Sparkler

Try this at your next party. Pour 4 fl oz (120 ml) soda water over 3 ice cubes in a 6-oz (180-g) glass. Add 1 teaspoon sherry flavouring and a slice of lemon or lime.

Grapefruit Fizz

4 ice cubes

8 fl oz (240 ml) grapefruit juice, no sugar added

1 bottle soda water

slices of lemon

Crush ice cubes and divide between 2 tall glasses. Add grapefruit juice and top up with soda water. Serve at once with lemon slices floating on top. Divide evenly.
Makes 2 servings.

OPTIONAL

Orange and Lemon Cooler

8 fl oz (240 ml) water

artificial sweetener to taste

mint leaves

8 fl oz (240 ml) orange juice, no sugar added

4 fl oz (120 ml) lemon juice

8 fl oz (240 ml) low-calorie ginger ale

crushed ice

Combine water, sweetener and mint leaves. Bring to the boil, strain and cool. Add to the other ingredients. Divide between 4 tall glasses and add crushed ice.
Makes 4 servings.

Orange Flip

2 to 3 ice cubes

8 fl oz (240 ml) low-calorie carbonated orange drink

1 oz (30 g) non-fat dry milk

Place 2 to 3 ice cubes in a tall glass. Mix orange drink and milk powder together thoroughly and pour over ice cubes.
Makes 1 serving.

Gingered Lime

2 fl oz (60 ml) low-calorie lime drink, undiluted

ice cubes

8 fl oz (240 ml) low-calorie ginger ale

Put lime drink and ice cubes into a tall glass and top up with ginger ale.
Makes 1 serving.

Fresh Peach Ice Cream Soda

5 fl oz (150 ml) soda water

3 tablespoons skim milk

2 oz (60 g) vanilla ice cream

1 medium peach, peeled, stoned and chopped

few drops maraschino or kirsch flavouring

3 to 4 ice cubes

Place soda water, milk and vanilla ice cream in blender. Blend for 1 minute; add the rest of the ingredients and blend for approximately 1 minute longer. Serve at once.
Makes 1 serving.

'Sweet Treat'

1 digestive biscuit

1 level teaspoon chocolate spread

1 level teaspoon shredded coconut

Spread digestive biscuit with chocolate spread and sprinkle with shredded coconut.
Makes 1 serving.

Banana Sundae

½ medium banana

½ teaspoon lemon juice

2 oz (60 g) vanilla ice cream

1½ teaspoons chocolate sauce

½ digestive biscuit

Peel and cut banana in half lengthwise into two equal portions; sprinkle cut surfaces with lemon juice. Form ice cream into scoop with a spoon, arrange banana and ice cream on a sundae dish and decorate with chocolate sauce. Cut biscuit in half and decorate.
Makes 1 serving.

'Knickerbocker Glory'

1 digestive biscuit, crumbled

2 oz (60 g) canned sliced peaches, no sugar added

2½ oz (75 g) strawberries (reserve one for garnish)

2 oz (60 g) vanilla ice cream

In a tall sundae glass, layer biscuit crumbs, peaches, strawberries and ice cream—repeat layers finishing with ice cream and garnish with strawberry.
Makes 1 serving.

Tropical Cocktail

8 fl oz (240 ml) low-calorie carbonated bitter lemon drink

12 fl oz (360 ml) grapefruit juice, no sugar added

few drops rum flavouring

artificial sweetener to taste

8 fl oz (240 ml) low-calorie ginger ale

juice of ½ lemon

1 medium orange, peeled and diced

mint leaf

Place all ingredients, except mint, in blender. Blend, strain and divide evenly between 4 glasses. Decorate with mint leaf.
Makes 4 servings.

Left: Tropical Cocktail
Centre: 'Knickerbocker Glory'
Right: Fresh Peach Ice Cream Soda

OPTIONAL

Honey-Orange Sauce

1 teaspoon honey

2 teaspoons water

1 tablespoon lemon juice

½ teaspoon grated orange rind

Heat honey and water together in a small saucepan. Add lemon juice and orange rind, reheat gently and use with puddings and desserts. Divide evenly.
Makes 2 servings.

Pan-Cooked Chicken with Tarragon

2 teaspoons margarine

1 teaspoon vegetable oil

2 lb (960 g) skinned chicken breasts, split

1½ teaspoons dried tarragon

1½ oz (45 g) onion, chopped

1½ oz (45 g) carrot, chopped

4 oz (120 g) mushrooms

4 fl oz (120 ml) dry white wine

4 tablespoons chopped fresh parsley

Melt margarine and oil in large frying pan or saute pan, which has a lid. Turn chicken breasts in hot oil mixture over fairly high heat until well browned on both sides. Sprinkle chicken with the tarragon and add the onion and mushrooms. Pour wine over chicken and cover frying pan. Reduce heat to gentle simmer and cook for 25 to 30 minutes or until chicken is tender. Remove chicken to a serving dish and keep hot. Add 3 tablespoons parsley to the frying pan and cook briskly, stirring well, until the liquid has reduced slightly.

Pour over the chicken and sprinkle with the rest of the parsley. Divide evenly.
Makes 4 midday or evening meal servings.

Beetroot with Honey Dressing

12 oz (360 g) peeled cooked beetroot

10 fl oz (300 ml) natural unsweetened yogurt

4 fl oz (120 ml) orange juice, no sugar added

1 tablespoon lemon juice

1½ teaspoons honey

salt and pepper to taste

1 head lettuce, washed

rind of ½ lemon, cut into thin strips

Slice beetroot. Combine yogurt, fruit juices, honey, salt and pepper and mix well. Line a salad plate with lettuce leaves, arrange beetroot on top and pour dressing over. Garnish with lemon rind. Divide evenly.
Makes 4 servings.

Toasted Honey Crumpet

1 x 1½ oz (45 g) crumpet

2 teaspoons low-fat spread

1 teaspoon honey

Toast crumpet, each side. Whilst still hot, spread with low-fat spread and honey.
Makes 1 serving.

Chicken Soup

6 fl oz (180 ml) chicken stock, made with 1 stock cube

1 oz (30 g) cooked carrot, diced

1 oz (30 g) cooked celery, diced

1 teaspoon dried onion flakes

½ teaspoon chopped fresh parsley

salt and pepper to taste

Combine all ingredients in small saucepan and heat through.
Makes 1 serving.

Creamy Apricot Fizz

4 canned apricot halves with 2 tablespoons juice, no sugar added

3 to 4 ice cubes

½ oz (15 g) non-fat dry milk

4 fl oz (120 ml) low-calorie ginger ale

Reserve one apricot half and place the rest of the ingredients in a blender container. Blend until the ice cubes have disappeared. Serve immediately in a tall glass. Garnish with apricot threaded on a cocktail stick and place across the rim of the glass.
Makes 1 serving.

Beef Drink

6 fl oz (180 ml) beef stock, made with ½ stock cube

pinch garlic powder

pinch chopped fresh parsley

dash Worcester sauce

Combine all ingredients in small saucepan and heat through.
Makes 1 serving.

Pep Up Your Meals With Spices And Herbs

Allspice—Delicate West Indian spice. Flavour resembles a blend of nutmeg, cinnamon and cloves. Whole, it's a favourite seasoning for pickles, stews and boiled fish.

Basil—Means 'king' and this herb adds the crowning touch to all tomato dishes. Gives zest to eggs, fish, soups, stews and salads.

Bay Leaf—The classic seasoning for stews, soups, pickles, sauces and fish. Remove the leaf before serving.

Bitters—A liquid blend of herbs and spices, often used in drinks. Add a few drops to tomato juice. For unusual flavour, try a few drops in scrambled eggs.

Bouquet Garni or Bouquet of Herbs—A combination of herbs either tied together or wrapped in muslin and tied into bags. Usually added during the last half hour of cooking and removed before serving.

Capers—Pickled buds of the caper bush. They taste like sharp gherkins. Use in sauces and salads.

Cardamon—Native to India. The seeds are delicious in coffee and are also used in pickling. Powdered or ground, it is nice sprinkled on melon and other fruits.

Celery Seed—Pungent seed, used in stews, cole slaw, potato salad and salad dressings.

Chervil—Delicate herb of the carrot family. Combines well with other herbs. Delicious fresh or dry, in salads, soups, egg and cheese dishes.

Chili Powder—The ancient Aztecs are credited for this blend of chili, allspice, red peppers, cumin seed, oregano, garlic powder and salt. Use sparingly in cocktail sauces, eggs, stews and meat loaf.

Chive—Has a mild onion-like flavour. Adds colour and flavour to cottage cheese, eggs, potatoes, vegetable dishes and soups.

Cinnamon—Bark of the cinnamon tree. Ground and mixed with artificial sweetener, it's a favourite on French toast, pancakes and puddings.

Cloves—Nail-shaped dried flower bud. Once available only to the rich, today it can be enjoyed by everyone. Whole, it is used in baking ham, in picklings and in drinks. Many desserts call for it in ground form.

Coriander—Use this pungent herb sparingly. Gives character to pickles and stuffing to be served with poultry. It is one of the many spices found in curry powder.

Cumin—Aromatic seeds used whole or ground in egg and cheese dishes, sauerkraut, meats, rice, pickles and Mexican foods.

Curry Powder—A blend of spices from India. Used in curries of meat, fish, eggs and chicken and to perk up leftover stews.

Dill—The tender fresh or dried leaves, as well as the seeds, add a delightful flavour to eggs, cheeses, salads and potatoes. A favourite in Scandinavian cookery.

Fennel—Has a slight liquorice taste. Gives special flavour to apples and steamed fish.

Garlic—The fresh root is a staple of Oriental cookery. Dried and ground it is used in soups, stews and desserts.

Ground Red Pepper—Small hot red pepper, ground and used sparingly to season eggs, meats and fish.

Italian Seasoning—You can buy this blend of herbs or you can make your own by combining basil, oregano, rosemary, red pepper, garlic, marjoram, thyme and sage. Used over fish, meats, poultry, liver, rice and pasta.

Mace—The lacy covering of the inner shell holding the nutmeg. Delicious in spinach.

Marjoram—One of the best-known herbs. Gives nice flavour to peas and beans.

Mint—Everyone knows this aromatic herb. Delicious with lamb and in cool drinks and hot tea.

Mustard—The whole seed is used in pickling; ground, with a little water added. it's the hot mustard used in Oriental cookery. Prepared mustard is the favourite with all sausages and is delicious in sauces and salad dressings.

Nutmeg—Traditionally used in desserts. Also adds a special flavour to spinach and Brussels sprouts.

Oregano—Wild marjoram, stronger in flavour than its cultivated cousin. Widely used in Mexican and Italian dishes.

Paprika—A member of the pepper family. Available in mild and fiery flavour. Used for colour and flavour.

OPTIONAL

Parsley—Used in foods for flavour and for garnish. Fresh parsley is available with either a curly or a flat leaf. Save the stems to use when preparing soup stock.

Pepper—Available black or white. Used whole in pickling and soups; ground in most meat, poultry, fish, egg and vegetable dishes.

Poultry Seasonings—A mixture of several spices used to season poultry and meats.

Rosemary—Rosemary is for remembrance, and its sweet fresh flavour makes lamb stews, boiled potatoes, turnips and cauliflower memorable.

Saffron—The world's most expensive spice, so make a little go a long way. Place a pinch in boiling water, before adding rice, to develop golden colour and appetising flavour. Turmeric may be used as a substitute.

Sage—Used in poultry seasoning, it is the perfect complement to chicken, pork and fish dishes.

Savory—Lightly aromatic; good with green beans, meats, chicken and scrambled eggs.

Tarragon—Add this anise-flavoured herb to vinegar, salad dressings and sauces for meat, poultry and seafood.

Thyme—Has a pungent flavour. Use sparingly with onions, aubergine, tomatoes and celery.

Turmeric—This slightly bitter-tasting herb adds a saffron-like natural colouring to rice, chicken and seafood.

Vanilla Beans—For the true vanilla flavour, add a whole vanilla bean to the milk when heating it for custards, puddings and drinks. The beans may be washed, dried and used again and again.

Directions for Using Gelatine Powder

In saucepan sprinkle 1 tablespoon unflavoured gelatine over 4 fl oz (120 ml) cold liquid. Place over low heat and stir until gelatine is dissolved. Remove from heat and add remaining liquid called for. Pour mixture into mould. Chill for 3 to 4 hours or until firm. To turn out, dip mould in warm water to depth of gelatine. Loosen round edge with the tip of a small knife. Place serving dish on top of mould and turn upside down. Shake, holding dish tightly to the mould. If gelatine does not unmould, repeat process.

Profiterole and Chocolate Sauce

8 teaspoons low-fat spread
2 fl oz (60 ml) water
1½ oz (45 g) self-raising flour
2 small eggs
4 teaspoons chocolate spread

Filling

12 tablespoons single cream
3 teaspoons cornflour
2 tablespoons water
½ teaspoon vanilla flavouring

Preheat oven to 400°F, 200°C, Gas Mark 6. Melt low-fat spread in medium saucepan. Add water and bring to the boil. Add flour, all at once, and stir vigorously until mixzture leaves the sides of the saucepan. Cool slightly and then add eggs, one at a time, beating thoroughly after each addition until mixture is smooth. Spray a baking sheet with a non-stick cooking spray. Spoon mixture in 8 portions on to tray. Bake for 15 minutes and then reduce oven temperature to 350°F, 180°C, Gas Mark 4; bake for a further 15 minutes. Remove buns from oven and turn off heat. Pierce buns to release steam; return to oven for 10 minutes leaving oven door ajar. Transfer to cooling tray. Make filling by bringing cream to the boil in a saucepan. Mix cornflour with the water and add to the cream with vanilla flavouring. Bring to the boil, stirring constantly, and cook for 1 minute. Pour into basin and leave until cold. Fill buns with the cream and top with the chocolate spread. Divide evenly.

Makes 4 midday or evening meal servings. Add protein as required.

Profiterole and Chocolate Sauce

INDEX

INDEX

INDEX